BOOKS BY
RICHMOND LATTIMORE

POETRY
Poems 1957
Sestina for a Far-off Summer
The Stride of Time
Poems from Three Decades

LITERARY HISTORY AND CRITICISM
Themes in Greek and Latin Epitaphs
The Poetry of Greek Tragedy
Story Patterns in Greek Tragedy

TRANSLATIONS
The Odes of Pindar
The Iliad of Homer
The Odyssey of Homer
Greek Lyrics
Aeschylus, Oresteia
Euripides, The Trojan Women
Euripides, Alcestis
Euripides, Helen
Euripides, Rhesus
Euripides, Iphigeneia in Tauris
Aristophanes, The Frogs
Hesiod
The Revelation of John
The Four Gospels and the Revelation
Acts and Letters of the Apostles

ACTS

AND LETTERS

OF THE

APOSTLES

ACTS
AND LETTERS
OF THE
APOSTLES

Newly translated
from the Greek by
Richmond Lattimore

Farrar · Straus · Giroux
New York

Copyright © 1982 by Richmond Lattimore

All rights reserved

First printing, 1982

Printed in the United States of America

Published simultaneously in Canada by

McGraw-Hill Ryerson Ltd., Toronto

Designed by Cynthia Krupat

Library of Congress Cataloging in Publication Data

Bible. N.T. Acts. English. Lattimore. 1982.

Acts and letters of the Apostles.

I. Lattimore, Richmond Alexander.

II. Bible. N.T. Epistles. English. Lattimore.

1982. III. Title.

BS2617.5.A3L37 1982   227'.05209   82-10199

Contents

Preface

¶THE FOUR GOSPELS ARE FOLLOWED
in the New Testament by the *Acts of the Apostles* which,
though far from being a complete account, is the earliest
consecutive story of early Christianity that we have. It
can be regarded as a continuation of *The Gospel According to Luke.* This is implied in the opening sentence, addressed, as is the Gospel, to Theophilus; and there is little or no doubt among scholars that the author is the
Luke of the Gospel.

Acts begins with the ascension of Jesus Christ to
heaven and the formation of the church in Jerusalem.
From there, Christianity is preached abroad by various
ministers. In the early part of the story the dominant
figure is Saint Peter. The second half of the work, however, becomes almost exclusively the tale of Saint Paul:
his missions to the Greek cities of the Roman Empire
(the Gentiles), the oppositions he encountered, his arrest
in Jerusalem, and his arrival in Rome. Not long after that
arrival, Luke somewhat abruptly (as it seems to me) ends
his story. Paul spent some time as a prisoner in Rome.
He is usually thought to have been martyred during the
persecutions of Christians when Nero was Emperor, per-

haps in A.D. 64, or on an individual charge before that, but the evidence is not conclusive.

Acts is usually dated with and immediately after *Luke*, about A.D. 85. That would put it considerably later than Paul's own writings. Still, it is useful to read it first, so as to have a more or less continuous background for Paul's letters.

These, the Epistles of Paul as they are canonically called, are his letters to various Christian communities or churches. They sometimes address themselves to particular problems, but also set forth, again and again, Paul's own theological doctrines and his principles for Christian behavior. There are also four letters to individuals.

For the letters of Paul I have followed a traditional order, but a better sense of time would be gained by reading them in some such order as this: First, letters written before the journey to Rome: *First* and *Second Thessalonians, Galatians, First* and *Second Corinthians, Romans;* and then the letters from Rome: *Colossians* (with *Philemon,* to a member of that community), *Ephesians,* and *Philippians.*

The two letters to Timothy and the one to Titus are commonly grouped together and known as the *Pastoral Letters.* Timothy and Titus are well known as associates of Paul, and the letters bear his characteristic self-identification at the beginning. But their authenticity has been seriously questioned. The style and language differ in places from what is characteristic of Paul's other writing, while the three do resemble one another in those respects. *First Timothy* and *Titus* speak of the institution of bishops and elders, which seems to point to a later stage in the development of the Church.

The Letter to the Hebrews is included with the letters of Paul, but the name of Paul does not appear in the text. There have been many speculations about date and authorship, but no final answer (except, perhaps, that it is not by Paul).

Next comes the group known as *The General Letters* (or *Catholic Epistles, Epistoloi Katholikoi*). The name signifies that they are addressed (most of them at least) to the whole Christian community rather than to separate churches, as Paul's letters were. *The Letter of James* is believed by some to be the work of James the brother of Jesus Christ, one of the chief men in the original church in Jerusalem. *The First Letter of Peter* is often credited to the great apostle himself. Not so *The Second Letter of Peter*, which has close affinities with *The Letter of Jude*. This, in turn, may just possibly be from the hand of the Jude (Judah, Judas) who was also a brother of Jesus Christ. As for the three letters ascribed to John, the second two are brief real letters apparently by the same writer. The *First Letter of John*, though it, too, may be by the same author, is quite different. It is a tract or homily, which shows strong resemblances to the Fourth Gospel, and is thought by some to be the work of the same John. Not one of these attributions can be called certain.

The Revelation of John concludes the New Testament. I published my translation of this along with *The Four Gospels*.

In general, I have translated *Acts and Letters* as a companion piece to *The Four Gospels*, following the same principle of trying to let the authors of the Greek speak for themselves in English. In the case of Saint Paul, that has not always been so easy.

I have also made far greater use of the great dictionary which can be cited, briefly, as W. F. Arndt and F. W. Gingrich (and now F. W. Danker), *A Greek-English Lexicon of the New Testament and other Early Christian Literature,* 2nd edition (Chicago and London: University of Chicago Press, 1958).

ACTS

The Acts
of the Apostles

¶THE FIRST BOOK I WROTE, O THEOPH-
ilus, was about all the acts and teachings of Jesus until
that day when, after giving instructions through the Holy
Spirit to the apostles whom he had chosen, he was taken
aloft. It was to these that he showed himself after his
ordeal with many proofs that he was alive, and for forty
days he would appear to them and tell them about the
Kingdom of God. And while he was staying with them
he told them not to remove from Jerusalem, but said:
Await my father's promise which you have heard of from
me; because John baptized with water, but after not many
days you will be baptized with the Holy Spirit. So those
who were with him questioned him, saying: Lord, are
you restoring the Kingdom of Israel in this time? He said
to them: It is not yours to know the times and occasions
which the Father has appointed by his own authority;
but when the Holy Spirit comes upon you, you will be
given power, and you will be my witnesses in Jerusalem
and all Judaea and Samaria and as far as the end of the
earth. When he had said this and as they watched he was
raised aloft and a cloud hid him from their eyes. And as
they stared into heaven where he went, behold, two men

clothed in white stood near them and said: You men of Galilee, why do you stand there looking toward heaven? This same Jesus who was taken up from you to heaven will come back in the same way that you saw him going to heaven. Then they returned to Jerusalem from the hill which is called the Mount of Olives; it is near Jerusalem, a sabbath's walk away. And when they were indoors, they went to the upper story where they were staying. They were Peter and John and James and Andrew, Philip and Thomas, Bartholomew and Matthew, James the son of Alphaeus and Simon the zealot and Judas the son of James. All these together were devoting themselves to prayer, along with some women, and Mary the mother of Jesus, and his brothers.

On one of those days Peter stood up in the midst of the brothers. There was a crowd of about a hundred and twenty persons assembled. And Peter said: Men and brothers, the scripture was bound to be fulfilled which the Holy Spirit gave us as prophecy through the mouth of David, concerning Judas, who acted as guide for the men who seized Jesus. For he was numbered among us and had his share of this ministry. Judas bought a piece of property with the money he got for his crime, and there he fell on his face and burst open in the middle and all his bowels spilled out of him. This became known to all who live in Jerusalem, so that that property is called in their language *Akeldamach*, which means the Field of Blood. For it is written in the Book of Psalms: May his dwelling place be desolate, and may there be no one living in it; and again: Let someone else take over his office. Therefore, out of those men who were with us in all the time when the Lord Jesus came and went among us, beginning from his baptism by John until the day when he was taken aloft from us, out of all these men one should join us as witness to his resurrection. Then they put forward two men, Joseph called Barsabbas, who was surnamed Justus, and Matthias. Then they spoke, praying: Lord, you who know the hearts of all, show us which one of these two you have chosen to take the place in this ministry and mission which Judas forsook for his own place. And they gave them the lots, and the lot fell on Matthias, and he was added by vote to the eleven apostles.

¶ Now as the day of Pentecost had come, they were all together in one place; and suddenly there came from the sky a noise like the blowing of a great wind, and it filled all the house where they were sitting. And they saw what was like separate tongues of fire, and one settled on each of them, and they were all filled with the Holy Spirit, and they began to speak in different languages according as the Spirit gave each one the gift of speaking them.

Now there were Jews living in Jerusalem who were devout men from every nation under heaven; and at the sound of these voices the crowd came together, and they were confused, because each one heard them speaking in his own language; and they were full of astonishment and wonder, and said: See, are not all these speakers Galileans? And how is it that each of us hears them speaking in the language he was born to? Parthians and Medes and Elamites, and inhabitants of Mesopotamia, Judaea and Cappadocia, Pontus and Asia, Phrygia and Pamphylia, Egypt and the parts of Libya by Cyrene; and the Romans who are here in town, Jews and proselytes, Cretans and Arabs: we all hear them speaking in our own languages of the greatness of God. They were astonished and puzzled and said, one to another: What can this mean? But others scoffed and said: They are drunk on new wine.

But Peter stood forth with the eleven and raised his voice and said to them: Men, Jews and all who live in Jerusalem, let this be understood by you and listen to my words. These men are not drunk as you suppose, for it is only the third hour of the day, but this is what was spoken of by the prophet Joel: And it will come about in the final days, says God, that I will inspire all flesh with my spirit, and your sons and your daughters will prophesy, and your young men will see visions, and your old men will dream dreams; and in those days I will inspire my slaves and my slave women with something of my spirit, and they will prophesy. And I will present portents in the sky above, and signs upon the earth below, blood and fire and clouds of smoke. The sun will turn to darkness and the moon to blood before the coming of the day of the Lord, the great and glorious day. And it will come about that everyone who calls upon the name of the Lord will be saved.

Men of Israel, listen to these words. There was Jesus of Nazareth, a man attested to you by God through powers and portents and the miracles God wrought through him in your presence, as you yourselves know. This man was delivered up by the definite plan and purpose of God, and you nailed him to the cross by the hands of heathen men, and killed him. But God destroyed the pangs of death and resurrected him, because it was not possible for him to be overcome by death. For David says, meaning him: Throughout all I see the Lord close by me, since he is on my right to keep me unshaken. Therefore my heart is gladdened and my tongue rejoices, and my flesh will still live with hope; because you will not abandon my soul to Hades, nor make him who is sacred to you look upon destruction. You have made me know the ways of life, and with your countenance will fill me with gladness.

Men and brothers, it is possible to speak confidently about the patriarch David because he did die and was buried and his tomb is with us, down to the present day. He was a prophet, and knew that God had sworn to him an oath that he would seat upon his throne one sprung from the issue of his loins; and he said with foreknowledge of the resurrection of the Christ that he was not abandoned to Hades, and that his flesh knew no corruption. God resurrected this Jesus; to that we are all witnesses. And raised to the right hand of God, and having received the promise of the Holy Spirit from his father, he inspired this which you see and hear. For David did not go up to heaven; he himself says: The Lord said to my Lord: Sit on my right, so that I may make your enemies a footstool for your feet. Then let every house in Israel know for sure that God made him Lord and Christ, this Jesus whom you crucified.

When they heard it they were stricken to the heart, and they said to Peter and the rest of the apostles: Men and brothers, what shall we do? Peter said to them: Repent, and let each one of you be baptized in the name of Jesus Christ for the remission of your sins, and you will receive the gift of the Holy Spirit; since for you is the promise, and for your children and for all those far away whom the Lord our God summons to him.

And in many more words he charged them and exhorted them, saying: Be saved from this crooked generation. And those who accepted his word were baptized, and something like three thousand souls were brought over on that day. And they held fast to the teaching of the apostles, their life in common, their breaking of bread, and their prayers. And there was fear in every soul, and many portentous things and miracles were wrought by the apostles. And all those who believed had everything in one place and in common, and they sold their property and belongings and shared all as each one might have need; and every day they would attend at the temple together, and break their bread at home, and share their food in cheerfulness and innocence of heart, praising God and in favor with the whole population. And every day the Lord added more who were saved to their number.

¶ Peter and John went up to the temple at the hour for prayer, the ninth hour; and there was a man being carried there who had been lame from his mother's womb. Every day they would lay him down by the gate of the temple which is called the Beautiful Gate, to beg for charity from the people going into the temple. When this man saw Peter and John about to enter the temple, he asked for charity. Peter, together with John, stared at him and said: Look at us. The man turned toward them, expecting to get something from them. But Peter said: I have no silver or gold. But what I do have, I give you. In the name of Jesus Christ of Nazareth, walk. And he gripped him by the right hand and pulled him up; and suddenly his feet and his ankles became strong, and he sprang up and stood and walked, and went into the temple with them, walking and bounding and praising God. And all the people saw him walking and praising God, and they knew that this was the man who had sat begging by the Beautiful Gate of the temple, and they were filled with wonder and amazement at what had happened to him.

As he clung to Peter and John, all the people, in wonderment, ran up to them at the porch which is called the Porch of Solomon. When Peter saw them he spoke forth to the people, saying: Men of Israel, why do you wonder at this? Or why do you stare at us as if by our own power or piety we had made this man walk? The God of Abraham and Isaac and Jacob, the God of our fathers, glorified his son Jesus, whom you betrayed and denied before Pilate, when Pilate judged that he should be released; but you denied the holy and righteous man, and demanded that a murderer be given you as your gift; and you killed the author of life, whom God raised from the dead. To this we are witnesses. And by faith in his name, his name gave strength to this man whom you see before your eyes, and the faith, through him, gave this man full health in the sight of you all.

Now I know, brothers, that you acted in ignorance, and so did your leaders; but God thus fulfilled the sufferings of his Christ which he had foretold through the mouths of all the prophets. Repent, therefore, and turn yourselves to wiping out your sins, so that times may come for relief from the face of the Lord and for him to send Jesus, appointed to be your Christ, whom heaven must receive until the time of the restoration of all things, time of which God has spoken from eternity through the mouths of his holy prophets. Moses said: The Lord God will raise up a prophet from among your brothers; as he did me. Listen to everything he says to you.

And every soul which does not listen to that prophet

shall be eradicated from the people. And all the prophets who have spoken, from Samuel and his successors, have predicted these days. You are the sons of the prophets and of the covenant which God made with your fathers, saying to Abraham: And in your seed all the nations of the earth shall be blessed. It was for you first that God raised up his son and sent him to you to bless you by turning each one of you away from his wickedness.

¶ As they were speaking to the people, the high priests and the captain of the temple and the Sadducees were upon them, angry because they were teaching the people and announcing in the name of Jesus the resurrection from the dead; and they laid hands on them and put them in prison until the next day, since it was now evening. But many of those who had heard the word believed, and the number of these men came to about five thousand.

And it happened that on the next morning the chief men and the elders and the scribes assembled in Jerusalem; and also Annas the high priest, and Caiaphas and John and Alexander and all who were of the high priest's family; and they stood them in their midst and questioned them, saying: By what power and in what name have you done this? Then Peter, filled with the Holy Spirit, said to them: Chief men of the people and elders, if, in the matter of helping a sick man, we are being asked today by whom he has been saved, let it be known to you all and to all the people of Israel that it was in the name of Jesus Christ of Nazareth, whom you crucified, whom God raised from the dead; it is through him that this man stands before you, a healthy man. He is the stone that was despised by you, the builders, which has come to be at the head of the corner. And salvation is not in anyone else, for there is no other name given to men under heaven by which we must be saved.

And seeing the boldness of Peter and John, and realizing that they were plain, unlettered men, they marveled, and they knew that they had been with Jesus, and when they saw the man standing with them, healed, they had nothing to say in reply. So they told them to leave the council, and they consulted together, saying: What shall we do with these men? Since a proved miracle has been done by them which is plain to all who live in Jerusalem, and we cannot deny it; but to keep this from being spread about further among the people, let us order them under threat to say no more to anyone in this name. Then they called them back in and ordered them absolutely not to speak and not to teach in the name of Jesus. But Peter and John answered and said to them: Judge whether it is right before God to listen to you rather than to God; since we are not able to keep from speaking of what we have seen and heard. They threatened them and let them go without finding any way to punish them, because of the people, since all were glorifying God over what had happened; for the man whom this miracle of healing had befallen was over forty years old.

When they were let go they went back to their own people and reported to them what the high priests and the elders had said. When they heard, of one accord they raised their voices to God and said: Lord, you who made the sky and the earth and the sea and all things that are in them, you said through the Holy Spirit by the mouth of David, our father and your servant: Why were the nations enraged and the peoples full of vain designs? The kings of the earth came on, and their leaders were gathered together against the Lord and against his Christ. For in truth in this city there were gathered against your holy son Jesus, whom you anointed, Herod and Pontius Pilate with the nations and peoples of Israel, to do what your hand and your will had foreordained to be done. And now, Lord, take note of their threats and grant to your slaves that they may speak your word with freedom, through your stretching out your hand to make healing and miracles and portents take place through the name of your holy son Jesus. And when they prayed, the place in which they were assembled was shaken, and they were all filled with the Holy Spirit and spoke the word of God with freedom.

There was one heart and one spirit in the whole body of the believers, nor did any one of them call any of his possessions his own, but they had everything in common. And with great force the apostles bore witness to the resurrection of the Lord Jesus, and there was great good will among them all. Nor was anyone among them in need, for all those who happened to own lands or houses would sell them and bring in the proceeds of what had been sold and lay them at the feet of the apostles; and they were distributed, to each one as he had need. And there was Joseph, surnamed by the apostles Barnabas, which means, translated, Son of Consolation, a Levite and a Cyprian by birth, who owned an estate. He sold it, and brought the money and laid it at the feet of the apostles.

¶ But a certain man, Ananias by name, whose wife was Sapphira, sold some property but, with the connivance of his wife, withheld some of the proceeds and brought only a part and laid it at the feet of the apostles. But Peter said to Ananias: Why was it that Satan put it into your heart to lie to the Holy Spirit and withhold some of the proceeds from the property? If you had let it remain, would it not have remained yours and, even when sold, still been at your disposal? Why did you let this deed be put in your heart? You lied, not to men but to God. When Ananias heard these words he fell down and died; and great fear came upon all those who heard. Then the younger men rose up and covered him and carried him out and buried him. There was an interval of about three hours and his wife came in, not knowing what had happened. Peter said to her: Tell me, was this the amount for which you sold the property? She said: Yes, this amount. Peter said to her: Why did you both agree to make trial of the Spirit of the Lord? See! The feet of those who buried your husband are at the door; and they will carry you out. And immediately she fell at his feet and died; and the young men came in and found her dead, and they carried her out and buried her by her husband. And great fear came upon the whole congregation and on all who heard about these things.

And many miracles and portentous things were wrought among the people by the hands of the apostles. And they all kept gathering in the Porch of Solomon; but none of the other people dared try to join their number, but the people thought them very great, and more and more a multitude of men and women came over to the Lord, believing in him; so that they even carried their sick out into the streets and set them there on cots and beds so that Peter's shadow at least might fall on them as he went by. And also a multitude from the cities round about Jerusalem gathered there, bringing their sick and those troubled by unclean spirits; and they were all healed.

Then the high priest and all who were with him, that
is, the sect of Sadducees, rose up and were filled with
jealousy and laid hands on the apostles and put them in
the public prison. But an angel of the Lord opened the
doors of the prison by night, and as he led them out he
said: Go and stand in the temple and tell the people all
the words of this life. When they heard this they went
into the temple at dawn and began teaching. But the high
priest and those with him came and called together the
council and the whole board of elders of the sons of Israel, and sent to the prison to fetch them. But when the
servingmen arrived, they did not find them in the prison,
and came back and reported, saying: We found the prison
locked quite securely and the guards standing at the
doors, and we opened them and found no one inside.
When the captain of the temple and the high priest heard
these words they were puzzled about them, as to how
this could be. But a man arrived and told them: See, the
men you put in prison are standing in the temple and
teaching the people. Then the captain went with his
servingmen and took them, not forcibly, for they were
afraid of the people and that they might be stoned, and
they brought them and stood them before the council.
And the high priest questioned them, saying: We gave
you a formal order not to teach in this name, and see,
you have filled Jerusalem with your teaching; and you
want to put the blood of that man upon us. Peter and
the apostles answered and said: We must obey God rather
than men. The God of our fathers raised Jesus, whom
you killed by hanging him on the cross. God elevated
him to his right hand as ruler and savior, to give Israel
repentance and remission of sins. And we are witnesses

to these things, we and the Holy Spirit which God gave to those who obey him.

When they heard this, they were convulsed with rage and wanted to kill them. But a certain Pharisee who was in the council, Gamaliel by name, a teacher of the law honored by all the people, stood up and urged them to have the men removed for a little while, and said to the others: Men of Israel, be careful how you go about dealing with these people. For before these days Theudas set himself up, claiming to be important, and men inclined to him to the number of about four hundred; he was killed, and all who believed in him were dispersed and came to nothing. And after him Judas of Galilee set himself up in the days of the census and won people over to his following; and he, too, was killed, and all those who believed in him were scattered. And as for now, I tell you, let these men be and release them. For if this purpose and this work come from men, they will come to nothing; but if they come from God, you will not be able to bring them to nothing. Do not be caught fighting against God.

They were persuaded by him, and they called back the apostles and had them lashed and ordered them not to speak in the name of Jesus, and released them. And they went away from the presence of the council rejoicing because they had been found worthy to suffer outrage for the sake of the name; and every day, in the temple and at home, they never stopped teaching and preaching the Christ, Jesus.

¶ During those days, as the number of disciples grew, loud complaints developed from the Hellenists against the Hebrews, that in the daily distribution the widows among their number were being overlooked. Then the twelve summoned the general body of disciples and said: It is not to our liking that we should neglect the word of God in order to see to the distribution of food. But, brothers, select from among yourselves seven men who are well recommended and who are full of the Spirit and wisdom, whom we shall put in charge of this service; and we shall devote ourselves to prayer and the ministry of the word. And this word was pleasing to all the people, and they chose Stephen, a man filled with faith and the Holy Spirit, and Philip and Prochorus and Nicanor and Timon and Parmenas and Nicolaus, a proselyte from Antioch, and these they set before the apostles, who said a prayer and laid their hands on them.

And the word of God increased, and the number of disciples in Jerusalem grew greatly, and a great number of the priests submitted to the faith.

And Stephen, filled with grace and power, accomplished portentous things and miracles among the people. But some people from the synagogue which is called that of the freedmen, and some of the Cyreneans and Alexandrians, and some from Cilicia and Asia, set themselves up against Stephen and disputed with him, but they were not able to stand up against the wisdom and spirit with which he spoke. Then they suborned certain men, who said: We have heard him speaking blasphemous words against Moses and God. And they stirred up the people and the elders and the scribes, and they set upon him and seized him and brought him before the council, and they set up false witnesses who said: This fellow never stops speaking against this holy place and the law, for we have heard him say that Jesus of Nazareth will destroy this place and change the customs which Moses handed down to us. And all who were sitting in the council stared at him and saw his face, which was like the face of an angel.

¶ Then the high priest said: Is this so? He replied: Men, my brothers and fathers, listen. The God of glory appeared to our forefather Abraham when he was in Mesopotamia, before he settled in Harran; and God said to him: Go out from your own country and your own people and come here to a country which I will show you. Then he left the country of the Chaldeans and settled in Harran. And from there, after his father died, God moved him to this land where you now live; and he did not give him any property in it, not one foot of land; but he promised to give it into his possession and to his seed after him. He had then no child. And God spoke to him thus, saying that his descendants would be alien in the land of others, and these would enslave them and afflict them for four hundred years. And I, he said, will judge that nation whom they will serve as slaves, and after that they will go from it and serve me in this place. And he gave him the covenant of the circumcision; and thus Abraham begot Isaac and circumcised him on the eighth day, as did Isaac to Jacob and Jacob to the twelve patriarchs.

The patriarchs were jealous of Joseph and sold him into Egypt; but God was with him and rescued him from all his afflictions, and gave him favor and wisdom in the eyes of Pharaoh the King of Egypt; and Pharaoh established him as governor over Egypt and all his household.

But there came a famine in all of Egypt and Canaan, and great affliction, and our fathers could find no food.

But Jacob, hearing that there was food in Egypt, sent our fathers on their first visit; and on the second visit Joseph was recognized by his brothers, and the origin of Joseph was made known to Pharaoh. And Joseph sent and summoned Jacob his father and all his family, some seventy-five souls, and Jacob went to Egypt. And he died, and so did our fathers, and they were transported to Shechem and buried in the tomb which Abraham had bought for a sum of silver from the sons of Hamor in Shechem.

When the time drew near for the promise which God had agreed to with Abraham, his people in Egypt increased and multiplied, until another king was set over Egypt, one who had not known Joseph. This one contrived against our people and did evil to our fathers by causing their babies to be exposed so that they should not survive. In this time Moses was born, and he was pleasing to God. He was reared for three months in the house of his father; and when he was exposed, the daughter of Pharaoh took him up and raised him as her own son. And Moses was educated in all the wisdom of the Egyptians, and he was powerful, in words and actions.

And when he was fully forty years old, it came into his heart to visit his brothers, the sons of Israel. And when he saw one of them being injuriously treated he came to the defense of the man abused, by striking the Egyptian down. He thought that his brothers understood that God through his hand was rescuing them; but they did not understand. And the next day he appeared to them as they were fighting each other, and he tried to reconcile them and make peace, saying: Sirs, you are brothers. Why are you injuring each other? But the man who had been injuring his neighbor thrust him away, saying: Who set you up as leader and judge over us? Could it be that

you want to kill me the way you killed the Egyptian yesterday?

At that word Moses went into exile and lived as an
alien in Midian, where he had two sons. And when forty
years had passed, an angel appeared to him in the desert
of Mount Sinai, in the flame of the burning bush. When
Moses saw him he wondered at the vision, but as he approached to look, there came the voice of the Lord: I am
the God of your fathers, the God of Abraham and Isaac
and Jacob. Moses trembled and did not dare look; but the
Lord said to him: Take off your shoes from your feet, for
the place where you stand is holy. I looked and saw the
evil done to my people in Egypt, and I heard their groan-
ing, and I came down to bring them out; and now, come,
I send you back to Egypt.

This was that Moses whom they had denied, saying:
Who set you up as leader and judge? This was he whom
God sent as leader and deliverer, helped by the hand of
the angel who appeared to him at the bush. He led them
out, after accomplishing portentous things and miracles
in Egypt and in the Red Sea and in the desert for forty
years. This is the Moses who said to the sons of Israel:
God will raise up a prophet for you from among your
brothers; as he did me. This is he who was in the congregation in the desert, with the angel who talked with
him on Mount Sinai and with our fathers.

He received living oracles to give you. But our fathers
would not obey him, but they thrust him away and
turned in their hearts toward Egypt, saying to Aaron:
Make us gods who will go before us; for as for this Moses
who led us out of Egypt, we do not know what became
of him. And they made the calf in those days, and they
sacrificed to the idol, and they were pleased with the

[19]

work of their hands. But God turned them about and committed them to the worship of the host of the sky, as it is written in the book of the prophets: House of Israel, did you bring me victims and sacrifices for forty years in the desert? No, but you took up the tabernacle of Moloch, and the star of the god Rhompha, the figures you made, to worship them. And I will move you beyond Babylon.

Our fathers had the tabernacle of testimony in the desert, as he who talked with Moses told him to make it in the image of what he had seen; and our fathers inherited it and also brought it here when with Joshua they dispossessed the Gentiles, whom God drove from the sight of our fathers. Until the days of David; and David found favor in the eyes of God and asked leave to devise a tabernacle for the God of Jacob. But Solomon built him a house. But the Highest does not live in what has been made by hands; as the prophet says: Heaven is my throne, and the earth is a footstool for my feet; what kind of house will you build for me, says the Lord, or what place will be my resting place? Did not my hand make all these things?

Stiff-necked, like the uncircumcised in your hearts and ears, you struggle always against the Holy Spirit. As your fathers did, so do you. Which one of the prophets did your fathers not drive out? And they killed those who foretold the coming of the righteous one whose betrayers and murderers you are now shown to be. You received the law on the orders of angels, and you did not keep it.

When they heard this they were convulsed with rage in their hearts and gnashed their teeth at him. But, filled with the Holy Spirit, he gazed into the sky and saw the glory of God, and Jesus standing on the right hand of

God, and he said: See, I behold the heavens opened and the son of man standing on the right hand of God. They cried aloud in a great voice and covered their ears, and they made a concerted rush at him and threw him out of the city and began to stone him. And the witnesses laid their coats at the feet of a young man named Saul. And they stoned Stephen as he made his invocation and said: Lord Jesus, receive my spirit. Then he fell on his knees and cried out in a great voice: Lord, do not hold this sin against them. And as he said this, he fell asleep.

¶ And Saul approved of their killing him.

And on that day a great persecution began against the church in Jerusalem; and all, except the apostles, were scattered about the countryside of Judaea and Samaria. Certain devout men buried Stephen and made a great lament over him. But Saul continued to outrage the church, breaking into houses, dragging out men and women, and sending them to prison.

Those who had been scattered went about proclaiming the word of the gospel. Philip went to the city of Samaria and preached the Christ to the people. And the masses followed the sayings of Philip with enthusiasm as they listened to him and saw what miracles he was working. For many who had unclean spirits were relieved of them, crying aloud as they went, and many who were paralysed and many who were lame were made whole. And there was great joy in that city.

But a certain man named Simon had been in the city before Philip, practicing sorcery and astonishing the people of Samaria, claiming to be a great man, and all followed him, from the small to the great, saying: This is the power of God which is called great. They followed him because for some time he had been astonishing them with his sorceries. But when they believed Philip as he preached the gospel of the Kingdom of God and the name of Jesus Christ, they were baptized, both men and women. And Simon himself believed, and when he was baptized he attached himself to Philip, and when he saw the miracles and great powers that were shown, he was astonished.

The apostles in Jerusalem, hearing that Samaria had accepted the word of God, sent Peter and John to them. When these arrived, they prayed for their sake that they might receive the Holy Spirit. For this had not yet come to any of them, but they had been baptized only in the name of the Lord Jesus. Then they laid their hands upon them and they received the Holy Spirit. When Simon saw that the Holy Spirit was given by the laying on of the hands of the apostles, he brought them money, saying: Give me also this power, so that anyone on whom I lay my hands may receive the Holy Spirit. But Peter said to him: May your silver go to perdition and you along with it, since you thought you could buy the gift of God for money. You have no part or rightful share in this word, since your heart is not straightforward in the sight of God. Then repent of this baseness and beg of the Lord that the intention of your heart will be forgiven; for I see that you are in the gall of bitterness and the bondage of unrighteousness. Simon answered and said: Yourselves pray to the Lord for my sake, that nothing of what you have spoken of will happen to me.

They then, bearing witness and speaking the word of the Lord, turned back toward Jerusalem, and they brought the gospel to many villages of the Samaritans.

An angel of the Lord spoke to Philip, saying: Rise up and go south to the road that comes down from Jerusalem to Gaza. This is desert. And he rose up and went on his way, and behold, there was an Ethiopian man, a eunuch, influential with Candace the Queen of the Ethiopians, who was in charge of all her treasure. He had come to worship in Jerusalem, and now he was on his way back, sitting in his carriage and reading the prophet Isaiah. And the Spirit said to Philip: Go and attach yourself to that carriage. Then Philip ran up to him, and he heard him reading the prophet Isaiah aloud, and said: Do you understand what you are reading? He answered: Why, how could I be able to, unless someone were to guide me? And he invited Philip to mount up and sit by him. And this is the passage of scripture which he had been reading: He was led like a sheep to slaughter, and as a lamb is speechless before his shearer, even so he does not open his mouth. He was condemned to humiliation. Who can tell of his posterity? His life is taken off the earth.

And the eunuch spoke forth and said: Please tell me, about whom does the prophet say this? About himself or someone else? Then Philip opened his mouth and, beginning from this scripture, told him the whole gospel of Jesus. And as they went on along the road they came to some water, and the eunuch said: See, water. What prevents me from being baptized? So he ordered the carriage to stop, and both of them, Philip and the eunuch, went into the water, and Philip baptized him. But when they came out of the water, the Spirit of the Lord caught Philip up and away, and the eunuch did not see him any more, for he was continuing on his way, rejoicing. But Philip found himself in Ashdod, and he brought the gospel to all the cities as he passed through until he came to Caesarea.

¶ But Saul, still breathing threats and slaughter against the disciples of the Lord, went to the high priest and asked him for letters to the synagogues in Damascus, so that if he could find any disciples of the Way, man or woman, he could bring them in bonds to Jerusalem. And on his journey it befell him that he was approaching Damascus, and suddenly there was a flash of light from the sky around him, and he fell to the ground and heard a voice saying to him: Saul, Saul, why do you persecute me? And he said: Who are you, Lord? And he said: I am Jesus; whom you persecute. But rise up and go into the city, and you will be told what you must do. And the men who were traveling with him had been standing there speechless; they heard the voice but they saw no one. Saul got up from the ground but when his eyes were opened he could see nothing, and they led him by the hand and brought him into Damascus. And he was three days without seeing, and he ate nothing and drank nothing.

There was a disciple in Damascus named Ananias, and the Lord said to him in a vision: Ananias. And he said: Here I am, Lord. The Lord said to him: Rise up and go to the street which is called Straight and look in the house of Judas for one, Saul by name, from Tarsus; for behold, he is praying, and he saw in a vision a man named Ananias coming in and laying his hands upon him, to make him see again. But Ananias answered: Lord, I have heard from many people about this man, and all the evil things he has done to your saints in Jerusalem; and he has such authority from the high priests that he can imprison all who call upon your name. The Lord said to him: Go on, because this man is my chosen instrument to carry my name before the nations and the Kings and sons of Israel, for I will show him all that he must suffer for the sake of my name. So Ananias went off and entered the house, and laid his hands upon him and said: Brother Saul, the Lord has sent me; Jesus, who appeared to you on the road where you were going; so that you may see again and be filled with the Holy Spirit. And immediately there fell from his eyes what was like scales, and he saw again, and rose up and was baptized; and when he had taken some nourishment, he got his strength.

He was with the disciples in Damascus for some days; and immediately he began proclaiming Jesus in the synagogues, and saying that he was the son of God. And all who heard were startled and said: Is not this the man who in Jerusalem preyed on those who called upon that name, and did he not come here to bring them in bonds before the high priests? But Saul grew all the stronger and confounded the Jews who lived in Damascus, demonstrating that this was the Christ. And after a number of days had passed, the Jews plotted to kill him; but their plot was made known to Saul. They were watching the gates, night and day, to kill him; but his disciples got him across the wall at night and eased him down in a basket.

Arriving in Jerusalem, he tried to attach himself to the disciples, but all were afraid of him, not believing that he was a disciple. But Barnabas took him by the hand and led him before the apostles and told them how he had seen the Lord on the road and talked with him, and how he had spoken out in Damascus in the name of Jesus. And he was with them, going in and out of Jerusalem, and speaking out in the name of the Lord; and he spoke and argued against the Hellenists. These were trying to kill him; but when the brothers learned of this, they got him down to Caesarea and sent him off to Tarsus.

So now in all Judaea and Galilee and Samaria the church had peace and was building up, and proceeding in the fear of the Lord, and the comforting of the Holy Spirit, it increased.

It happened that Peter traveled about among them all and came to the saints who lived in Lydda. And there he found a man named Aeneas who had been lying in bed for eight years. He was paralysed. And Peter said to him: Aeneas, Jesus Christ heals you. Get up and make your bed. And at once he stood up. And all those saw him who lived in Lydda and Sharon, those who had turned to the Lord.

In Joppa there was a disciple named Tabitha, which translated means Dorcas. She was full of good works and the acts of charity which she did. And it happened that in those days she fell sick and died; and they washed her and laid her out in an upper room. Lydda is close to Joppa, and the disciples, hearing that Peter was there, sent two men to him who said to him in entreaty: Do not hesitate, come to us. Peter rose up and went with them; and when he arrived they took him to the upper room, and all the widows came to him, weeping and displaying the tunics and mantles which Dorcas had made when she was with them. Peter put everyone out and went on his knees and prayed and turned to the body and said: Tabitha, rise up. She opened her eyes and when she saw Peter she sat up. He gave her his hand and raised her up, and called to the saints and the widows and set her before them, alive. This became known throughout Joppa, and many believed in the Lord. And it happened that he stayed for some days in Joppa with a certain Simon, a tanner.

¶ There was a man in Caesarea named Cornelius, a centurion of the cohort called the Italian cohort; a pious man who feared God, together with all his household, who did many acts of charity for the people and prayed to God in everything he did. In a vision about the ninth hour he saw plainly an angel of God who came into his house and said to him: Cornelius. He gazed at him and was full of fear and said to him: What is it, Lord? He said to him: Your prayers and your acts of charity have gone up and come to the attention of God. Now send men to Joppa, and invite a man named Simon, surnamed Peter; he is the guest of Simon the tanner, whose house is by the sea. And when the angel who spoke to him left him, he called in two of his servants, and a pious soldier out of those who were under his command, and told them everything and sent them to Joppa.

On the next day, as these men were on their way and approaching the city, Peter went up to the roof to pray at about the sixth hour. And he was hungry and wished to eat; and as people were preparing something for him, a trance came over him, and he saw the sky opened, and coming down from it an arrangement that was like a great sheet let down by its four corners upon the earth; and on it were all the four-footed beasts and creeping things of the earth, and the birds of the sky. And a voice came to him: Rise up, Peter; kill, and eat. But Peter said: Surely not, Lord; since I have never eaten anything profane and unclean. And the voice spoke to him again: What God has made clean do not you make profane. This happened three times; and immediately the arrangement was taken back up into the sky.

As Peter was wondering to himself over the meaning of the vision he had seen, behold, the men sent by Cornelius had found their way to the house of Simon and stood before the gate, and called out to ask whether Simon, surnamed Peter, were a guest there. And as Peter was still pondering his vision the Spirit said: Behold, here are three men looking for you; rise, and go down, and go along with them without hesitation; because I sent them. Peter came down to the men and said: Here I am, the one you were looking for. What is the reason for your being here? They said: Cornelius the centurion, a man who is righteous and fears God, as is attested by all the Jewish people, was told by a holy angel to invite you to his house and listen to what you have to say. So Peter asked them in and made them his guests.

On the next day he rose up and went with them, and some of the brothers from Joppa went with him. And on the day after that he entered Caesarea; and Cornelius was expecting them and had called in all his relatives and his close friends. And at the time when Peter entered, Cornelius went to meet him and threw himself at his feet and did obeisance to him. But Peter raised him and said: Stand up. I myself am also a man. And he went inside, talking with him, and found many gathered together, and said to them: You understand that it is not lawful for a Jewish man to approach or mingle with an alien. But God has shown me that I must not call any person profane or unclean. Therefore I came without objection when I was invited. So I ask, for what reason did you invite me? And Cornelius said: Four days before this time I was praying at the ninth hour in my house, and behold, a man stood before me in shining clothes, and said: Cornelius, your prayer has been heard and your acts of charity have come to the attention of God. Send therefore to Joppa and invite Simon, who is surnamed Peter; he is the guest of Simon the tanner, by the sea. So I sent men to you at once, and you have been kind enough to come. Here then we are all gathered in the sight of God to hear all that the Lord has commanded you to say.

Then Peter opened his mouth and said: I understand the truth, that God has no favorites, but in any nation he who fears him and practices righteousness is acceptable to him. He sent out the word to the sons of Israel, bringing the gospel of peace through Jesus Christ. He is the Lord of all. You know the word that went through all Judaea, beginning from Galilee after the baptism which John preached: Jesus, from Nazareth, when God anointed him with the Holy Spirit and with power, who went about doing good and healing those who were in the power of the devil, because God was with him. And we are witnesses to all that he did in the land of the Jews and in Jerusalem. And they killed him by hanging him on the cross. God raised him on the third day and granted that he should become visible, not to all the people but to witnesses who were foreordained by God; to us, who ate and drank with him after his resurrection from the dead; and he told us to preach to the people and testify that this is the one appointed by God as judge of the living and the dead. And all the prophets testify to him, that through his name everyone who believes in him shall have forgiveness of his sins.

While Peter was still speaking these words, the Holy Spirit descended upon all who were listening to his discourse. And the faithful from among the circumcised who had come with Peter were astonished that the gift of the Holy Spirit had been diffused upon the Gentiles also; for they heard them speaking with tongues and glorifying God. Then Peter spoke forth: Surely no one can forbid the water for the baptism of those who have received the Holy Spirit, as we also have done. And he ordered that they should be baptized in the name of Jesus Christ. Then they asked him to stay with them for a few days.

¶ The apostles and the brothers who were in Judaea heard that the Gentiles also had received the word of God. And when Peter went up to Jerusalem, the circumcised took issue with him, saying that he had visited uncircumcised men and eaten with them. But Peter explained everything in order from the beginning, saying: I was in the city of Joppa, praying, and in a trance I saw a vision: an arrangement like a great sheet let down by its four corners from the sky, and it came close to me. And I gazed at it and studied it, and I saw the four-footed beasts of the earth and the wild animals and the creeping things and the birds of the sky. And I heard a voice saying to me: Rise up, Peter; kill, and eat. But I said: Surely not, Lord; since nothing profane or unclean has ever entered my mouth. But the voice answered me again from the sky: What God has made clean do not you make profane. This happened three times and then everything was drawn up again into the sky. And behold, presently three men stood before the house where we were, sent to me from Caesarea; and the Spirit told me to go along with them without hesitation. These six brothers went with me and we entered the man's house. And he described to us how he had seen the angel standing in his house and saying: Send to Joppa and invite Simon, surnamed Peter, who will tell you words which will be the salvation of yourself and all your household. And as I began to speak, the Holy Spirit descended upon them as it did upon us at the outset. And I remembered the words of the Lord, how he said: John baptized in water, but you shall be baptized in the Holy Spirit. If, then, God has given them a gift equal to that which he gave us when we believed in the Lord Jesus Christ, who was I to be able to stand in the way of God?

When they heard this, they held their peace and glorified God, saying: In truth then, God has granted repentance to the Gentiles, to give them life.

Those who had been scattered abroad after the persecution that came over the matter of Stephen traveled to Phoenicia and Cyprus and Antioch, announcing the word to no one except Jews. But some of them were men from Cyprus and Cyrene, and these when they came to Antioch spoke also to the Greeks, preaching the gospel of the Lord Jesus. And the hand of the Lord was with them, and a great number believed and turned to the Lord. Word of them came to the ears of the church which was in Jerusalem, and they sent Barnabas to Antioch. When he arrived and saw the grace of God there, he was filled with joy, and he urged them all to remain true to the Lord in the devotion of their hearts; since he was a good man and full of the Holy Spirit and faith. And a considerable number was brought over to the Lord. Then he went to Tarsus to look for Saul, and when he found him he brought him to Antioch. And it befell them that they met for a whole year in the church and taught a considerable number of people; and it was in Antioch that, for the first time, the disciples came to be called Christians.

In those days prophets came down from Jerusalem to Antioch; and one of them, by name Agabus, stood up and, through the Spirit, foretold that there would be a great famine over all the world. This took place in the time of Claudius. And they ordained that each of the disciples, according to his means, should send something to take care of the brothers who lived in Judaea. This they did, sending it to the elders through the agency of Barnabas and Saul.

¶ At that time Herod the King laid hands upon some members of the church to destroy them. He had James, the brother of John, killed with the sword. And seeing that this was pleasing to the Jews, he added the arrest of Peter. It was during the days of Unleavened Bread. He seized Peter and put him in prison, and gave four squads of soldiers the duty of guarding him, meaning to bring him before the people after the Passover. So Peter was kept under guard in the prison, and there was continual prayer to God from the church for his sake.

When Herod was about to produce him, Peter was sleeping that night between two soldiers, bound with two chains, and guards were keeping watch before the door. And behold, an angel of the Lord stood there, and light flashed in the cell; and he struck Peter in the side and wakened him, saying: Rise up in speed. And his chains fell off his hands. Then the angel said to him: Dress and put on your shoes. And he did so. Then he said to him: Put on your mantle and follow me. And he followed him out, and he did not know that this was really being done by the angel, but thought he was seeing a vision. They passed through the first guard and the second and came to the iron gate which leads to the city, and this opened to them of its own accord; and they went out and walked to the next street, and suddenly the angel left him. And Peter came to himself and said: Now I know that the Lord really did send his angel and rescue me from the hand of Herod and all that the Jewish people had been hoping to do against me. And when he realized this, he went to the house of Mary, the mother of John, who was surnamed Mark, where a number of people were gathered together and praying. When he knocked on the courtyard door a maid named Rhoda came to answer, and when she recognized the voice of Peter, in her joy instead of opening the door she ran inside and announced that Peter was standing before the courtyard. They said to her: You are mad; but she insisted that it was so. But they said: It is his angel. But Peter continued to knock, and when they opened they saw him and were astonished. But motioning with his hand for them to be quiet, he described to them how the Lord had led him out of the prison, and said: Report this to James and the brothers. Then he went out and removed to another place.

When day came, there was no little consternation among the soldiers over what had become of Peter. And Herod, having searched for him and not found him, interrogated the guards and ordered them to be taken away and executed, and then went down from Judaea to Caesarea and stayed there. He was furious with the Tyrians and Sidonians; but they came to him in a body, after persuading Blastus, the king's chamberlain, and sued for peace, because their country was supported from the royal territory. And on an appointed day Herod put on his royal robes and sat on the platform and made a speech to them; and the people cried aloud: The voice of God, not of man. And suddenly an angel of the Lord struck him down because he had not given the glory to God, and he was eaten by worms and died.

And the word of the Lord grew and increased.

And Barnabas and Saul returned from Jerusalem after fulfilling their mission, taking along with them John, who was surnamed Mark.

¶ At the church which was in Antioch, there were prophets and teachers, Barnabas and Simeon surnamed Niger, and Lucius of Cyrene, and Manaen, a close friend of Herod the Tetrarch, and Saul. And while they were serving the Lord and fasting, the Holy Spirit said to them: Appoint Barnabas and Saul to do for me the work I have called them to. Then after fasting and prayer and laying their hands upon them they sent them on their way.

So these men, sent forth by the Holy Spirit, arrived at Seleucia, and from there sailed to Cyprus, and in Salamis preached the word of God in the synagogues of the Jews. And they had John with them as a helper. And after traveling through the entire island as far as Paphos they found there a certain man, a magician and false prophet, a Jew, whose name was Barjesus, who was in the company of the proconsul Sergius Paulus, an intelligent man. This man invited Barnabas and Saul in and desired to hear the word of God. But the magician Elymas, for this is how his name is translated, opposed them, trying to turn the proconsul away from the faith. But Saul, who is also Paul, was filled with the Holy Spirit and stared at him and said: O full of every trick and every deception, son of the devil, enemy of everything righteous, will you not stop trying to twist the straight ways of the Lord? And now, behold, the hand of the Lord is against you, and you will be blind and not see the sunlight for a while. And immediately a mist and darkness fell upon him, and he went about looking for people to lead him by the hand. Then the proconsul, seeing what had happened and struck by the teaching of the Lord, believed.

Sailing from Paphos, Paul and his party came to Perge in Pamphylia, but John left them and returned to Jerusalem. And traveling from Perge, they arrived at the Pisidian Antioch, and entered the synagogue on the day of the sabbath and sat down. After the reading of the law and the prophets, the heads of the synagogue sent them a message saying: Men and brothers, if you have any word of exhortation before the people, speak. Then Paul stood up and gestured with his hand and said: Men of Israel, and all who fear God, listen. The God of this people, Israel, chose our fathers, and exalted their people in their stay in Egypt, and with his mighty arm he brought them out of there; and when for a period of forty years he had nursed them in the desert, then by overcoming seven nations in the land of Canaan he made that land their heritage for some four hundred and fifty years. And after that he gave them judges, until Samuel the prophet; and after that they asked for a King, and God gave them Saul the son of Kish, a man from the tribe of Benjamin, for forty years. Then putting him aside he raised up David to be their King, to whom he bore witness and said: I have found David the son of Jesse, a man after my own heart, who will carry out all my wishes.

It was from his seed, according to his promise, that he brought Israel its savior, Jesus, before the coming of whose presence John had preached the baptism of repentance to all the people of Israel. And as John ran his course, he would say: What do you suppose I am? I am not he. But behold, there is one coming after me, and I am not fit to take his shoes off his feet.

Men and brothers, sons of the stock of Abraham, and all among you who fear God, the word of this salvation was sent to us. For the dwellers in Jerusalem and their chiefs did not recognize him, and by judging him they fulfilled the utterances of the prophets which are read aloud on every sabbath; and without finding any true cause for his death they demanded that Pilate should have him killed. And when they had fulfilled everything that was written about him, they took him down from the cross and laid him in a tomb. But God raised him from the dead; and he appeared for some days to those who had come up with him from Galilee to Jerusalem, who are his witnesses before the people. And we bring you the gospel of the promise that was made to our fathers, that God has fulfilled this for us their children by resurrecting Jesus, as it is written in the Second Psalm: You are my son, this day I begot you.

And that he raised him from the dead to be one who would never more return to corruption, this he has said, thus: I will give you the sacraments of David, which are to be believed. Since in another place he says: You shall grant your holy one that he shall not know corruption. For David, after serving the will of God, in his own lifetime died and was laid beside his fathers and knew corruption, but he whom God raised did not know corruption.

Therefore let it be understood by you, men and brothers, that remission of sins through him is promised to you, and for all those matters where you could not be justified by the law of Moses, everyone who believes is justified by him. Look to it then that what was spoken of by the prophets may not come upon you: Look, you scoffers, and marvel and be brought to nothing, because in your days I will do a deed, a deed which you would not believe if someone described it to you.

When Paul and Barnabas went out, they requested that these matters should be spoken of on the next sabbath. And when the meeting broke up, many Jews and faithful proselytes followed Paul and Barnabas; and they talked to them and urged them to remain true to the grace of God. And on the next sabbath almost the entire city was gathered together to listen to the word of God. But the Jews, when they saw the crowds, were filled with envy and attacked the speeches of Paul, reviling him. But Paul and Barnabas spoke out boldly and said: It was necessary that the word of God should be told first to you; but since you reject it and judge yourselves to be unworthy of everlasting life, we are turning to the Gentiles. For thus the Lord has commanded us: I have appointed you to be the light of the Gentiles, and for you to bring salvation as far as the end of the earth. When the Gentiles heard this they were joyful and glorified the word of God, and all those who were destined to life everlasting believed; and the word of the Lord was spread through the entire country. But the Jews stirred up the prominent women who were worshippers and the foremost men of the city, and they started a persecution of Paul and Barnabas and drove them out of their territory. And they shook the dust from their feet against them and went to Iconium, and their disciples were filled with joy and the Holy Spirit.

¶ In the same way it happened in Iconium that they went into the synagogue of the Jews and spoke in such a way that a great number of Jews and Greeks believed. But the Jews who would not believe stirred up the minds of the Gentiles and poisoned them against the brothers. They spent some time there, speaking boldly, trusting in the Lord, who testified to the word of his grace by granting that miracles and portentous things should be brought about at their hands. But the population of the city was split, and some were with the Jews and some were with the apostles. But when there was a movement among the Gentiles and Jews, together with their leaders, to use violence and stone them, they got wind of it and fled to the cities of Lycaonia, Lystra and Derbe and their vicinity; and there they went on bringing the gospel.

Now there was a certain man, crippled in his feet, who sat in Lystra. He was lame from his mother's womb and had never walked. This man was listening to Paul as he spoke; and Paul gazed at him, and seeing that he had faith that he could be saved, he said in a great voice; Get on your feet and stand upright. And he sprang up and walked. And when the crowds saw what Paul had done, they cried aloud in their own Lycaonian language, saying: The gods have made themselves like men and come down to us. And they called Barnabas Zeus and Paul Hermes, because he was the chief speaker. And the priest of the Zeus whose temple was before the city brought bulls and garlands into the courtyard and, together with the crowds, wanted to sacrifice to them. When the apostles Barnabas and Paul heard of this, they tore their robes and leaped into the crowd, crying out and saying: Men, why are you doing this? We also are men who feel and suffer as you do, who are bringing you the gospel to turn you away from these idiocies, to the living God, who made the sky and the earth and the sea and all that is in them. In past ages he let all nations go their own ways; and yet he has not let himself be without proof for his good works, giving you rains from the sky and fruitful seasons, filling your hearts with sustenance and good cheer. And by saying these things they finally managed to stop the crowds from sacrificing to them.

But Jews arrived from Antioch and Iconium, and won over the masses, and stoned Paul and dragged him out of the city, believing that he was dead. But his disciples made a circle around him and he got up and went into the city. And on the next day he set out with Barnabas for Derbe. And after bringing the gospel to that city and making a number of converts they returned to Lystra and Iconium and Antioch, strengthening the spirits of the disciples, urging them to endure in their faith, and telling them that it is only through much suffering that we can enter the Kingdom of God. And they selected elders for them, church by church, and with prayer and fasting committed them to the Lord in whom they had put their faith.

Then, passing through Pisidia, they came to Pamphylia, and after preaching the word in Perga they came to the sea at Attalia and sailed from there to Antioch; from which place they had by the grace of God been appointed to the work which they had now completed. And arriving there and convening the church they reported all that God had done through them, and that he had opened the door of faith to the Gentiles. And they spent a considerable amount of time with the disciples there.

¶ Then certain men came down from Judaea and began to teach the brothers, saying: Unless you are circumcised by the rite of Moses, you cannot be saved. And when considerable dissension and debate arose between Paul and Barnabas and these men, they decreed that Paul and Barnabas and some others of their number should go up to see the apostles and elders in Jerusalem to discuss this question. So those who were sent by the church passed through Phoenicia and Samaria describing the conversion of the Gentiles, and brought great joy to all the brothers. And arriving in Jerusalem, they were received by the church and the apostles and the elders, and they reported all that God had done through them. But some believers from the sect of the Pharisees rose up, saying that they must circumcise them in order to keep the law of Moses.

The apostles and the elders assembled to look into this question. And after much discussion Peter stood up and said to them: Men and brothers, you know well that in our early days God made his choice among us that from my lips the Gentiles should hear the word of the gospel and believe; and God, who knows the heart, proved it to them by giving the Holy Spirit to them, as he did to us, and did not discriminate between us and them, purifying their hearts through faith. Why then do you make trial of God by putting on the necks of the disciples a yoke that neither our fathers nor ourselves were strong enough to bear? Rather through the grace of the Lord Jesus we believe that we are saved in the same way as they. Then all the congregation fell silent, and they listened to Barnabas and Paul describing all the portentous acts and miracles that God had worked through them among the Gentiles.

And when they had fallen silent, James answered, saying: Men and brothers, listen to me. Simon has told how the Lord was first concerned to accept a people in his name from among the Gentiles. And the words of the prophets accord with this; as it is written: After this I will return, and I will rebuild the fallen tabernacle of David and restore its ruins and raise it up again, so that the rest of mankind may seek out the Lord, and all the nations to whom my name has been spoken. Thus says the Lord, making all this known, since eternity.

Therefore I believe we should not make difficulties for those of the Gentiles who turn to God, but instruct them to abstain from the pollution of idols, and from lechery, and from what has been strangled, and from blood. For Moses has had since ancient generations those who preach him in every city, and he is read in the synagogues every sabbath.

Then the apostles and elders, together with the whole church, resolved to send men picked from among them to Antioch along with Paul and Barnabas. They were Judas, surnamed Barsabbas, and Silas, prominent men among the brothers. And they wrote a letter, for them to deliver by hand, saying: The apostles and elders, brothers, to the Gentile brothers in Antioch and Syria and Cilicia; greetings. Since we have heard that some of us have disturbed and distracted your minds by their words, without instructions from us, we have unanimously resolved to select two men and send them to you together with our beloved Barnabas and Paul, men who have risked their lives for the name of the Lord Jesus Christ. We have sent, then, Judas and Silas, who will give you the same message by word of mouth. It seemed best to the Holy Spirit, and to us, not to burden you with any commandments except these, which are fundamental: to abstain from idol offerings, and blood, and what has been strangled, and lechery. If you keep yourselves from these, you will be acceptable. Farewell.

So they were sent on their way and went down to Antioch, and they assembled the congregation and delivered the letter; and when they read it they rejoiced over the advice. And Judas and Silas, who were themselves also prophets, talked much with them and advised and strengthened the brothers; and after staying some time they went in peace from these brothers to those who had sent them. But Paul and Barnabas stayed on in Antioch, teaching and, with many others, carrying the gospel of the word of the Lord.

Then after some days Paul said to Barnabas: Let us return and visit our brothers in every city in which we preached the word of the Lord, to see how they are faring. Barnabas wished to take John Mark along; but Paul thought it would be wrong to take that man who had deserted them in Pamphylia and not gone on with them to their work. And some bitterness arose, so that they separated from each other, and Barnabas sailed for Cyprus, taking Mark with him. But Paul chose Silas and left, commended to the grace of the Lord by the brothers, and journeyed through Syria and Cilicia strengthening the churches.

¶ He also visited Derbe and Lystra. And behold, there was a disciple there named Timothy, the son of a Jewish woman believer and a Greek father, and he was recommended by the brothers in Lystra and Iconium. And Paul wished to have him travel with him, and he took him and circumcised him, on account of the Jews who were in those parts, since all knew that his father was a Greek. And as they journeyed through the cities, they delivered to the people the commandments decreed by the apostles and elders in Jerusalem, for them to obey. And the churches were strengthened in their faith and grew in number day by day.

They passed through Phrygia and the Galatian territory, being prevented by the Holy Spirit from preaching the word in Asia; and going by Mysia they tried to go on to Bithynia, but the Spirit of Jesus would not let them; and passing by Mysia they landed at Troas. And a vision appeared in the night to Paul; a Macedonian man was standing there inviting him and saying: Cross over into Macedonia and come to our aid. And when he had seen the vision, we sought to go to Macedonia, concluding that God had invited us to bring the gospel to those people.

So sailing from Troas we ran a straight course to Samothrace, and on the next day to Neapolis, and from there to Philippi, which is the first city in the district of Macedonia, a colony. We spent some days in this city. And on the day of the sabbath we went outside the gate beside the river where we thought there was a place of prayer, and we sat down and talked to the women who gathered there. And one woman named Lydia, a seller of purple cloth, from the city of Thyatira, one who worshipped God, listened, and the Lord opened her heart to receive what was said by Paul. And when she and her household had been baptized, she invited us, saying: If you have judged me to be faithful to the Lord, come into my house and stay with me. And she made us do so.

And it happened that as we were on our way to the place of prayer, we encountered a maidservant who pos-

sessed a spirit of prophecy; she made a great deal of
money for her masters by her divining; and she followed
Paul and the rest of us and cried aloud, saying: These
people are slaves of the highest God, and they announce
to you the way of salvation. She did this for many days.
But Paul was annoyed and turned on the spirit and said:
I command you in the name of Jesus Christ to go forth
from her. And it went forth in that same hour. But when
her masters saw that their hope for profit was gone, they
seized on Paul and Silas and dragged them into the market place before the authorities, and led them up to the
chief magistrates and said: These people, who are Jews,
are upsetting our city and preaching usages which we,
who are Romans, cannot accept. And the mob joined in
the attack against them, and the chief magistrates tore
the men's clothing to pieces and ordered them to be
beaten, and after inflicting many blows they threw them
in prison, ordering the warden to keep them under close
guard; and he on receiving such an order threw them into
the innermost part of the prison and fastened their feet
in the stocks. But in the middle of the night Paul and
Silas were praying and singing hymns to God, and the
prisoners were listening to them; and suddenly there was
a great earthquake, so that the foundations of the prison
were shaken, and all the doors came open, and the chains
fell off all of them. The warden woke up, and when he
saw that the doors of the prison were open, he drew his
sword and was about to kill himself, believing that the
prisoners had escaped. But Paul called out in a great voice,
saying: Do not do yourself an injury, for we are all here.
And the man called for a light and leaped inside, and
threw himself down trembling before Paul and Silas, then
led them outside and said: Lords, what must I do to be

saved? And they said: Believe in the Lord Jesus and you and your household will be saved.

And they preached the word of God to him, with all who were in his house; and he took them at that hour of the night and washed their wounds, and he himself and all who were in his house were baptized on the spot; and he took them into his house and set a table before them, and rejoiced with all his household that he had come to believe in God.

When day came the chief magistrates sent their lictors, saying: Release those men. The warden brought the message to Paul, to this effect: The chief magistrates have sent to have you released; so now come out and go on your way in peace. But Paul said to them: After lashing us publicly without trial, us who are Roman citizens, they threw us in prison. And now they are putting us out secretly? Not so; let them come themselves and conduct us out. The lictors reported these words to the chief magistrates; and they were frightened when they heard that they were Romans, and came and apologized and conducted them out and asked them to leave the city. And they left the prison and went to Lydia's house; and they saw the brothers and encouraged them and left.

¶ Making their way through Amphipolis and Apollonia, they came to Thessalonica, where there was a synagogue of the Jews. And following his custom, Paul visited them and for three sabbaths lectured to them on the scriptures, demonstrating and proving that the Christ had to suffer and rise from the dead, and saying, This is the Christ, Jesus, whom I proclaim to you. And some of them believed and attached themselves to Paul and Silas, a great number of Greek believers, and not a few prominent women. But the Jews became jealous, and they enlisted the help of some tough men from the market place rabble and started a riot and threw the city into confusion; and they besieged the house of Jason and demanded that he bring them out before the people. But not finding them, they dragged Jason and some of the brothers before the authorities, shouting: These men who are upsetting the Empire are here now, and Jason has taken them in; and all of them are acting against the decrees of Caesar, saying that there is another who is King, Jesus. And they stirred up the mob and the authorities, but after getting bail from Jason and the others they let them go.

The brothers immediately took Paul and Silas to Beroea by night, and arriving there they went to the synagogue of the Jews. These people were more honorable than the ones in Thessalonica, and they received the word in all eagerness, studying the scriptures day by day to see if this were really so. And many of them believed, and not a few of the prominent Greek women and men. But when the Jews of Thessalonica learned that the word of God had been proclaimed in Beroea by Paul, they went there also, upheaving and disturbing the masses. But then the brothers promptly sent Paul on his way to the sea; and Silas and Timothy stayed there. Then those who had Paul in their charge brought him to Athens and, after receiving his instructions to Silas and Timothy that they should come to him with all speed, they returned.

In Athens, while Paul was awaiting them, his spirit was exasperated within him as he saw that the city was full of idols. And he would have discussions with the Jews and the worshippers in the synagogue and in the market place every day with anyone he happened to meet. And some of the Stoic and Epicurean philosophers encountered him, and some of them said: What might this vagabond be trying to tell us? And others said: He seems to be an announcer of foreign divinities. Because he brought the gospel of Jesus and the resurrection. So they took him in hand and led him up to the Areopagus, saying: Can we discover what is this new teaching of which you are telling us? You are bringing something new to our ears. So we wish to learn what this means. All the Athenians and their visitors from abroad spent their time on nothing except saying or hearing something novel.

Then Paul, standing on the middle of the Areopagus, said: Gentlemen of Athens, I perceive that you are in every way more god-fearing than others; for as I went about and observed your sanctuaries I even found an altar inscribed: To the Unknown God. What you worship, without knowing what it is, this is what I proclaim to you. God, who made the world and everything in it, being Lord of heaven and earth, does not live in hand-built temples, nor, as one who needs anything, is he ministered to by human hands, since he himself gave life and breath and everything else to all. And out of one he made every nation of men to live on every face of the earth, decreeing the seasons in their order and the boundaries of their habitations; and he made them search for God, to try to feel their way to him, since indeed he is not far from any one of us. For in him we live and move and are, since, as some of your own poets have said: We are his offspring.

Being then as we are the offspring of God, we ought not to believe that divinity is like gold or silver or stone, the carving of art and the thought of man. God, then, overlooking our times of ignorance, now announces to men that all men everywhere must repent; because he has set a day on which he will judge the inhabited world in justice through a man whom he has appointed to do this, after giving sure proof to all by resurrecting him from the dead.

When they heard about the resurrection from the dead, some scoffed but some said: We will listen to you again concerning this matter.

So Paul went from their midst; but some men attached themselves to him and believed, among them Dionysius the Areopagite and his wife, who was named Damaris, and some others with them.

¶ After that he left Athens and went to Corinth. There he found a Jew named Aquila, from Pontus by origin, who had recently come from Italy with his wife, Priscilla, because Claudius had decreed that all Jews must leave Rome. He went to them and, because they shared the same craft, he stayed with them and they all worked together. Their craft was tent-making. And every sabbath he would speak in the synagogue, and he converted both Jews and Greeks.

But when Silas and Timothy arrived from Macedonia, Paul gave himself over to preaching the word, testifying to the Jews that the Christ was Jesus. And when they opposed him and abused him, he shook out his clothing and said: Your blood be upon your own heads. My hands are clean. From now on I shall go to the Gentiles. And leaving the place, he went to the house of a man named Titius Justus, who worshipped God, and whose house was next to the synagogue. And Crispus, the head of the synagogue, believed in the Lord, together with all his household; and many Corinthians when they heard him believed and were baptized. And in a vision by night the

Lord said to Paul: Do not fear, but speak on and do not be silent; because I am with you, and no one will attack you to do you harm; because I have many people in this city.

And he stayed for a year and six months teaching them the word of God. But when Gallio was proconsul of Achaea, the Jews made a concerted attack on Paul and brought him to the tribunal, saying: This man persuades people to worship God contrary to the law. But as Paul was about to open his mouth to speak, Gallio said to the Jews: If there were some crime or flagrant villainy, you Jews, I would reasonably have put up with you; but if your complaints concern a word or names or the law that you have, you must see to it yourselves. I do not wish to be judge of these matters. And he drove them from the tribunal. Then they all seized on Sosthenes, the head of the synagogue, and beat him in front of the tribunal; but none of all this was of any concern to Gallio.

Paul stayed on for a number of days and then, after saying farewell to the brothers, sailed for Syria, and Priscilla and Aquila went with him, and he cut his hair short in Cenchreae, for he had taken a vow. They put in at Ephesus, and he left the others there and went himself into the synagogue and talked with the Jews. And when they asked him to stay for a longer time, he refused, but after saying farewell and telling them: I will return to you again, God willing, he sailed from Ephesus; and went ashore at Caesarea and went up and greeted the church, and went down to Antioch, and after spending some time there left; and passed from place to place through the territory of Galatia and Phrygia, strengthening the disciples.

There was a certain Jew, Apollos by name, an Alexandrian by origin, who came to Ephesus: an eloquent man, strong in the scriptures. This man was a student in the way of the Lord and, seething with enthusiasm, he spoke and taught accurately the facts about Jesus, but he knew only the baptism of John. And he began to speak freely in the synagogue; but when Priscilla and Aquila heard him, they took him aside and explained to him more exactly about the Way of God. When he wished to go to Achaea, the brothers encouraged him and wrote to the disciples that they should accept him. And when he arrived, he was very helpful to those who, through grace, had become believers; for he strenuously confuted the Jews, proving in public, through the scriptures, that the Christ was Jesus.

¶ While Apollos was in Corinth, it happened that Paul, after traveling through the interior, came to Ephesus, and there found some disciples and said to them: When you believed, did you receive the Holy Spirit? They said: We have not even heard whether there is a Holy Spirit. Paul said: Then in what were you baptized? They answered: In the baptism of John. Paul said: John baptized in the baptism of repentance, telling the people to believe in the one who was coming after him, that is, in Jesus. When they heard this, they were baptized in the name of the Lord Jesus; and after Paul had laid his hands upon them, the Holy Spirit came over them, and they began to speak with tongues and prophesy. There were about twelve men in all.

Then he went into the synagogue and spoke freely for three months, lecturing and arguing about the Kingdom of God. But when some men began to scoff and disbelieve, speaking ill of the Way of God before the congregation, Paul left them and took away his disciples, lecturing every day in the school of Tyrannus. And this went on for two years, so that all the inhabitants of Asia heard the word of the Lord, Jews and Greeks alike. And God displayed no ordinary powers through the hands of Paul, so that even if only handkerchiefs or towels he had touched were brought to the sick, their diseases would leave them and the evil spirits would go out of them. And some of the traveling Jewish exorcists tried naming the name of the Lord Jesus to those who possessed evil spirits, saying: I adjure you by Jesus, the one Paul preaches. There were seven sons of a certain Sceva, a Jewish high priest, who did this. But the evil spirit answered and said to them: Jesus I know, and I know about Paul, but who are you? And the man who had been controlled by the evil spirit leaped upon these men and overpowered and defeated them so that they fled from the house naked and bleeding. This became known to all the Jews and Greeks living in Ephesus, and fear fell upon them all, and the name of the Lord Jesus was exalted. And many of those who had come to believe began confessing and reporting their magical practices, and a number of those who had been practicing magic brought their books together into one place and burned them in the sight of all; and they counted the value of these and found that they came to fifty thousand pieces of silver. Thus powerfully did the word of the Lord grow and gain strength.

After these matters were concluded, Paul took it into his mind to make a tour through Macedonia and Achaea and go on to Jerusalem, saying: After I have been there,

I must also see Rome. Then he sent off two of his assistants, Timothy and Erastus, to Macedonia, and himself stayed for some time in Asia.

And at that time there arose a considerable disturbance over the Way of the Lord. For there was a certain man, Demetrius by name, a silversmith, who built shrines of Artemis and so gave considerable employment to the craftsmen. He assembled those and others who did this kind of work, and said: My men, you understand that our prosperity comes from this work; and you can see, and hear, that this man Paul has converted by his persuasion a large crowd not only in Ephesus but in almost all of Asia, saying that gods who are made by hands are not gods. This threatens not only to make our trade fall into disrepute, but also to make the temple of the great goddess Artemis be set at naught, and to put her, whom all Asia and the world worships, in danger of being brought down from her greatness. When they heard this, they were filled with anger and shouted: Great is Artemis of the Ephesians. And the whole city was filled with confusion, and they made a concerted rush to the theater, seizing and carrying along with them Gaius and Aristarchus, Macedonians and traveling companions of Paul. Paul wanted to go before the people, but the disciples would not let him; and also some of the Asiarchs who were friendly to Paul sent to him and urged him not to present himself in the theater.

Now some were shouting one thing and some another, for the meeting was in confusion, and most people did not know why they had been assembled. And some from the crowd told Alexander what to say; the Jews had pushed him forward. And Alexander, gesturing with his hand, tried to speak in defense before the people; but when they recognized that he was a Jew, a single voice came from them all as they shouted for something like two hours: Great is Artemis of the Ephesians. But the secretary of the city quieted the crowd and said: Men of Ephesus, what living person does not know that the city of the Ephesians is the temple keeper of the great Artemis and the image that fell from heaven? Since all that is indisputable, you should remain quiet and not do anything reckless. For you brought these men here when they had neither blasphemed against our goddess nor injured her temple. So now if Demetrius and his fellow craftsmen have anything to say against anyone, the courts are in session and the proconsuls are there, let them bring their charges. If you demand anything more, it will be settled in the regular assembly. For we are in danger of being charged with lawlessness over today; since there is no excuse we can give for this disturbance. And so saying, he closed the meeting.

¶ After the excitement was over, Paul sent for his disciples and encouraged them and said his farewells and set off on his journey to Macedonia. And after passing through those parts and encouraging the people with much speaking, he arrived in Greece. When he had spent three months there and was about to sail to Syria, he decided to return by way of Macedonia because of a plot against him by the Jews. Along with him went Sopater the son of Pyrrhus, from Beroea, Aristarchus and Secundus of the Thessalonians, Gaius and Timothy of Derbe, and the Asians Tychicus and Trophimus. These went on ahead and awaited us at Troas; and we sailed from Philippi after the days of Unleavened Bread, and we came to them at Troas after five days, and for seven days we remained there.

On the first day of the week when we were gathered together to break bread, Paul was discoursing, and since he intended to leave the next day, he drew out his discourse until midnight. There were plenty of lamps in the upper room where we were gathered together. But a young man named Eutychus was sitting in the window, and he fell into a deep sleep as Paul talked on at length, and overcome as he was by sleep, he fell all the way from the third story and was picked up dead. Paul went down and lay over him and embraced him, then said: Do not be alarmed, his life is there within him. Then he went up and broke bread and ate it and talked until sunrise, and then left. And they took away the boy, and he was alive; and they were greatly comforted.

We went on board the ship and sailed for Assos, intending to take Paul on board there, for so he had directed; he himself was going to go there by land. And when he met us at Assos, we took him aboard and went to Mitylene, and sailed from there, and on the next day we were off Chios; on the day after that we crossed over to Samos, and on the following day came to Miletus. For Paul had decided to bypass Ephesus so as not to lose time in Asia, since he was hastening to be in Jerusalem on the day of the Pentecost if that might be possible.

From Miletus he sent to Ephesus and summoned the elders of the church. And when they were in his presence he said to them: You know well, from the first day I set foot in Asia, what I was like all the time I was with you, serving the Lord in all humility and through the tears and trials that befell me from the plots of the Jews against me; how I never gave up doing what was to your advantage, bringing the news to you and teaching you, both in public and in your houses, attesting, to Jews and Hellenes alike, repentance and faith in our Lord Jesus. And now, behold, I am on my way to Jerusalem, in bondage to the Holy Spirit; not knowing what will happen to me there, except that the Holy Spirit testifies to me in every city that imprisonment and afflictions await me. But I do not count my life as of any great value to me, so long as I finish my course and the ministry which I accepted from the Lord Jesus, to testify to the gospel of the grace of God. And now, behold, I know that you will never see my face again: not any of you among whom I went about preaching the Kingdom.

Therefore I testify to you, upon this very day, that I am clean of the blood of all of you; for I never gave up announcing all God's will to you. Take heed, then, for yourselves and for all the flock in which the Holy Spirit has set you as guardians, to be shepherds of the church of God which he brought about with his own blood. I know that after I leave you, fierce wolves will come among you who will not spare the flock; and men from your own number will rise up and speak perversely, to pull the disciples into their own following. Therefore be watchful, remembering how for three years I never ceased, night and day, from counseling each one of you, with tears. And now I give you into the charge of the Lord and the word of his grace, which has power to restore you and give you your inheritance among all who have been consecrated. I never wanted anyone's silver or gold or clothing; you yourselves know that these hands of mine provided for my needs and for my companions. I have always shown you that thus you should toil to help those who are weak and remember the words of the Lord Jesus Christ which he himself spoke: It is more blessed to give than to receive.

So saying, he knelt with all of them and prayed. And there was much lamentation by all, and they fell on Paul's neck and kissed him. What had grieved them the most was when he said that they would never see his face again. And they escorted him to his ship.

¶ When we had to tear ourselves away from them and put out to sea, we made a straight run to Cos, and on the next day to Rhodes, and from there to Patara; and finding there a ship that was crossing to Phoenicia we went aboard and sailed. After sighting Cyprus and leaving it behind on the left, we sailed to Syria and came ashore at Tyre, for it was there that the ship unloaded her cargo. We found the disciples and stayed there seven days; and they warned Paul, because of what the Spirit had told them, not to go on to Jerusalem. But when we had come to the end of our days there, we left and started on our way, and they all escorted us, with their wives and children, outside the city; and we all knelt down on the beach and prayed and said our farewells; and then we boarded the ship, and they turned back to their homes.

We ended our sea voyage from Tyre by reaching Ptolemais, and there we greeted the brothers and stayed with them for a day. And on the next day we set forth and reached Caesarea and went to the house of Philip the evangelist, one of the seven, and stayed with him. He had four maiden daughters, who were prophetic. After we had stayed there for a number of days, there came down from Judaea a prophet named Agabas, who came up to us and took off Paul's belt and bound his own feet and his hands, saying: Thus says the Holy Spirit. The Jews will thus bind the man, whose belt this is, in Jerusalem, and they will give him over into the hands of the heathens. When we heard this, we, together with the people who lived there, implored him not to go up to Jerusalem. Then Paul answered: Why are you doing this, crying and breaking my heart? I am ready not only to be bound but to die in Jerusalem for the name of the Lord Jesus. So when he would not be persuaded we held our peace, saying: The Lord's will be done.

After these days we made our preparations and went up to Jerusalem; and some of the disciples from Caesarea went with us and took us where we could be the guests of a certain Mnason of Cyprus, a disciple of long standing, and when we arrived in Jerusalem the brothers welcomed us gladly. On the next day Paul went with us to the house of James, and all the elders were there. And Paul greeted them and recounted to them one by one all the things that God had made happen among the Gentiles through his ministry. When they heard, they glorified God; but they said to Paul: You can see, brother, how many tens of thousands there are among the Jews who have come to believe; and all of them are zealots for the law. And they have been told concerning you that you are teaching all the Jews who live among the Gentiles to turn away from Moses, telling them not to circumcise their children and not to follow his customs.

What to do, then? They will surely learn that you are here. So do as we tell you, thus. There are four men among us who have taken a vow, of their own free will. Take them along with you and be purified along with them, and pay their expenses so that they can shave their heads; and all will realize that what they were told about you is not true, but you also hold to serving the law. Concerning the Gentiles who have come to believe, we have sent word decreeing that they must keep themselves from idol offerings, and blood, and what has been strangled, and lechery.

Then on the next day Paul took the men with him, and was purified along with them and entered the temple, giving notice of the time when the days of purification would be completed, at which time the offering should be made for each one of them. But when the seven days were about to be completed, the Jews from Asia, who had seen him in the temple, stirred up the whole populace, and they laid hands on him, shouting: Men of Jerusalem, help us. This is the man who teaches all men everywhere, going against the people and the law and this place; and now he has even brought Greeks into the temple and profaned this holy place. For they had previously seen Trophimus of Ephesus with him in the city, and they thought Paul had brought him into the temple. The whole city was aroused, and the people made a rush and seized Paul and dragged him out of the temple; and immediately the doors were shut. And as they were demanding his death, word got to the tribune of the Roman cohort that all Jerusalem was rioting; and he, taking with him his soldiers and their centurions, ran at once to where they were, and when they saw the tribune and the soldiers they stopped beating Paul. Then the tribune went to Paul and seized him and ordered him to be bound with double chains, and asked who he was and what he had done. Some in the crowd said one thing and some said another. And when the tribune could not find out for sure because of the uproar, he ordered him to be taken into the barracks. But when he got to the steps, he had

to be carried by the soldiers, because of the violence of
the mob, for most of the population followed him crying:
Kill him.

When he was about to be taken into the barracks, Paul
said to the tribune: May I say something to you? He said:
You know Greek? Then you are not that Egyptian who
started a riot some days ago and went off into the desert
with four thousand of the assassins? Paul said: I am a
Jew, from Tarsus in Cilicia, a citizen of no insignificant
city; and I request of you, give me leave to speak to the
people. When he gave him leave, Paul stood on the steps
and motioned with his hand to the people; and when
there was mostly silence, he spoke to them in Hebrew,
saying:

¶ Brothers, fathers, listen to the defense I make before
you now. And when they heard him speaking to them in
Hebrew they were the more quiet. And he said: I am a
Jew, born in Tarsus in Cilicia, and brought up in this
city at the feet of Gamaliel, instructed in the strict style
of the law of our fathers, and I was a zealot for God as
all of you are today. I persecuted this Way to the death,
binding men and women and delivering them to the pris-
ons, as the high priest and the entire council of elders
will testify. From them I received letters to the brothers
in Damascus and I was on my way to bring those who
were there in bonds to Jerusalem to be punished. And it
befell me that as I was on my way and approaching Damascus, about noon, a great light from the sky suddenly
flashed about me, and I fell to the ground and I heard a
voice saying: Saul, Saul, why do you persecute me? And
I answered: Who are you, Lord? And he said to me: I am
Jesus of Nazareth; whom you persecute. And the men

who were with me saw the light but they did not hear the voice which spoke to me. And I said: What shall I do, Lord? And the Lord said to me: Rise up and go on to Damascus, and there you will be told about all the things that you have been appointed to do.

But since from the glory of that light I could not see, I came to Damascus with my companions leading me by the hand. Then a certain Ananias, a man devout in the law and well spoken of by all the Jews who live in Damascus, came and stood over me and said: Brother Saul, regain your sight; and in that moment I saw him. And he said: The God of our fathers has chosen you to learn his will, and to see the Just One and to hear the voice from his mouth; because you will be his witness, to all men, of what you have seen and heard. And now, why delay? Rise up and be baptized and wash away your sins, calling upon his name.

Then it befell me that when I returned to Jerusalem and was praying in the temple I fell into a trance, and I saw him and he was saying to me: Make haste and go from Jerusalem quickly, because they will not accept your testimony concerning me. And I said: Lord, they themselves know that I kept imprisoning and flogging those in one synagogue after another who believed in you; and when the blood of Stephen your martyr was shed, I myself was standing by and approving and keeping the coats of the men who were killing him. But he said to me: Go, because I shall send you far from here, among the Gentiles.

They had been listening to him up until this word, but then they cried aloud, saying: Rid the earth of him; such a man has no right to live. And as they clamored and threw off their coats and raised a cloud of dust in the air the tribune ordered him to be taken into the barracks, telling them to whip him so as to get it out of him and find out why they cried out so against him. But when they stretched him out for the lashes, Paul said to the centurion who stood by: Are you permitted to whip a Roman citizen, and that without a trial? When the centurion heard this, he went and told it to the tribune, saying: What do you mean to do? This man is a Roman citizen. The tribune went to him and said: Tell me, are you a Roman citizen? He said: Yes. The tribune said: I paid a great deal to get this citizenship. Paul said: I was born to it. Then those who had been going to interrogate him immediately withdrew from him; and the tribune was frightened, realizing that he was a Roman, and that he had put him in chains.

The next day, wishing to find out precisely what he was accused of by the Jews, he released him, and ordered the high priests and the entire council to assemble, and then brought Paul in and set him before them.

¶ Paul looked hard at the council and said: Men and brothers, I have been God's citizen in full good conscience down to this very day. Then the high priest Ananias ordered the men who stood beside him to strike him on the mouth. Then Paul said to him: God will strike you, you whitewashed wall. And do you sit there and judge me according to the law while you unlawfully order me to be struck? The men who stood beside him said: Do you revile the high priest of God? Paul said: I did not know, brothers, that he was the high priest; for it is written: You shall not insult the leader of the people.

Then Paul, knowing that one part of them was Sad-

ducees and the other Pharisees, cried aloud in the council: Men and brothers, I am a Pharisee, the son of Pharisees; I am being tried for my hope for the resurrection of
the dead. When he said this, there was strife between the
Pharisees and the Sadducees, and the assembly was split
in two. For the Sadducees say that there is no resurrection, and neither angel nor spirit, but the Pharisees believe in both of these. And there was a great uproar, and
some of the scribes of the Pharisaean sect rose up and
dissented, saying: We find no evil in this man. It may be
that a spirit has spoken to him, or an angel. And as the
quarrel grew violent, the tribune, fearing that Paul might
be torn to pieces by them, ordered his soldiers to go down
and snatch him out of their midst and take him into the
barracks.

On the following night the Lord stood over him and
said: Take heart; for as you testified concerning me in
Jerusalem, so you must also testify in Rome.

When day came, the Jews formed a gang and bound
themselves by oath neither to eat nor drink until they
had killed Paul. There were more than forty men in this
conspiracy; and these went to the high priests and elders
and said: We have bound ourselves by oath to taste nothing until we kill Paul. Do you now explain to the tribune, along with the council, that he should bring the man
before you, since you wish to learn more accurately about
him; and we are ready to kill him before he gets to you.

But the son of Paul's sister heard of the ambush, and
he went to the barracks and got in and reported it to
Paul. Paul called over one of the centurions and said:
Take this young man to the tribune, since he has something to report to him. So the centurion took him to the
tribune and said: The prisoner Paul called me over and

asked me to bring this young man to you; he has something to tell you. The tribune took him by the hand and led him to a place apart and asked him: What is this you have to tell me? He said: The Jews have decided to ask you to bring Paul before the council tomorrow, as if for the purpose of learning more accurately about him. But do not do as they say; for more than forty of them are lying in wait for him, and they have bound themselves by oath neither to eat nor drink until they kill him; and now they are ready and waiting for the word from you.

The tribune let the young man go, saying to him: Do not tell anyone that you gave me this information. Then he called in two of his centurions and said: Have two hundred infantrymen, and seventy horsemen, and two hundred light troops ready to start for Caesarea at the third hour of the night; and have horses for Paul to ride, and get him safely to Felix, the governor. And he wrote a letter which read as follows: Claudius Lysias to Felix the most mighty governor, greetings. When this man had been seized by the Jews and was on the point of being killed by them, I went with an armed force and rescued him, having learned that he is a Roman citizen, and I brought him before their council, wishing to learn what was their case against him. And I found that he was accused because of questions concerning their law, but not on any charge that would deserve death or imprisonment. And being informed of a plot against the man I immediately sent him to you, having also ordered his accusers to charge him in your presence.

So the soldiers, as ordered, took Paul by night and brought him to Antipatris; and the next day, leaving the horsemen to go on with him, they returned to the barracks. And the cavalry went on to Caesarea and deliv-

ered the letter to the governor and also brought Paul to
him. When he had read it, and asked from what province
he came and learned that he was from Cilicia, he said: I
will hear you when your accusers are also here. And he
ordered him held in the residence of Herod.

¶ After five days the high priest Ananias came down from
Jerusalem with some of the elders and a certain orator,
Tertullus, and they brought a charge against Paul before
the governor. And when Paul had been summoned, Tertullus began to accuse him, saying: We have had much
peace because of you, and reforms of every kind have
come from everywhere in this country through your
forethought, which, most mighty Felix, we acknowledge
in all gratitude. But, not to weary you, I beg you in your
graciousness to give us a brief hearing. For we have found
this man to be a plague, one who stirs up dissensions
among all the Jews in the empire, and the ringleader of
the heretical sect of Nazarenes. He even tried to profane
the temple. We seized him, and wanted to try him by
our own law, but the tribune Lysias came and forcibly
took him out of our hands and said that his accusers must
go to you. You yourself will be able to learn by question-
ing him about all that we accuse him of. And the Jews
joined in the attack, saying that this was true.

Then Paul answered, when the governor nodded his
permission to speak: Knowing that for many years you
have been judge over this nation, I will speak in my own
defense with a good will; since you can verify that it is
not more than twelve days since I went up to Jerusalem
to worship, and they have not found me talking to anyone or attracting a mob either in the temple or the syn-

agogues or about the city; nor are they able to prove any of the things of which they now accuse me. But I do admit this to you, that the Way which they call heresy is the Way in which I serve the God of our fathers (for I believe all that is written in the law and the prophets) with hope in God, a hope these men also share, that there will soon be a resurrection of the just and the unjust. In this matter I myself make it my study to have a clear conscience before God and man throughout.

Now, after a number of years, I went to Jerusalem to effect some charities for my people and to bring offerings; during which they found me in the temple after my purification, but not with any crowd or causing disturbance. But there are some Jews from Asia, who ought to be here before you and accusing me, if they have anything against me; or else let these men say what wrongdoing they found in me when I stood before the council other than that one cry that I uttered when I stood among them: I am being judged by you today over the resurrection of the dead.

Then Felix, who knew a great deal about the Way, put them off, saying: When the tribune Lysias comes here I will decide your case. And he ordered the centurion to have him kept under guard, but to give him some freedom, and not to prevent any of his own people from ministering to him.

And after a few days, Felix came with Drusilla, his own wife, who was Jewish, and sent for Paul, and heard him tell about belief in Christ Jesus. But when Paul discoursed about righteousness and continence and the judgment to come, Felix was frightened and said: For the present, go, but I will send for you again when I find another occasion. Also, he was hoping to be given money by Paul, for which reason he sent for him and talked with him the more frequently.

After a full two years, Felix was succeeded by Porcius Festus; and wishing to store up some favor with the Jews, Felix left Paul still a prisoner.

¶ Three days after setting foot in his province Festus went up from Caesarea to Jerusalem; and the high priests and the foremost men of the Jews brought charges against Paul; and they urged Festus, asking to be favored against Paul, to have him transferred to Jerusalem. They were planning to lie in wait for him and kill him on the way. But Festus answered that Paul was being held in Caesarea, and that he himself was about to leave for there very soon. So, he said, let your chief men come down with me, and if there is anything wrong about the man, charge him with it.

Then, after spending no more than eight or ten days among them, he went down to Caesarea; and the next day he sat in the tribunal and ordered Paul brought in. When he arrived the Jews who had come down from Jerusalem surrounded him and brought many serious charges against him, which they could not prove; since Paul said in his defense: I have not sinned in any way against the law of the Jews, nor against the temple, nor against Caesar.

But Festus, wishing to store up some favor with the Jews, answered and said to Paul: Are you willing to go up to Jerusalem and there be tried on these charges, before me? But Paul said: I have taken my stand at the tribunal of Caesar, and there I must be tried. I have done the Jews no wrong, as you yourself know quite well. If I am guilty and have done something that deserves death, I do not protest against dying; but if there is nothing in what they charge against me, no one can give me to them as a favor. I appeal to Caesar. Then Festus, after talking with the council, answered: You have appealed to Caesar; to Caesar you shall go.

After a few days had gone by, King Agrippa and Bernice visited Caesarea to welcome Festus. And as they spent some days there, Festus referred Paul's case to the King, saying: There is a man whom Felix left behind as a prisoner; and concerning him the high priests and the elders of the Jews brought charges when I was in Jerusalem, demanding his condemnation. To these I answered that it is not the Roman way to hand any man over as a favor; not until the accused has his accusers before his face and is given some chance to defend himself against the accusation. So when they assembled here I made no delay but the next day I sat in the tribunal and ordered the man brought in. When his accusers stood up they did not accuse him of any of the evildoings I had expected, but they had against him only some questions concerning their own religiosity, and concerning one Jesus; who is dead but who, as Paul says, is alive. Not knowing what to do about investigating these matters, I asked him if he would be willing to go to Jerusalem and there be tried on these charges. But Paul appealed to be held for the attention of Augustus; so I ordered him held until I can send him to Caesar. Agrippa said to Festus: I would like to hear the man myself. Tomorrow, said Festus, you shall hear him.

So on the next day Agrippa arrived, and Bernice, with much circumstance, and they entered the audience room along with the tribunes and the men of prominence in the city; and at the command of Festus, Paul was brought in. And Festus said: King Agrippa, and all you gentlemen who are here with us, you are looking at the man for whose sake the whole population of the Jews has been after me, both in Jerusalem and here, crying that he should not go on living. I myself judged that he had done nothing to deserve death; but since he himself appealed to Augustus, I decided to send him. But I have nothing definite to write to our master about him; which is why I have brought him before all of you, and above all before you, King Agrippa, so that when he has been questioned I can have something to write; for it seems absurd to me to send a prisoner without indicating the charges against him.

¶ Then Agrippa said to Paul: You have leave to speak for yourself. Then Paul extended his hand and began his defense, saying: I count myself most fortunate, King Agrippa, that I am to defend myself against the charges of the Jews in your presence today; for I know that you are supremely well informed in all the customs and questions which are the concern of the Jews. Therefore I beg you to listen to me with patience.

All Jews know about my life, from youth onward, both in my own country and in Jerusalem, and they know from the past, if they will admit it, that I lived according to the strictest sect in our religion, as a Pharisee. And now I stand on trial for hope in that promise which was given by God to our fathers, that expectation which our twelve tribes hope to realize by serving strenuously night and day. It is for this hope, O King, that I am being accused by the Jews. If God wakens the dead, why is that accounted incredible by you Jews?

Now, I thought to myself that I had to do much to oppose the name of Jesus of Nazareth. And this I did in Jerusalem, and with authority granted me by the high priests I confined many of the saints in prison, and when they were killed I cast my vote for it, and in all the synagogues by frequent punishment I tried to force them to blaspheme; and in my immoderate rage against them I even pursued them into cities abroad.

One of these was Damascus, where I was on my way with authority and a commission from the high priests when in the middle of the day on the road I saw, O King, a light surpassing the brightness of the sun which flashed about me and my fellow travelers. And as all of us fell to the ground I heard a voice saying to me in Hebrew: Saul, Saul, why do you persecute me? It is hard for you to kick against the goads. And I said: Who are you, Lord? And the Lord said: I am Jesus, whom you persecute. But rise up and stand on your feet; since it was for this that I appeared to you, to choose you as my minister and my witness to the things which you have seen and to the times I shall be seen by you; choosing you out of my people and the Gentiles, to whom I shall send you, so as to open their eyes, to turn them from darkness to light and from the power of Satan to God; for them to receive remission of sins and a share among those who have been sanctified by their belief in me.

Therefore, King Agrippa, I have not disobeyed the heavenly vision, but to those in Damascus first and Jerusalem, to the whole land of Judaea, and to the Gentiles I have preached repentance and turning to God and the doing of acts to match their repentance. For these reasons the Jews seized me in the temple and tried to kill me. But having been given the help of God until this day, I stand here and testify to great and small, saying nothing but what the prophets and Moses said must be going to happen, that the Christ must suffer, that after the resurrection of the dead he will be the first to proclaim the light to his people and to the nations.

When he made this defense, Festus said in a great voice: Paul, you are mad. Too many books are driving you mad. But Paul said: No, I am not mad, most mighty Festus; my words are those of truth and good sense. The King, to whom I speak openly, knows about these matters; I think there is not one thing that has escaped him, for it was not done in a corner. Do you, King Agrippa, believe in the prophets? I know that you believe. Agrippa said to Paul: Soon you will persuade me to become a Christian. Paul said: Late or soon, I would pray to God that not only you but all who listen to me today would become like me—except for these chains.

Then the King and the governor and Bernice and those who had sat with them got up, and talked with each other as they went out, saying: This man is doing nothing to deserve death or imprisonment. And Agrippa said to Festus: This man could have gone free, if he had not appealed to Caesar.

¶ When it was decided that we should sail for Italy, they turned Paul and some other prisoners over to a centurion named Julius, from the Augustan cohort. We went aboard a ship of Adramyttium which was to sail to places in Asia, and put out to sea. Aristarchus, a Macedonian from Thessalonica, was with us. On the next day we put in at Sidon, and Julius, who treated Paul humanely, allowed him to visit his friends and receive some kindnesses from them. Then putting out from there, we sailed under the lee of Cyprus because the winds were against us, and crossing the open sea by Cilicia and Pamphylia we came to Myra in Lycia. There the centurion found an Alexandrian ship bound for Italy and put us aboard it. Then, sailing slowly for a number of days and barely getting to Cnidus, when the wind would let us go no farther, we sailed under the lee of Crete, by Salmone, and barely managed to coast along until we came to a place called Fair Haven, with the city of Laseia near by.

Since a good deal of time had been spent and sailing was now dangerous, with the Day of Atonement already past, Paul advised them, saying: I can see, gentlemen, that our sailing will be stormy, with much damage not only to the cargo and the ship but to our own lives. But the centurion trusted the steersman and the captain more than Paul's advice. Since the harbor was unsuitable for wintering, most were in favor of leaving there and, if they could somehow make Phoenix, a harbor of Crete which looks both northwest and southwest, they would spend the winter there. And with the south wind blowing gently they thought they had achieved their purpose and put out and coasted along Crete. But not much later the hurricane wind which is called the northeaster struck from the land, and the ship was caught up in it and could not face the wind, so we gave in to it and were swept along. Then, running under shelter of a little island named Cauda, we were barely able to recover the lifeboat, which they hoisted aboard, and then undergirded the ship with cables; and then, fearing that they might be driven on to the shoals of Syrtis, they let down the sea anchor and so were carried along. But we were battered by the storm, and on the second day they began to jettison, and on the third they threw the ship's gear overboard with their own hands. But when neither sun nor stars could be seen for a number of days, and we were being beset by a great storm, all hope that we would survive was finally lost.

And there had been no eating for a long time. Then Paul stood in their midst and said: You should, gentlemen, have paid attention to me and not put out from Crete and so got yourselves this battering and damage. But now I advise you to be of good courage, for there will be no loss of life from among you, only of the ship. For last night the angel of God, to whom I belong, whom I serve, stood by me and said: Have no fear, Paul. You must stand before Caesar. And behold, God has granted you the lives of all who sail with you. Therefore be of good courage, gentlemen; for I believe in God and that it will be as he has told me. But we must be driven upon some island.

And when it was our fourteenth day of being adrift on the Adriatic, in the middle of the night the sailors thought that some land was near. And they took soundings and found twenty fathom, and after a little interval they took soundings again and found fifteen; and fearing that we might be driven on rugged shores they dropped four anchors from the stern and prayed for day to break. But when the sailors tried to abandon the ship and were lowering the lifeboat into the sea, pretending that they were going to set out anchors from the prow, Paul said to the centurion and the solders: Unless these men stay on the ship, you cannot be saved. Then the soldiers cut the ropes on the lifeboat and let it drop.

Now Paul urged everyone to take some food before the coming dawn, saying: This is the fourteenth day that you have gone without food in your anxiety, tasting nothing; therefore I urge you to take some food, since this has to do with your safety. For not one hair from any of your heads shall be lost. And so saying, he took a loaf and gave thanks to God before them all and broke it and began to eat. Then all became cheerful and they also took some food. We were seventy-six souls in all on the ship. When they had eaten their fill they lightened the ship by throwing the grain into the sea.

When day came, they did not recognize the land, but they could see a bay, with a beach where they planned to get the ship safely ashore, if they could. So they cast off the anchors and let them go, and at the same time loosening the bands on the rudders and hoisting the foresail they went before the wind toward the shore. But they struck upon a shoal surrounded by water and ran the ship aground, and the prow stuck and remained fixed, but the stern began to break up in the surf. There was a plan among the soldiers to kill the prisoners, to keep any from swimming away and escaping; but the centurion wished to keep Paul alive and prevented them from that purpose; and he ordered those who could swim to plunge in first and get to shore, and the rest to use boards or anything else from the ship. And so it came about that all got safe to shore.

¶ After our escape we learned that the island is called Malta. And the natives showed us no ordinary kindness, for they lit a fire and brought us all to it, because of the rain which had set in and the cold. And Paul had gathered a load of brushwood and laid it on the fire when a viper came out to escape the heat and fastened on his hand. And when the natives saw the creature dangling from his hand they said to each other: This man is surely a murderer; he was saved from the sea but justice would not let him live. But he shook off the creature into the fire and suffered no hurt; while they waited for him to begin to swell up or suddenly drop dead. But when they waited a long time and saw nothing extraordinary happening to him, they changed their minds and said that he was a god.

In the neighborhood of this place were the estates of the chief man of the island, Publius by name, who invited us in and entertained us hospitably for three days. It happened that the father of Publius was lying sick with a fever and dysentery, and Paul went in to him and prayed and laid his hands upon him and healed him. When that happened the other people on the island who had sicknesses came to him and were treated; and they honored us with many honors, and when we sailed away they gave us all that we needed.

After three months we sailed aboard an Alexandrian ship which had wintered at the island. It carried the insignia of Castor and Pollux. And we went to Syracuse and stayed there three days, and removing from there proceeded to Rhegium. And after one day, with the arrival of a south wind, we reached Puteoli on the second day. There we found brothers, and were invited to stay with them for seven days. And so we went to Rome. And from Rome the brothers, who had heard about us, came out to meet us as far as the Appian Forum, and the Three Taverns; and when he saw them Paul gave thanks to God, and took courage.

When we entered Rome, Paul was permitted to stay by himself, with the soldier who was guarding him.

It happened that after three days he called together those who were the chief men among the Jews; and when they were gathered together he said to them: Men and brothers, though I had done nothing against our people or contrary to the laws of our fathers, I was turned over as a prisoner from Jerusalem into the hands of the Romans; who after interrogating me wanted to set me free because there was nothing in my case that deserved death. But when the Jews objected I was forced to appeal to Caesar, though not as one who had any charge to bring against my own people. For this reason I have invited you, to see you and to talk with you; because it is on account of the hope of Israel that I wear these chains. They said to him: We have received no letters about you from Judaea, nor has any of the brothers arrived and reported or spoken any evil of you. But we desire to hear from you what you think; for concerning this sect, it is known to us that people everywhere speak against it.

Then they agreed on a day with him and came to him at his lodgings in greater numbers, and he lectured to them from dawn until evening, testifying to the Kingdom of God and trying to persuade them about Jesus from the law of Moses and the prophets. And some were persuaded by what was said, and others would not believe; and they broke up, at variance with each other, as Paul said one thing to them: Well did the Holy Spirit speak through the prophet Isaiah to your fathers, saying: Go to this people and say: With your hearing you shall hear and not understand, and you shall use your sight and look but not see. For the heart of this people is stiffened, and they hear with difficulty, and they have closed their eyes; so that they may never see with their eyes, or hear with their ears, and with their hearts understand and turn back, so that I can heal them.

Let it be known to you that this salvation of God was sent forth to the Gentiles; and they will listen.

He remained a full two years, in his own rented place, and he received all who came to him, preaching the Kingdom of God and teaching about the Lord Jesus Christ, quite openly, without any interference.

LETTERS

The Letter
to the Romans

¶PAUL, THE SLAVE OF JESUS CHRIST, called to be an apostle, set apart for the gospel of God which God proclaimed through his prophets in the holy scriptures concerning his son, who was born, in the way of the flesh, from the seed of David; but who is declared to be the son of God in power, which is according to the spirit of sanctity, by his resurrection from the dead; Jesus Christ our Lord, from whom we have received grace, and the rank of apostle to make the faith obeyed among all the nations for the sake of his name; among which nations you also are called by Jesus Christ; to all who in Rome are the beloved of God, chosen saints: grace to you and peace from God our Father and our Lord Jesus Christ.

First I thank my God through Jesus Christ concerning all of you, that your faith is proclaimed through all the world. For God, whom I serve in my spirit in the gospel of his son, is my witness how constantly I make mention of you always in my prayers, asking if somehow at last I may be guided by the will of God to come to you. For I long to see you, so that I may impart to you some spiritual gift for your strengthening, that is, for you to be comforted among yourselves through our faith in each other, yours and mine. I do not wish you not to realize, brothers, that I have often proposed to come to you (but I have been prevented until now), so that I may make some harvesting among you as among the rest of the nations. To Greeks and Barbarians, wise and unwise, I am indebted; thus for my part I am eager to bring the gospel to you in Rome also. For I am not ashamed of the gospel, for it is the power of God for the salvation of everyone who believes, Jew and Greek; since the justice of God is revealed in it from faith to faith, as it is written: The righteous man shall live by faith.

For from heaven is revealed the anger of God against all the impiety and unrighteousness of people who in their unrighteousness suppress the truth; since what can be known about God is plain to them because God made it plain to them. Since the creation of the world, what is his and invisible, his eternal power and divinity, has been perceived by the mind through what he has made, so that they have no excuse; because, while knowing God, they did not glorify or thank him as God, but they were beguiled in their reasonings and their uncomprehending hearts were made dark. They thought that they were wise but they were fools, and they gave up the glory of imperishable God in exchange for the likeness of an image, of perishable man, or of creatures that fly and walk on all fours and crawl.

Therefore God gave them up in the lusts of their hearts to immorality, to the disgracing of their own bodies among themselves. They exchanged the truth of God for falsehood, and they worshipped and served the creature rather than the Creator, who is to be praised forevermore. Amen. Because of this God delivered them over to disgraceful passions. For their females changed their natural relations into what is against nature; and so likewise the males, forsaking the natural intercourse with the female, were inflamed with desire for each other, males for males, acting shamefully and receiving the retribution due them for their misguided ways. And as they did not see fit to keep God in mind, so God delivered them over to a state of mind that was unworthy, and to unbecoming conduct; being filled with every wrong, wickedness, greed, badness; stuffed with envy bloodthirstiness contentiousness treachery malignity; whisperers gossips god haters violent proud pretentious; devisers of evil, disobedient to parents; mindless faithless loveless pitiless; who though they knew well about the verdict of God, that those who do such things deserve death, nevertheless not only do them but encourage others who do.

¶ Thus you, whoever you are, who are human, and judge, have no defense. In judging another you convict yourself, for you who judge do the same thing; but we know that the judgment of God is truly against those who do such things. Then you, who are human, and judge those who do such things while you do them yourself, do you count on escaping the judgment of God? Or do you misunderstand the wealth of his goodness and forbearance and patience, not realizing that the goodness of God means to lead you to repentance? Through your hardness and your unrepentant heart you are storing up for yourself anger on the day of anger and the revelation of the righteous judgment of God, who will give to each according to his actions: to those who, through steadfastness in doing good, strive for glory and honor and incorruptibility, he will give everlasting life; but for those who out of contentiousness are disobedient to the truth but obey unrighteousness there shall be rage and anger, affliction and anguish for every soul of a man who does evil, Jew first, but also Greek; but glory and honor and peace for everyone who does good, Jew first, but also Greek, for there is no discrimination with God.

For those who sinned outside the law will also perish outside the law: and those who sinned while within the law will be judged according to the law. For it is not those who listen to the law who are righteous in the sight of God, but it is those who do what is in the law who will be justified. For when Gentiles who do not have the law do by nature what is in the law, they, without having the law, are their own law; and they display the work of the law engraved on their hearts; with their conscience bearing them witness, as their arguments attack or defend each other, on that day when God will judge the secrets of men, as it is said in my gospel, through Jesus Christ.

But if you call yourself a Jew, and rely on the law, and glory in God and know his will, and pass judgment on what is important, being educated in the law; and are confident that you are the guide of the blind, light for those in the dark, instructor of the ignorant, teacher of the simple, possessing, in the law, the shape of knowledge and truth; do you then, who teach someone else, not teach yourself? You who preach no stealing, do you steal? You, who forbid adultery, do you commit it? And you, who loathe idols, do you steal from temples? Do you, who glory in the law, dishonor God by breaking the law? Because, as it is written, the name of God is ill spoken of among the Gentiles, because of you.

Circumcision is helpful if you do obey the law, but if you transgress the law, your circumcision becomes uncircumcision. If, then, the uncircumcised man keeps the requirements of the law, shall not that uncircumcision be counted as circumcision? And the uncircumcised, who by nature fulfill the law, shall judge you who have the circumcision and the letter of the law, but break it. For one is not a Jew by what can be seen, nor is circumcision in what can be seen in the flesh; but one is a Jew in what cannot be seen, and circumcision is a thing of the heart, in the spirit, not in the letter, for one whose approval comes not from men but from God.

¶ What then is the Jew's advantage, and what is the use of circumcision? Great, in every way. In the first place, to them were entrusted the oracles of God. But what then? If some were unfaithful, will not their unfaithfulness make void the good faith of God? Never! God must be truthful and every man a liar, as it is written: So that you may be justified in your words and triumph when you are brought to judgment. But if our unrighteousness demonstrates the righteousness of God, what are we to say? Can God be unfair in visiting his anger? (I speak in human terms.) Never: since then how shall God judge the world? But if, through my falseness, God's truthfulness redounds to his glory, why am I condemned as a sinner? Am I not what my detractors call me, when certain people say that I say: Let us do evil so that good may come of it? Their condemnation is just.

What then? Are we Jews better? Not altogether, for we have already charged all Jews and Greeks with being subject to sin, as it is written: There is not one righteous man, not one, there is not one who understands, not one who seeks out God. They have all gone off the course, and with that they have become useless; there is none who practices honesty, there is not so much as one. Their throat is an open grave, with their tongues they are deceitful; the poison of asps is on their lips, their mouth is full of cursing and bitterness. Their feet are swift toward bloodshed. Ruin and wretchedness are in their ways, and they have not learned the way of peace. Their eyes know no fear of God.

We know that the law says what it says to those who are within the law, so that every mouth may be stopped and all the world be subject to the judgment of God; because it is not from the works of the law that all flesh will be justified in his presence, since through the law comes consciousness of sin. But now the righteousness of God has been made evident apart from the law. It was testified to by the law and the prophets, but the righteousness of God is through belief in Jesus Christ; for all who believe, for there is no distinction. For all sinned and come short of the glory of God, but are justified by the gift of his grace through their redemption by Christ Jesus, whom God put forward for propitiation through faith in his blood, for the demonstration of his righteousness by the forgiveness of sins committed before, through the indulgence of God; for the demonstration of his righteousness in the present time, that he is righteous himself and justifies one who believes in Jesus.

Where then is the exultation? It is excluded. By what law? The law of actions? No, but by the law of faith. For we hold that a man is justified through faith without the actions of the law. Is God the God of the Jews alone? Not of the Gentiles also? Yes, of the Gentiles also, since God is one, and he will justify the circumcised from faith and the uncircumcised through faith. Are we then making the law void through faith? Never. We are confirming the law.

¶ What then shall we say of Abraham, our forefather in the way of the flesh? If Abraham was justified because of his actions, he has reason for glorying; but not before God, since what does the scripture say? Abraham believed God, and it was counted as righteousness in him. For one who does something, repayment is counted not as grace but as his due; but for one who does nothing, but believes in him who justifies the impious man, his faith is counted as righteousness. So David also says of the blessedness of the man whom God counts as righteous, apart from his actions: Blessed are they whose lawless acts have been forgiven and whose sins have been hidden away. Blessed is the man whose sin the Lord does not count.

Now, is this blessedness for the circumcised or also for the uncircumcised? Since we say the faith of Abraham was counted as righteousness. How then was it counted? In his circumcised or uncircumcised state? It was when he was not yet circumcised, but still uncircumcised. And he received the mark of circumcision, the seal upon the righteousness of that faith he had when he was still uncircumcised; to be the father of all those who are believers through their uncircumcised state so that righteousness could be counted for them, and also to be the father of the circumcised for those who not only have been circumcised but also walk in his footsteps through the faith, which our father Abraham had when he was still uncircumcised. For the promise to Abraham, or his seed, that he should be the inheritor of the world, was not on account of the law, but of the righteousness of his faith. For if the inheritors are those who belong to the law, then the faith is made void and the promise is gone; for the law causes anger, but where there is no law there is no lawbreaking.

Thus (it is) because of faith, and thus by grace, that the promise should hold good for all his seed; not only for him who has the law but for him who has the faith of Abraham. He is the father of us all, as it is written: I have made you the father of many nations. It held good in the sight of God, in whom he believed, the God who puts life into the dead and summons into existence the things that do not exist. He against hope believed in the hope that he would become the father of many nations according to what had been said, that is: Thus shall your seed be. And Abraham, without weakening in his faith, knew that his own body was that of a dead man, since he was about a hundred years old, and he knew the dead state of Sarah's womb, but he was not distracted with unbelief in God's promise but was strengthened in his belief, giving glory to God and assured that God was able to do as he had promised.

Thus it was that faith counted as righteousness in him. But it was not written for him alone that it was so counted for him, but also for us for whom it is to be counted, for us who believe in him who raised from the dead Jesus our Lord, who was betrayed for our sins and raised up again for our justification.

¶ Justified therefore through faith, let us keep peace with God through our Lord Jesus Christ, through whom we have got by faith access to that grace in which we stand, and let us exult in the hope of the glory of God. Not only that, let us even exult in afflictions, knowing that affliction causes endurance, and endurance quality, and quality, hope, and hope does not disappoint us. Because God's love is diffused in our hearts through the Holy Spirit who was given to us; if indeed when we were sick Christ died in time for the sake of us, who were sinful. Indeed, one will scarcely die for a righteous man. Perhaps one does even dare to die for a good man. But God shows his love for us; because it was when we were still sinners that Christ died for us. All the more then, being justified now by his blood, shall we be saved from the anger to come. For if when we were enemies we were reconciled through the death of his son, all the more, now reconciled, shall we be saved by his life; not only that, but exulting in God through our Lord Jesus Christ, through whom we have now got this reconciliation.

Therefore, just as sin came into the world through one man, and through sin, death, so also death went about among all men, because all sinned. Before there was the law there was sin in the world, but when there was no law it was not reckoned as sin. But death was king from Adam until Moses, even over those who did not sin after the example of the transgression of Adam, who is the type of what was to come.

But the gift of grace is not like the transgression; for if by the transgression of one many died, far more has been the abundance, for the many, of the grace of God and his gift in the grace of one man, Jesus Christ. And the gift is not as when one man sinned; for the judgment from one leads to condemnation, but the gift of grace, after many transgressions, leads to justification. For if by the transgression of one man death was king because of the one, so all the more shall they be kings in life, who have received the abundance of grace and righteousness, through one, Jesus Christ.

So then, just as one blunder meant condemnation for all men, so also one righteous act shall mean the vindication of life for all men; for just as through the disobedience of the one man the many were made sinful, so also through the obedience of the one man the many shall be made righteous. The law came in to increase the transgression; but where the sin has increased, grace has increased even more, so that just as sin was king in death, so also grace shall be king through righteousness for life everlasting, because of Jesus Christ our Lord.

¶ What then shall we say? Shall we persist in our sin, so that the grace may be multiplied? Never. How shall we, who died to sin, still live in it? Or do you not know that we, who were baptized for Christ, were baptized for his death? So we were buried with him through the baptism for death; so that, as Christ was raised from the dead through the glory of his father, so we too may walk in a renewal of life. For if we were united with him in the same kind of death, so shall we share his resurrection; knowing that the old person who was in us was crucified with him, so the body of our sin might be destroyed, and we shall no longer be the slaves of sin, since one who has died is absolved of sin. But if we died with Christ, we believe that we shall also live with him, knowing that Christ, raised from the dead, dies no more, for death no longer has lordship over him. When he died, he died to sin, once for all; but when he lives, he lives for God. Thus do you also count yourselves as dead for sin, but living for God, in Jesus Christ.

Do not then let sin be king in your mortal body so that

you obey its desires, and do not give your limbs to sin as the weapons of wrongdoing, but give yourselves to God, as living people who have been dead, and give your limbs to God as the weapons of righteousness. For sin will have no lordship over you, for you are subject not to law but to grace.

What then? Shall we sin because we are subject not to the law but to grace? Never. Do you not know that when you give yourselves as slaves to someone, to obey him, you are the slaves of him whom you obey, either of sin, for death, or of obedience, for righteousness? Thanks be to God, though you were the slaves of sin, you obeyed from the heart that form of teaching which had been made traditional for you; and when set free from sin you were enslaved to righteousness. I speak in human terms because of the weakness of your flesh. For as you gave your bodies over as slaves to debauchery and lawlessness, so now give over your bodies as slaves to righteousness, to be sanctified. For when you were the slaves of sin, you were free for righteousness. What was then the harvest you reaped from those acts of which you are now ashamed? Their end is death. But now, set free from sin and enslaved to God, you have your harvest, to be sanctified, and the end is life everlasting. For the stipend of sin is death, but God's gift of grace is life everlasting through Christ Jesus our Lord.

¶ Are you not aware, brothers—I am speaking to those who know the law—that the law has power over a person only as long as he is alive? Thus a married woman is bound by the law to her husband while he is alive; but if her husband dies, she is set free from the law of her husband. So while her husband lives she will be called an adulteress if she goes to another man; but if her husband dies, she is free from the law, so that she is not an adulteress if she goes to another man. Thus, my brothers, you also have died for the law through the body of the Christ, to belong to another, to him who was raised from the dead so that we may bear harvest to God. For when we were in the flesh, the passions of our sins, because of the law, worked in our bodies to make us bear harvest to death. But now, by dying, we have been set free from the law, to which we had been subjected, so as to be slaves, in a new way, of the Spirit, and not, in the old way, of the letter.

What then shall we say? That the law is sin? Never. But I never would have known sin except through the law, for I never would have known desire if the law had not said: You shall not desire what is not yours. But it was by getting a starting point through the commandment that sin caused every kind of desire in me, since without the law sin is a dead thing. I once did live without the law; but when the commandment came the sin came to life, and I died, and my commandment for life was found to be for my death. So it was by getting a starting point through the commandment that sin distracted me and, through the commandment, killed me.

Thus the law is holy, and the commandment is holy and just and good. Then was this good thing death for me? Never. But it was sin, so that sin might be shown, through the good, to be accomplishing my death; so that sin might be surpassingly sinful, because of the commandment. For we know that the law is spiritual; but I am carnal, sold into subjection to sin. I do not know what I am doing. I do not do what I want, but what I hate;

that is what I do. But if what I do is what I do not want,
I agree that the law is good. But now it is no longer I
who do this but the sin that lives in me. For I know that
good does not live in me, not, that is, in my flesh; for it
is in my power to wish for the good, but not to do good.
I do not do the good that I want, but the bad that I do
not want. That is what I do. But if I do what I do not
want, it is no longer I who do it but the sin that lives in
me.

I find that the law, for me, who wish to do good, comes
as an evil. I rejoice, in my inner person, in the law of
God, but I see another law in my body arrayed for battle
against the law of my mind, and it takes me captive by
means of the law of sin which is in my body. I am a
wretched human being. Who will rescue me from this
body which belongs to death? Thanks be to God, it will
be through Jesus Christ our Lord. I myself am slave by
the mind to the law of God, but slave by the flesh to the
law of sin.

¶ Thus there is no condemnation for those who are in
Christ Jesus; for the law of the Spirit of life in Christ
Jesus set you free from the law of sin and death. God did
what the law could not do, because it was weakened by
the flesh; he sent his own son in the likeness of the sinful flesh, and found sin in the flesh guilty of sin; so that
the requirements of the law might be fulfilled in us who
walk not in the way of the flesh but in the way of the
Spirit. For those who are in the flesh think the thoughts
of the flesh, but those who are in the spirit think the
thoughts of the Spirit. The thinking of the flesh is death,
but the thinking of the Spirit is life and peace; because

the thinking of the flesh is hostility against God, since it is not obedient to the law of God, for it cannot be. Those who are in the flesh cannot please God.

But you are not in the flesh but in the Spirit if the Spirit of God lives in you. One who does not have the Spirit of Christ is not his. But if Christ is in you, your body is a dead thing, because of sin, but your spirit is life, because of righteousness. But if the Spirit of him who raised Jesus from the dead lives in you, then he who raised Christ Jesus from the dead will make your mortal bodies live through his Spirit that dwells in you.

So then, brothers, we are under obligation, but not to the flesh to live according to the flesh, since if you live according to the flesh you will die; but if by spirit you make the activities of the body die, you will live. For all who are led by the Spirit of God are the sons of God. You did not receive the spirit of slavery, to be afraid again, but you received the spirit of adoption as sons, in which we cry aloud: Abba, Father! This spirit bears witness to our spirit, that we are the children of God. If we are children, we are also heirs: heirs of God, co-heirs with Christ, if we are suffering with him so that we may be glorified with him.

I reason that the sufferings of the present time are not comparable to the glory that is going to be revealed to us. For the expectation of the world awaits the revelation of the sons of God. For the world is subjected to vanity not because it wishes to be but because of him who subjected it; but there is hope, because this world will be set free from slavery to decay into the freedom of the glory of the children of God. For we know that the whole world groans and is in labor together, until now; not only that, but even we who have some foretaste of the Spirit also groan within ourselves as we await adoption and the redemption of the body. It was by hope that we were saved; but hope that sees is not hope, since who hopes for what he sees? But if we hope for what we do not see, we await it steadfastly.

So also the Spirit takes a hand to help our weakness. We do not know what we should rightly pray for, but the Spirit itself intercedes for us with inarticulate groans, and he who scrutinizes our hearts knows the will of the Spirit, that by the will of God it intercedes for the saints. We know that God helps make everything good for those who love God, those who are summoned by preference. Those whom he foreknew, he foreordained to share the likeness of his son so that that son should be the first-born among many brothers; and those whom he foreordained, he also summoned; and those whom he summoned, he also justified; and those whom he justified, he also glorified.

What then shall we say to that? If God is for us, who is against us? For he did not spare his own son, but sacrificed him for the sake of us all. How, with his help, will not every grace be given us? Who will speak against the chosen of God? It is God who justifies us. Who will condemn us? It is Christ who died, or rather was raised from the dead, who is on the right hand of God, it is he who intercedes for us. Who will take us away from the love of the Christ? Will it be affliction or distress or persecution or starvation or nakedness or peril or the sword? It is written: For your sake we are killed all day long, we are counted like sheep for the slaughter. But in all this we are more than winners because of him who loves us. For I believe that neither death nor life; neither angels nor authorities; neither things that are nor things to come; not powers, nor height nor depth nor any other state of the world will be able to take us away from the love of God which is in Christ Jesus our Lord.

¶ I am speaking the truth, in Christ, I am not lying, and my conscience in the Holy Spirit bears me witness: there is great sorrow and incessant pain in my heart. I could have wished to be outcast from the Christ myself for the sake of my brothers, who are my blood kindred. They are Israelites. Theirs is the adoption and the glory, theirs the covenants and the giving of the law and the service and the promises. From them are the fathers, from them, in the way of the flesh, the Christ, who is over all, God to be praised forever. Amen. But it is not possible that the word of God has failed. For not all who are from Israel are Israel; nor, because they are the seed of Abraham, are they all his children, but: Your seed shall be named through Isaac. That is, it is not the children of the flesh who are children of God, but the children of his promise are counted as his seed. For this is what the promise says: I will come at that time, and Sarah shall have a son. Not only that, but there was Rebeccah whose children were conceived from a single person, Isaac our forefather. Then, when her children had not yet been born, when they had done nothing either good or bad, so that the purpose in the choice of God might hold good, not because of what they had done but because of him who called them, she was told: The elder shall be the slave of the younger. As it is written: I loved Jacob and I hated Esau.

What then shall we say? Could there be any unfairness in God? Never! To Moses he says: I will pity whom I pity, and I will have mercy on him on whom I have mercy. But that is not a matter of wish or effort but of God's mercy. For scripture says to Pharaoh: For this I have raised you up, to show my power through you, and for you to make my name known in all the earth. He pities the one he wishes to pity, and he makes insensitive the one he wishes to be so.

Will you then ask me: What fault can he still find? Who ever stood up against his will? My good man, who are you to argue with God? Shall the work of art say to the artist: Why did you make me the way you did? Does not the potter have power over his clay to make, from the same material, one piece that is to be prized and another to be despised? But if God, while wishing to show his anger and make known his power, endured with great patience the vessels of anger which were made for destruction, it was to make known the abundance of his glory given to the vessels of mercy which he had foreordained for glory: ourselves, whom he summoned not only from among the Jews but also from among the Gentiles. So he says in Hosea: I will call what is not my people my people, and her who was not beloved, beloved; and in the place where it was said to them: You are not my people, they shall be called sons of the living God. Isaiah cries aloud concerning Israel: Though the number of the sons of Israel is as the sands of the sea, only a remnant will be saved; for the Lord will complete and conclude his sentence upon the earth. And as Isaiah said before: If the Lord of Hosts had not left us children, we would have been like Sodom, and we would have been in the likeness of Gomorrah.

What then shall we say? That the Gentiles, who did not pursue righteousness, found righteousness, but it was the righteousness which comes from faith; while Israel, pursuing the law of righteousness, did not achieve that law. Why so? Because it was not by faith but by actions, and they stumbled against the stone of stumbling, as is written: Behold, I place on Zion the stone of stumbling and the rock of misdirection; but he who has faith in him shall not be brought to shame.

¶ Brothers, the desire in my heart and my prayer to God are for them, that they may be saved. For I bear these brothers witness that they have the longing for God; but not in the way of understanding; for they are ignorant of the righteousness of God, and when they tried to set up their own righteousness, they did not submit to the righteousness of God. Christ is the fulfillment of the law and means righteousness for everyone who has faith. Moses writes that everyone who acts righteously according to the law shall live through that. But the righteousness which comes from faith speaks thus: Do not say in your heart: Who will go up to heaven? This is to bring Christ down. Or say: Who will go down into the bottomless pit? This is to bring Christ up from the dead. Then what does it say? That the word is close to you, it is in your mouth and in your heart. This is the word of the faith which we preach: that if you confess to the word that is in your mouth, that Jesus is Lord, and believe in your heart that God raised him from the dead, you will be saved. For faith in the heart means righteousness, and confession by the mouth means salvation; Since scripture says: No one who has faith in him shall be put to shame. There is no distinction between Jew and Greek, since the same Lord is Lord of all, and he is bountiful toward all who call upon him. For everyone who calls upon the name of the Lord shall be saved. How then shall they call upon one in whom they do not believe? How shall they believe in one of whom they have not heard? How shall they hear without one to preach him? How shall they preach unless they are sent forth? As it is written: How beautiful are the feet of those who bring the good news, the gospel.

But not all heeded the gospel. For Isaiah says: Lord, who believed in our report? Faith comes from what they hear, and what they hear is of the word of Christ. But do I say, they did not hear? Rather: Their voice went out over all the earth, and their words to the ends of the world. But I say, did Israel not understand? First Moses says: I will make you jealous of what is no nation, against a nation without understanding I will rouse your anger. And Isaiah is bold to say: I was found by those who did not seek me, I was made manifest to those who did not want to know me. And to Israel he says: All day I have stretched out my hands to a people who would not obey and contradicted me.

¶ Then I ask, could God have rejected his people? Never! I myself am an Israelite, of the seed of Abraham, of the tribe of Benjamin. God did not reject his people, not those whom he had chosen before. Or do you not know that the scripture says, in Elijah, how he pleads with God against Israel: Lord, they killed your prophets, they wrecked your altars, and I alone am left, and they are after my life. But then, what is the divine response to him? I have put aside for myself seven thousand men who did not bend the knee to Baal. So even in the present time there is a remnant by way of election for grace; but if by grace, not because of their actions, since such grace is grace no longer. How then? Israel did not find what Israel sought; but the elect found it. But the rest were made insensitive, as it is written: God gave them a spirit of stupidity, and eyes that would not see and ears that would not hear, even down to the present day. And David says: Let their table turn into a snare to entrap them, and a stumbling block, so that they will be punished. Let their eyes be darkened so that they may not see, and their backs forever bent double.

I ask then, did they stumble in order to fall? Never! But by their transgression came the salvation of the Gentiles, to make the Jews emulate them. But if their transgression meant good fortune for the world, and their defeat meant good fortune for the Gentiles, how much more will their success mean!

But this I say to you, the Gentiles: Insofar as I am the apostle of the Gentiles, I enlarge my ministry, to stir up if I can my own flesh and blood and so save some of them. For if their rejection means the reconciliation of the world, what will their acceptance mean? Surely, life after death. But if the first fruits are blessed, so is the main mass; and if the root is blessed, so are the branches.

But if some of the branches have been broken off, and you, a wild olive, have been grafted in their place and share with the root the richness of the olive tree, do not glory over those branches. Though you may glory, it is not you who support the root, the root supports you. You will say: The branches were broken off so that I could be grafted on. Very well. They were broken off for lack of faith and you took their places because of your faith. Do not be too confident; but be full of fear. For if God did not spare the branches that were naturally his, he will not spare you. Behold the goodness, and the severity, of God: his severity toward those who have fallen away, but for you the goodness of God, so long as you endure in that goodness; since you too could be cut off. And those others, unless they persist in their unbelief, will be grafted, for God has the power to graft them in again. For if you were cut away from your natural wild olive tree and grafted against your nature onto the good olive tree, how much the sooner will they be grafted onto the olive tree which is naturally their own.

For I would not have you think yourselves wise, brothers, through failure to understand this mystery: that a part of Israel has been made uncomprehending until such time as the number of the Gentiles is full; and thus all Israel shall be saved, as it is written: The deliverer will come from Zion, and he will turn impiety away from Jacob; this will be my covenant with them, when I take away their sins. In the matter of the gospel they are enemies because of you, but in the matter of being chosen they are beloved because of their fathers; for the favors and the summons of God are not to be reversed. Just as you once disbelieved in God, but now have been granted mercy through their disbelief; so now they have disbelieved, so that, by the mercy given to you, they may also receive mercy; since God has included all in one disbelief so that he may have mercy on all.

Oh, the depth of the riches and wisdom and understanding of God! How inscrutable are his judgments, how untraceable his ways! For who knows the mind of the Lord? Who was ever his counselor? Who ever advanced him anything, and will be repaid? Since from him and through him and to him come all things; his is the glory forever. Amen.

¶ I urge you, brothers, by God's mercy, to offer your bodies as a living holy sacrifice pleasing to God. This is your reasonable service. And do not pattern yourselves after this age, but transform yourselves through a renewal of the mind, to study the nature of the will of God, what is good, and pleasing, and perfect.

For through the grace that has been granted me I say to every one among you: Do not think thoughts beyond the thoughts you should have, but think to be moderate, according to the measure of faith God has given to each. As in our bodies we have many parts, but the parts do not all have the same function, so we many are one body in Christ, and individually parts of each other. We have different gifts which vary according to the grace that has been given us. If the gift is for prophecy, it should be based on faith. If one is gifted for service, he should serve; the teacher should teach, the comforter should bring comfort; the contributor should show his generosity, the leader his energy, the charitable man his graciousness. Let love be sincere. Hate the bad, hold fast to the good; love each other as brothers, prize each other more than yourselves; be unflagging in energy, seething with enthusiasm, serving the Lord, rejoicing in hope, steadfast against oppression, devoted in prayer; contribute to the needs of the saints, cultivate hospitality. Bless your persecutors, bless them, do not curse them. Rejoice with those who rejoice and weep with those who weep. Agree with each other in your thoughts, and do not be haughty but accommodate yourselves to modest thoughts. Do not be wise in your own estimation. Return no one evil for evil. Have good intentions in regard to all men. If it is possible, be for your part at peace with all men. Do not avenge yourselves, dear friends, but give way to God's anger, since it is written: Mine is the vengeance, mine the retribution, says the Lord. Then if your enemy is hungry, feed him; if he is thirsty, give him something to drink; so doing, you will heap coals of fire on his head. Do not let yourselves be overcome by evil, but overcome evil through good.

¶ Let every soul subject itself to the authorities that are set over it, for there is no authority except by God's will, and those which exist are appointed by God. Thus anyone who sets himself against authority is rebelling against the ordinance of God, and the rebels will bring judgment upon themselves. The men in power are nothing for good conduct to fear, only for bad conduct. Do you wish not to be afraid of authority? Then continue to do good, and you will have praise from it, for authority is God's minister for your good. But if you do evil, then be afraid, since it is not for nothing that that minister wears a sword, since he is God's minister, vindictive in anger against the evildoer. So it is necessary for you to subject yourself, not only because of the anger but because of your conscience. This is also why you pay your taxes. These are the servants of God devoted to this very purpose. Pay all men what you owe them; pay the tax to whom you owe the tax, the toll to whom you owe the toll; fear him you ought to fear, honor whom you ought to honor.

Do not be obliged to anyone for anything, except to love each other; he who loves has fulfilled all the rest of the law. For: You shall not commit adultery, you shall not murder, you shall not steal, you shall not covet, and any other commandment there may be, all are summed up in this statement: You shall love your neighbor as yourself. Love does your neighbor no harm, so love is the fulfillment of the law. And do this knowing what time it is, that now is the hour for you to waken from sleep, since our salvation is now much closer to us than when we got our faith. The night is advanced, the day is near. Let us put away the works of darkness and put on the armor of light. As in daylight let us go about decently, without reveling and drunkenness, without lovemaking and debauchery, without contentiousness and jealousy. But arm yourselves in the Lord Jesus Christ, and do not take thought for your body and its desires.

¶ Welcome the company of the man who is weak in faith, but not to dispute over fine points. For some have faith that they can eat anything, but the weak man eats only vegetables. Let the man who does eat not ridicule the one who abstains, and let the one who abstains not judge the one who eats, for God has accepted him. Who are you to judge the servant of another? He stands or falls by his own master. But he will stand, for the Lord has the power to make him stand.

One man prefers one day to another; another man approves of every day. Let each one be convinced in his own mind; for he who favors a day favors it for the Lord. The eater eats for the Lord, since he gives thanks to God; the abstainer abstains for the Lord, and he too gives thanks to God. For not one of us lives for himself, and not one of us dies for himself; if we live, we live for the Lord, and if we die, we die for the Lord. Whether we live or die, we belong to the Lord. For that was why Christ died and came to life, to be Lord over the dead and the living. You, why do you judge your brother? Or you, why do you, in turn, ridicule your brother? For we shall all stand before the judgment seat of God; since it is written: I live, says the Lord, that every knee shall bend to me, and every tongue shall confess to God. So each of us shall account for himself to God.

Then let us stop judging each other; rather, use your judgment to keep from offending your brother or putting a stumbling block in his way. I know and believe through the Lord Jesus that nothing is unclean in itself; only if one thinks that something is unclean, it is unclean for him. If your brother is hurt by what you eat, you are not walking in the way of love. Do not undo him, for whom Christ died, through what you eat. Do not let what is good for you be cause for ill repute. For the Kingdom of God is not food and drink, but righteousness and peace and joy in the Holy Spirit; and he who in this Spirit serves the Christ is pleasing to God and respected by men. Let us then pursue the ways of peace and the edification of each other. Do not undo the work of God for the sake of food. All things are pure, but it is bad for a man to eat in a way that will mislead. It is good not to eat meat or drink wine or do anything else if by this your brother is misled; as for you, keep your own faith before God. Happy is he who does not have to judge himself in the matter of what he approves. If one doubts but eats, he is guilty, because he does not do it from faith; and anything done without faith is a sin.

¶ We who are strong have a duty to put up with the weaknesses of those who are not strong, rather than pleasing ourselves. Let every man try to please his neighbor, to build up the community; for Christ also did not please himself, but, as it is written: The revilements of those who reviled you fell upon me. All that was written in days before was written for our instruction so that, through steadfastness and through the exhortation of the scriptures, we may have hope. May the God of steadfastness and exhortation grant you concord among yourselves after the example of Christ Jesus, so that together with one voice you may glorify God the Father of our Lord Jesus Christ.

So welcome each other, as Christ has welcomed us, for the glory of God. For I say that Christ was born to be the minister of the circumcised for the sake of God's truth, to confirm the promises made to our fathers; but also, for the Gentiles to glorify God for his mercy, as it is written: Therefore I shall acknowledge you among the Gentiles, and I will sing the praises of your name. And again it says: Rejoice, Gentiles, along with his people; and again: All nations, praise the Lord, and let all peoples praise him. And, once more, Isaiah says: There shall be a scion of Jesse who shall rise up to rule the nations, and in him the nations will have hope. May the God of hope fill you with all joy and peace, by your faith, so that your hope will be abundant through the power of the Holy Spirit.

Concerning you, my brothers, I am convinced that you yourselves are full of goodness, and complete in all understanding, and able to advise each other. But I have written to you rather boldly in part, to remind you, because God gave me the privilege of being the minister of Christ Jesus to the Gentiles, serving as priest the gospel of God; so that the offering up of the Gentiles to him may be acceptable and sanctified by the Holy Spirit. I am full of exultation before God because of Christ Jesus, for I will not dare speak of anything except Christ working through me to make the Gentiles obedient to his will;

by word and act, by the power of miracles and portents, by the power of the Holy Spirit. Thus I have toured about from Jerusalem as far as Illyria to complete the preaching of the gospel of Christ, so ambitious was I to bring the gospel where the name of Christ was not known, so as not to build on someone else's foundation but, as it is written: They who had not been told of him shall see him, and they who never heard of him shall know him.

Because of all this, I have been constantly prevented from coming to you. But now I no longer find any place for me in these regions, and for some years I have been longing to visit you, and then go on to Spain; for I hope to become acquainted with you as I pass through, and that you will see me on my way after I have first enjoyed something of your company. But now I am on my way to Jerusalem in the service of the saints. For Macedonia and Achaea have decided to make a contribution for the poor who are among the saints in Jerusalem. They have so decided and they are indebted to them; for since the Gentiles shared with them in matters of the spirit, they owe it to them to help them in a material way. When I have finished this business and set my seal upon this bounty for them, then I shall leave for Spain, stopping with you on the way; and I know that when I come to you I shall come with the full blessing of Christ.

Now I entreat you, by our Lord Jesus Christ and by the love of the Spirit, to aid me in my struggle, through your prayers to God, for me, so that I may be kept safe from the faithless in Judaea and my ministry in Jerusalem may prove acceptable to the saints, and so by God's will I may come to you in joy and take some rest with you. And may the God of peace be with you all. Amen.

¶I recommend to you Phoebe, our sister, who is deacon-ess of the church in Cenchreae; to receive her, in the Lord's name, in a manner befitting the saints, and help her in anything she needs from you, for she has been the benefactor of many, myself among them.

Give greetings to Prisca and Aquila, my fellow work-ers in Christ Jesus. They have risked their necks for my life, and not only am I grateful to them but so are all the churches among the Gentiles. Give greetings also to the church that is in their own house. Give greetings to my beloved Epaenetus, who is Asia's first offering to Christ. Give greetings to Mary, who has worked very hard for you. Give greetings to Andronicus and Junias, my fellow countrymen and fellow prisoners, who are distinguished among the apostles and were with Christ even before me. Give greetings to Ampliatus, my beloved in the Lord. Give greetings to Urbanus, our fellow worker in Christ, and to my beloved Stachys. Give greetings to Apelles, honored in Christ. Give greetings to the household of Aristobulus. Give greetings to Herodian, my fellow countryman. Give greetings to those of the household of Narcissus who are in the Lord. Give greetings to Try-phaena and Tryphosa, who have worked hard for the Lord. Give greetings to the beloved Persis, who has worked very hard for the Lord. Give greetings to Rufus, excellent in the Lord, and to his mother, who is a mother to me. Give greetings to Asyncritus, Phlegon, Hermes, Patrobas, Hermas, and the brothers who are with them. Give greetings to Philologus and Julia, Nereus and his sister, and Olympas, and all the saints who are with them. Give greetings to each other with the sacred kiss. All the churches of Christ give you greetings.

And I entreat you, brothers, to mark well those who

cause dissension and misguidance, which are counter to the doctrine you have learned; and avoid them. Such people are the slaves not of our Lord Christ but of their own bellies; but by fair speech and flattery they deceive the hearts of the simple. Your obedience has become known to everyone. Therefore I rejoice in you, and I wish you to be wise for good, but innocent for evil. The God of peace will crush Satan under your feet soon.

The grace of our Lord Jesus be with you.

Timothy, my fellow worker, sends you greetings, as do Lucius and Jason and Sosipater, my fellow countrymen. And I, Tertius, who wrote down this letter send you greetings in the Lord. Gaius, who is host to me and to the entire church, sends you greetings. And Erastus, the treasurer of the city, sends you greetings, as does Quartus, his brother.

To the one who has power to strengthen you, as in my gospel and the preaching of Jesus Christ; by the revelation of a mystery which was silenced through the ages but now has been brought to light, and has been made known through prophetic scriptures to all the nations by order of the everlasting God, to make them obedient to the faith; to the one God, who is wise, may the glory be given, through Jesus Christ, forever. Amen.

The First Letter
to the Corinthians

¶PAUL, CALLED TO BE AN APOSTLE OF
Jesus Christ by the will of God, and Sosthenes, his
brother, to the church of God which is in Corinth, to
those who are consecrated in Christ Jesus, called to be
saints; together with all those who invoke the name of
our Lord Jesus Christ in every locality, theirs and ours:
grace to you and peace from God our Father and the Lord
Jesus Christ.

I thank God at all times on your account for the grace
of God given you in Christ Jesus, that in every way you
have been made rich in him, in every word and all understanding, as the testimony to the Christ has been
confirmed among you, so that you do not come short in
any gift of grace, as you look for the revelation of our
Lord Jesus Christ. He will keep you firm until the end,
without reproach on the Day of our Lord Jesus. One must
believe in God, by whom you were summoned to the
fellowship of his son Jesus Christ our Lord.

Still, I entreat you, brothers, in the name of our Lord
Jesus Christ, all to agree with each other, so that there
will be no schisms among you, but you will be united in
the same mind and the same understanding. For, my

brothers, I have been told about you by Chloe and her people; that there are rivalries among you. I mean this: each of you says: I am for Paul; or else: I am for Apollos; or: I am for Peter; or: I am for Christ. Christ is partitioned! Was Paul ever crucified for you? Or were you baptized in the name of Paul? I am thankful that I baptized no one of you (except Crispus and Gaius), so that no one can say that you were baptized in my name. I did also baptize the household of Stephanas. For the rest, I do not know whether I baptized anyone else. For Christ did not send me forth to baptize, but to preach the gospel; not in accomplished oratory, but so that the cross of the Christ might not be made meaningless.

For the word of the cross is folly to those who go the way of perdition, but to us who go the way of salvation it is the power of God. Since it is written: I will destroy the wisdom of the wise, and I will make void the intelligence of the intelligent.

Where is the sage? Where is the scholar? Where is the student of this age? Did not God turn the wisdom of the world to folly? For since by the wisdom of God the world did not, because of its wisdom, know God, God saw fit to save the believers through the folly of what was preached to them. For the Jews demand miracles and the Greeks look for wisdom; but we preach Christ crucified, a stumbling block to the Jews and folly to the heathens, but to us who are chosen, Jews and Greeks alike, Christ the power of God and the wisdom of God. Since the folly of God is wiser than men, and the weakness of God is stronger than men.

For consider your calling, brothers: that not many of you are wise in the way of the flesh, not many are strong, not many are well born. But God chose out the fools of the world, to shame the wise, and God chose out the weak of the world, to shame the strong, and God chose out the humble and despised of the world; and what is not, to abolish what is; so that no flesh may take pride before God. For you are from him, in Christ Jesus, who was born our wisdom from God, and our righteousness and sanctification and redemption, so that, as it is written: Let him who takes pride take pride in the Lord.

¶ And I myself when I came to you, brothers, did not come to you with any superiority of speech or wisdom when I proclaimed to you the mystery of God; for I did not judge that, among you, I knew anything except only Jesus Christ, that is, Jesus Christ crucified. And I came to you in weakness and much fear and trembling, and my message and my preaching did not consist in persuasive words of wisdom but in the revelation of spirit and power, so that your faith might not rest on the wisdom of men but on the power of God. Still, what we say is wisdom, to the initiates, but not the wisdom of this age or of the leaders of this age, who are doomed; but what we say is the wisdom of God in a mystery, the hidden wisdom, which God foreordained before the ages for our glory; which not one of the leaders of this age understood, since if they had understood it they would not have crucified the Lord of glory. But, as it is written: All that God made ready for those who love him; which the eye did not see and the ear did not hear, nor did it enter into the heart of man.

For God made his revelation to us through the Spirit; for the Spirit explores everything, even the depths of God. Who among men knows what is in a man except the spirit of man which is in him? So also no one knows what is in God except the Spirit of God. And we did not receive the spirit of the world but the Spirit which is from God, so that we may know what grace we were given by God; which we also now speak of, not in words which are the teaching of human wisdom, but in words which are the teaching of the Spirit, combining the spiritual with the spiritual. The sensual man does not accept what belongs to the Spirit of God, since it is folly to him, and he cannot understand, because these things are judged spiritually; but the spiritual man judges all things, while he himself is judged by no man. For who knows the mind of the Lord, which will instruct him? But we do have the mind of Christ.

¶ And I, brothers, could not speak to you as to spiritual persons, but as fleshly ones, little children in Christ. I gave you milk to drink, not solid food, for you were not yet strong enough. Nor are you even now, since you are still of the flesh. For when there is jealousy and rivalry among you, are you not of the flesh, and going the way of mankind? When one of you says: I am for Paul, and another: I am for Apollos, are you not being human? What then is Apollos? And what is Paul? Servants, through whom you got belief, and each as the Lord gave it. I planted, Apollos watered, but God made it grow. So he who plants is nothing, nor he who waters; only God who makes it grow. He who plants and he who waters are one, but each will receive his own wages for his own labor. We are the fellow workers of God; you are God's field, God's architecture.

By the grace of God given to me I laid the foundation like a skilled architect, but another builds upon it. Let every man look to it how he builds; for no one can lay down any foundation beside the one that has been laid down, which is Jesus Christ. And if anyone builds upon the foundation in gold, silver, precious stones, wood, hay, straw, the work of each will become manifest, for the Day will make it plain; because revelation comes by fire, and the fire itself will prove the nature of each man's work. If the work a man has built endures, he will have his reward; if anyone's work burns up, he will be penalized, but he himself will be saved; but as if through fire.

Do you not know that you are God's temple and God's Spirit lives in you? If anyone destroys God's temple, God will destroy him. For the temple of God is holy. This you are.

Let no one deceive himself. If anyone thinks he is wise among you in this age, let him become a fool, so that he may become wise, for the wisdom of this world is folly with God. Since it is written: He who catches the wise in their shiftiness; and again: The Lord knows the reasonings of the wise; that they are vain. So let no one take pride among men; for all things are yours, whether it be Paul or Apollos or Peter or the world or life or death or present or future; all are yours, but you are Christ's and Christ is God's.

¶ So let a man think of us as servants of Christ and stewards of the mysteries of God. But it is required of any steward that he be found reliable. It means very little to me to be judged by you or by any human day of judgment; nor again do I judge myself, for I am not conscious of any guilt; but I am not justified by that, but he who judges me is the Lord. Do not, therefore, make any judgment before it is time, not until the Lord comes; and he will illuminate what is hidden in darkness and bring to light the counsels of men's hearts; and that will be the time for each man's praise from God.

I have put this in terms of Apollos and myself for your sake, brothers, so that in us you may understand the saying: Nothing beyond what is written; so that you may not become too emotional each in favor of one against another. For who marks you out for distinction? What do you have which you were not given? And if you did receive something, why do you take pride as if you had been given nothing? Have you had your fill yet? Have you grown rich yet? Have you been made kings, without us? I wish you had been made kings, so that we could be kings along with you.

For I believe God displayed us, the apostles, at the end of the show like men condemned to death; because we have turned into a spectacle for the world, for angels and men alike. We are fools for Christ but you are wise in Christ. We are weak, you are strong. You are respected, we are despised. For until this very day we have been hungry and thirsty and naked, and beaten and driven from place to place, and worn ourselves out working with our own hands. We are reviled and give blessings; we are persecuted and put up with it; we are abused and are conciliatory. We have become the outcasts of the world, the offscouring of everything; to this very day.

I write you this, not to make you ashamed, but as if I were admonishing my own beloved children; for even if you have ten thousand tutors in Christ, you do not have many fathers; but I am your father in Christ Jesus through the gospel. So I implore you: copy me. For this reason I have sent you Timothy, who is my child, beloved and faithful in the Lord, and he will recall to you my ways in Christ, as I teach everywhere in every church.

Some of you became inflated with pride as if I were not coming to you; but if the Lord is willing, I shall come to you soon, and learn of the proud ones not what they say but what they can do, since the Kingdom of God is not in speech but in power to act. Which do you want? Shall I come to you with a stick, or in love and the spirit of gentleness?

¶ In very truth, a case of immorality is reported in your community, and such immorality as is not found even among the heathens: a man has taken his father's wife. And are you pleased with yourselves, rather than so grieved that the man who did this thing must be removed from your presence? For I, absent in body but present in spirit, have already judged the man who did this as if I were really there; in the name of our Lord Jesus; with yourselves and my spirit gathered together, with the power of our Lord Jesus; to hand over a man like this to Satan for the destruction of the flesh, so that his soul may be saved on the Day of the Lord. Your pride is not good. Do you not know that a little leavening raises the whole mass of dough? Clean out the old leavening so that you may be a new baking, unleavened as you are. For even Christ, our paschal lamb, was sacrificed; so let us keep the festival, not in the old leavening, nor in the leavening of baseness and corruption, but in the unleavened bread of purity and truth.

I wrote in my letter to you that you should have nothing to do with lechers; not, that is, meaning the lechers of this world in general, nor the covetous or the rapacious or the idolatrous, since then you would have had to take leave of the world; but in fact I wrote to you that you should have nothing to do with one who is named a

brother if he is a lecher, or covetous or idolatrous or abusive or drunken or rapacious; not even to eat with such
a one. For what have I to do with judging those who are
outside our number? Do you not judge those who are
inside our number, while God judges those who are outside? Drive the evil one out from among you.

¶ Does any one of you, who has a case against any other
one of you, presume to have it judged before the unjust
rather than before the saints? Do you not know, then,
that the saints will judge the world? And if the world is
judged by you, are you then unfit for the most trivial
lawsuits? Do you not know that we shall be judging angels, let alone ordinary cases? And if you have ordinary
cases, do you seat in judgment those who are of no account in the church? I say this to your shame. Is there
among you no man wise enough to be able to decide between brother and brother? Does brother go to law with
brother, and before unbelievers too? It is a real fault in
you that you have lawsuits against each other at all. Why
not rather let yourselves be wronged? Why not rather let
yourselves be robbed? But you do wrong and rob, and to
brothers too. Or do you not know that wrongdoers shall
not inherit the Kingdom of God? Do not be deceived.
Neither lechers nor idolators nor adulterers nor effemi-
nates nor pederasts nor thieves nor the covetous, none
who are drunken or abusive or rapacious, shall inherit
the Kingdom of God. And some of you have been these
very things; but you have been washed clean and sanctified and justified in the name of our Lord Jesus Christ
and in the Spirit of our God.

All things are lawful for me; but not all things are advantageous. All things are lawful for me, but I shall not

be in the power of anything. Foods are for the belly, and the belly is for food; but God will put an end to both the one and the other. But the body is not for lechery but for the Lord and the Lord is for the body; and God both raised the Lord from the dead and also will raise us by his power. Do you not know that your bodies are the limbs of Christ? Then shall I take the limbs of Christ and make them the limbs of a whore? Never. Or do you not know that he who clings to a whore is one body with her; for, says scripture, the two shall be one flesh. But he who clings to the Lord is one spirit with him. Flee from lechery. Any other sin a man may commit is outside his body, but the lecher sins against his own body. Or do you not know that your body is the temple of the Holy Spirit in you, which you have from God? And you are not your own, since you were bought for a price. Then glorify God in your body.

¶ Concerning the matters you wrote me of, it is a good thing for a man not to touch any woman; but to save you from loose living, let each man have his own wife, and each woman have her own husband. Let the husband give his wife her due, and so likewise the wife to her husband. The wife does not have authority over her own body; her husband does; and so likewise the husband does not have authority over his own body; his wife does. Do not deny each other, except by agreement for a time when you can devote yourselves to prayer, and then be as you were before; for fear Satan may entice you through incontinence. I tell you this as a concession, not as a command. What I should like is for all people to be as I am; but each person has his own endowment from God, some of one kind and some of another.

And I say to the unmarried and the widows, that it is good to remain as I am; but if they cannot control themselves, let them marry, for it is better to marry than to be on fire. And to those who are married, I command; no, not I, but the Lord: that a wife should not separate from her husband; and if she does separate herself, she must remain single or else be reconciled with her husband; and a man should not divorce his wife.

And to the others I, not the Lord, say this: If any brother has a wife who is an unbeliever, and she consents to live with him, he should not divorce her; and a woman who has a husband who is an unbeliever and who consents to live with her should not divorce him. For the unbelieving husband is hallowed by his wife, and the unbelieving wife is hallowed by one who is a brother; since otherwise your children are impure, but this way they are hallowed. But if the unbeliever separates, let him or her be separate; the brother or sister is not bound in such cases; God called you in peace. For how do you know, wife, if you will save your husband? Or how do you know, husband, if you will save your wife?

Unless the Lord has so directed, let everyone go on as he was when God called him; and I so order in all the churches. Was one circumcised when he was called? Let him not try to undo it. Was one uncircumcised when he was called? Let him not be circumcised. Circumcision means nothing and uncircumcision means nothing; only keeping the commandments of God means anything. Let each remain in that condition in which he was called. Were you a slave when called? Let it not trouble you; but even if you can become free, make the best of your condition; for the slave called by the Lord is the Lord's freedman, and so likewise the free man called is the

Lord's slave. You were bought for a price; do not become the slaves of human beings. As each one was when called, brothers, so let him remain before God.

Concerning those who are unmarried I have no mandate from the Lord, but I give you my opinion as one who has been mercifully granted by the Lord to be trustworthy. I think that, because of the impending peril, it is good for a man to remain as he is. Are you bound to a wife? Do not seek freedom. Are you free of a wife? Do not seek a wife. But even if you do marry, you have not sinned. And if an unmarried girl marries, she has not sinned. But such people will have affliction in the flesh. I am trying to spare you. But this I do say, brothers: our time is now short. For the time that remains, let even those who have wives be as if they did not; let those who mourn be as if they did not mourn, and those who rejoice be as if they did not rejoice; and those who buy, as if they kept nothing; and those who use the world, as if they got no use of it. For the form of this world is passing away.

I want you to be free from care. The unmarried man cares about the things of the Lord and how he can please the Lord; but the married man cares about the things of the world and how he can please his wife, and he is of two minds. And the unmarried woman and the virgin care about the things of the Lord, how to be pure in body and spirit; but the married woman cares about the things of the world, and how she can please her husband. I say this for your own good, not to throw a noose around you, but for the sake of propriety, and undistracted devotion to the Lord.

But if a man thinks he is acting shamefully toward his girl if he becomes too impassioned, and it has to be so, let him do what he wants. He is not sinning; let them marry. But the man who stands firm in his heart, and is not constrained, but has control over his will and decides in his own heart to keep his girl a virgin, will be doing well. Thus the one who marries his girl does well, and the one who does not marry does better.

A wife is bound as long as her husband lives. If her husband dies, she is free to marry anyone she wishes, as long as it is marriage in the Lord. But she is happier if she remains as she is, in my opinion; for I think I myself have the spirit of God.

¶ Concerning idol offerings, we are sure that we all have knowledge. Knowledge inflates with pride; love builds. If a man thinks he knows something, he still does not know it as he ought to know it; but if one loves God, he is known by him. Concerning, then, the eating of idol offerings, we know that an idol has no existence in the world, and that there is no god but the one God. For if there are so-called gods, whether in heaven or on earth, as indeed there are many gods and many lords, for us there is one God, the Father, from whom all things are and we are his; and one Lord, Jesus Christ, through whom all things are and we exist through him.

But this knowledge is not in all; and some, through being accustomed hitherto to idols, eat food as if it were idol offerings, and their conscience, being weak, is soiled. But food will not bring us to God; nor, if we do not eat, do we have less; nor, if we do eat, do we have more. But see to it that your freedom does not become a cause of trouble to the weak. For if one sees you, the possessor of understanding, dining in an idol temple, will not his conscience, being weak, be encouraged to eat idol offerings? Then the weak man is undone by your understanding; your brother, for whom Christ died. Thus by sinning against your brothers and battering their weak conscience you are sinning against Christ. Therefore if my eating drives my brother astray, I will never eat meat any more, so as not to drive my brother astray.

¶ Am I not free? Am I not an apostle? Have I not seen Jesus, our Lord? Are you not my handiwork in the Lord? Even if to others I am not an apostle, at least I am to you, since you are the proof of my apostleship in the Lord.

This is my answer to those who call me to account. Do we not have the right to eat and drink? Do we not have the right to take one of our number with us as wife, like the rest of the apostles and the Lord's brothers and Peter? Do only Barnabas and I not have the right not to be laborers? Who ever serves in the army at his own expense? Who plants a vineyard and does not eat its fruit? Who herds a flock and does not drink milk from the flock? Do I speak as an individual or does the law also say this? For in the law of Moses it is written: You shall not muzzle the ox who threshes the grain. Can God be concerned with the oxen, or is he really speaking about us? For it is for us that it is written that the plower must plow in hope, and the thresher must be in hope, of getting his share. If we sowed the things of the spirit among you, is it too much if we reap material benefits from you? If others have this right from you, should we not even more?

But we have not used that right, but we suffer everything so as not to offer any obstruction to the gospel of the Christ. Do you not know that those who perform sacrifices eat some of what has been sacrificed, and those who serve at the altar have their share from the altar? Even so has the Lord instructed those who bring the gospel to live from the gospel. But I have not made use of any of these privileges. I did not write this so that it should be thus for me; for it is better for me to die than that anyone should make my pride an empty thing. For if I preach the gospel, that is no source of pride for me, since the necessity has been laid upon me; woe to me if I do not preach the gospel. For if I do this of my own will, I have my reward; but if I do it not of my own will, I have been entrusted with a duty. What then is my reward? That, as I preach the gospel, I may make the gospel be free of charge, so as not to use up the privilege which the gospel gives me.

For, being free from all, I have enslaved myself to all, so that I may win over the more people. And I have made myself like a Jew to the Jews so as to win over Jews; to those subject to the law like one subject to the law, though I am not myself subject to the law, so as to win over those subject to the law; to those outside the law like one outside the law, though I am not outside the law of God but within the law of Christ, so as to win over those outside the law. To the weak I have made myself weak, to win over the weak. I have made myself all things to all people, so that by some means or other I may save some. And I do all this for the sake of the gospel, so that I may have my share in the gospel.

Do you not know that when they run in the stadium they all run, but only one wins the prize? Run to win. And everyone who competes keeps in training in every way; but they, to win a perishable wreath; we, for an imperishable one. I myself do not race without a goal; I do not box to punish the air; but I batter my own body and enslave it; so that, while calling others to action, I may not myself be disqualified.

¶ Now I do not wish you to be unmindful of the fact, brothers, that our fathers all went under the cloud and all passed through the sea, and were all baptized into Moses under the cloud and in the sea, and all ate the same spiritual food and drank the same spiritual drink, for they drank from the spiritual rock which went with them, and the rock was the Christ. But God was not pleased with most of them; for they died in the desert. These things took place as examples for us, to keep us from desiring evil things as they desired them. Do not become idolaters like some of them; as it is written: The people sat down to eat and drink, and they stood up to play. And let us not be lecherous as some of them were lecherous, and twenty-three thousand fell in a single day. And let us not make trial of the Lord as some of them made trial of him, and they were killed by the snakes. And do not grumble as some of them grumbled, and they were killed by the angel of death. These things made an example of them, and were written of for our instruction, for us with whom the end of the world coincides.

So let him who thinks he is standing see to it that he does not fall. No trial has come upon you which is not human; and God is to be trusted, who will not let you be tried beyond your powers, but with the trial will give you a way out by your being able to endure.

Therefore, my dear friends, flee from idolatry. I speak to you as sensible people; judge for yourselves what I am saying. The cup of blessing which we bless, is that not participation in the blood of the Christ? The loaf which we break, is that not participation in the body of the Christ? Because we many are one loaf, one body, for we all partake of the one loaf. Consider Israel in the matter of the flesh. Do not those who eat the sacrifices share in the altar of sacrifice? What then am I saying? That what is sacrificed to idols amounts to something, or that the idol amounts to something? Rather, that what they sacrifice they sacrifice to demons and not to God, and I would not have you be partners of demons. You cannot drink the cup of the Lord and the cup of demons. You cannot share the table of the Lord and the table of demons. Or are we challenging the Lord? Surely we are not stronger than he?

All things are lawful; but not all things are advantageous. All things are lawful; but not all are helpful. Let no one look for his own good, but for that of the other man.

Eat anything that is sold in the butcher shop without discriminating because of conscience, for the earth with all that fills it belongs to the Lord. If one of the unbelievers invites you and you wish to go, eat everything that is set before you without discriminating because of conscience. But if someone says to you: This is sacrificial meat, do not eat it, for the sake of him who told you, and for conscience; the conscience, I mean, not of oneself but of the other man. For why is my freedom judged by the conscience of another? And if I partake in thankfulness, why am I insulted because of that for which I am thankful?

Then, whether you eat or drink or whatever you do, do it for the glory of God. Be inoffensive toward Jews and

Greeks and the church of God, as I also try to please all in all ways, looking not for my own advantage but for that of the many, so that they may be saved.

¶ Copy me, as I copy Christ.

I have praise for you because you remember everything I say and maintain traditions as I have handed them on to you. But I wish you to know that the head of every man is the Christ, and the head of a wife is her husband, and the head of the Christ is God. Any man who prays or prophesies with his head covered disgraces his head; and any woman who prays or prophesies with her head unveiled disgraces her head; for it is one and the same thing as having a shaven head. If a woman unveils her head, let it be shorn also; but if it is shameful for a woman to have a shorn or shaven head, let her cover it. A man does not need to cover his head, since he is the image and semblance of God; but a woman is the semblance of a man. For man is not from woman, but woman from man; since indeed man was not created for the sake of woman, but woman for the sake of man. Therefore a woman should take care of her head, because of the angels. But, in the Lord, woman does not exist apart from man, nor man apart from woman. For as woman came from man, so man is born of woman; and all is from God.

Judge for yourselves. Is it proper for a woman to pray to God with her head unveiled? Does not nature herself teach you that, if a man has long hair, it is his disgrace, but if a woman has long hair, it is her glory? Since her hair is given to her for a covering. But if I seem to be arbitrary, it is because we do not have that custom, nor do the churches of God.

In giving you my instructions, I have this fault to find with you, that your meetings do more harm than good. For in the first place, I hear that, when you meet together in church, there are dissensions among you; and this in part I believe. For there must be factions among you, so that those who are the true ones may become known among you. Then again, when you meet together, it is not possible to eat the Lord's supper; because each one at dinner seizes his own portion first; and one man goes hungry, another man gets drunk. Do you not have your homes for eating and drinking? Or do you despise the church of God, and put to shame those who are needy? What am I to say to you? Shall I praise you? In this I do not praise you.

For I received from the Lord this tradition which I handed on to you: that the Lord Jesus, on the night when he was betrayed, took a loaf and gave thanks and broke it and said: This is my body, which is for your sake; do this in remembrance of me. So also with the cup after supper, saying: This cup is the new covenant in my blood; do this, whenever you drink, in remembrance of me. For whenever you eat this loaf and drink the cup, you are commemorating the Lord's death; until he comes.

Thus anyone who eats the loaf or drinks the cup of the Lord unworthily is guilty against the body and blood of the Lord. Let a person prove himself worthy, and thus eat from the loaf and drink from the cup. For anyone who eats and drinks is eating and drinking his own damnation if he does not recognize the Body. For that reason many among you are weak and sick, and a good many have even died. If we judged ourselves, we would not be judged; but when we are judged by the Lord, we are being disciplined, so as not to be condemned with the world.

So, my brothers, when you come together to eat, wait for each other. If anyone is hungry, let him eat at home; so your gathering together will not be for your damnation.

I will give you my other instructions when I come.

¶ But concerning matters of the spirit, brothers, I would not have you ignorant. You know that when you were heathens you were led helplessly at random to dumb idols. I make it known to you, therefore, that no one who is speaking in the Spirit says: A curse on Jesus; and no one can say: Jesus is Lord, unless he is speaking in the Holy Spirit.

But there are varieties of gifts; but the same Spirit; and there are varieties of services, and the same Lord; and there are varieties of activities, and the same God, who activates them all among all. To each is given disclosure by the Spirit of what is to his advantage. To one, through the Spirit, it is given to speak with skill; to another, to speak with understanding, through the same Spirit; to another, faith, by the same Spirit; to another, the gifts of healing, by that one Spirit; to another, miraculous powers; to another, prophecy; to another, the power to discern spirits; to another, the varieties of speaking with tongues; and to another, the interpretation of the tongues. One and the same Spirit activates all these things, distributing them separately to each person as it will.

For just as the body is one and has many parts, but all the parts of the body, being many, are one body, so likewise is the Christ; for we were all baptized in one Spirit into one body, whether we were Jews or Greeks, whether slaves or free; and we have all been given one Spirit to drink. For the body is not one part but many. If the foot says: Because I am not a hand, I am not part of the body; it is not for that reason not part of the body. And if the ear says: Because I am not an eye, I am not part of the body; it is not for that reason not part of the body. If all the body were eye, where would our source of hearing be? If all were hearing, where would be our source of smell? But as it is, God has set the parts, each of them, in the body, according to his will. And if all were one part, where would the body be? But as it is, there are many parts, and one body. The eye cannot say to the hand: I have no need of you; nor again can the head say to the feet: I have no need of you. But by so much the more are those parts of the body necessary, which seem to be weak; and those parts of the body which we think are less regarded are those to which we give extra regard; and the unseemly parts of us are treated with more decorum, which our decorous parts do not need. But God has combined the body, giving extra attention to what is inferior, so that there may be no dissension in the body but all parts may be equally concerned for each other. And if one part suffers, all parts suffer with it; and if one part is honored, all parts rejoice with it. You are the body of Christ and its parts, individually.

And those whom God has established in the church are: first, apostles; second, prophets; third, teachers; then, miraculous powers; then, gifts for healing, helpful actions, talents for governing, varieties of tongues. Surely we are not all apostles? Not all prophets? Not all teachers? Not all with miraculous power? Surely not all have gifts for healing? Not all speak with tongues? Not all can interpret these? Aspire to the gifts which are greater.

¶ But now I show you a way that is even better. If I speak with the tongues of men and angels, but have no love, all I am is sounding bronze or a clashing cymbal. And if I have the gift of prophecy and know all mysteries and all understanding, and if I have faith entire so as to move mountains, and have no love, I am nothing. And if I give all I have in alms, and if I give my body to be burned, and have no love, it does me no good. Love is patient, is kind, love has no jealousy, does not swagger, has no pride, is not immodest, does not look for its own advantage, is not stirred to anger, does not keep count of evil done, is not happy over wrongdoing, shares the happiness of the truth; all-sustaining, all-faithful, all-hopeful, all-enduring. Love never fails. If there are prophecies, they will come to nothing; if there are speeches, they will be stopped; if there is understanding, it will come to nothing. For we understand in part and we prophesy in part; but when completeness comes, what is in part will vanish away. When I was a child, I spoke as a child, and thought as a child, and reasoned as a child; now that I am a man, I am through with childish things. For now we see by a mirror, obscurely; but then face to face. Now I know in part; but then I will know in full, as I myself am fully known. And now there remain faith, hope, love; these three; but the greatest of these is love.

¶ Pursue love, aspire to things spiritual, all the more so that you may prophesy. For one who speaks with tongues speaks not to men but to God, since no one understands him, and he talks mysteries by the Spirit; but one who prophesies to men speaks edification and exhortation and consolation. One who speaks with tongues edifies himself; one who prophesies edifies the church. I would like you all to speak with tongues, but would like still more for you to prophesy. He who prophesies is greater than he who speaks with tongues, unless the latter translates it so that the church may be edified. But as it is, brothers, if I come to you speaking with tongues, what good shall I do you; unless I speak to you by way of revelation, or understanding, or prophecy, or teaching? In the same way, if the inanimate things which produce sound, whether flute or lyre, have no distinction in their tones, how will what is played on the flute or lyre be recognized? And again, if the trumpet gives out an unrecognizable call, who will make ready for battle? So too with you, if you do not with your speaking offer orderly discourse, how will what is said by you be understood? You will be talking to the air. Who knows how many kinds of language there are in the world? And none without its own sound. If, then, I do not know the meaning of the sound, I shall be a stupid barbarian to him who speaks it, and he who speaks it will be a stupid barbarian to me. Thus, as for you, since you are eager for the things of the spirit, try to excel in the edification of the church.

So let him who speaks with tongues pray that he may be able to translate it. If I pray speaking with tongues, my spirit prays but my mind adds nothing. What then? I will pray with my spirit, but I will pray also with my mind. I will sing praises with my spirit, but I will sing praises also with my mind. Since if you give thanks and praise in the spirit only, how will one who is in the position of an uninitiate add his amen to your thanksgiving, since he does not know what you are saying? You give thanks very well, but the other man is not edified. I thank God that I speak with tongues more than all the rest of you; but in the church, I would rather say five words rationally and so communicate with others, than ten thousand words with speaking with tongues.

Brothers, do not be children in your thinking; in evil-doing be like little innocents, but in thinking be grown-up. In the law it is written: In strangers' tongues and by the lips of strangers I will speak to this people, and not even so will they listen to me, says the Lord. Thus speaking in tongues is portentous not for believers but only for unbelievers; but prophecy is not for unbelievers, but only for believers. If, then, the whole congregation assembles in one place, and all speak with tongues, and uninstructed persons or unbelievers come in, will they not say you are mad? But if all are prophesying, and an unbeliever or uninstructed person comes in, he is examined by all, and questioned by all, and the secrets of his heart are laid open; and thus he will fling himself down on his face and worship God, announcing: God is really among you.

What then, brothers? When you meet together, each has a song of praise, or a lesson, or a revelation, or speech with tongues, or interpretation. Let all be for edification. If there is speaking with tongues, let it be two at a time or at most three, and in turn, and let one person interpret it. And if there is none who can interpret, let each man be silent in church, and talk to himself and to God. And let two or three speak as prophets, and the rest pass judgment; and if a revelation comes to someone else who is sitting there, let the first speaker be silent. For you can all prophesy, one by one, so that all may learn and all be encouraged; and the spirits of prophets are under the control of the prophets, for God is not the God of disorder but of peace.

As in all the churches of the saints, women must be

silent in church meetings; they are not allowed to speak,
so let them submit as the law dictates. If they wish to
learn about something, let them ask their own husbands
at home; for it is disgraceful for a woman to talk in
church.

Did the word of God originate from you? Or did it come
to you alone? If any one of you thinks that he is a prophet
or gifted with spirit, let him understand that what I write
you is the commandment of God; one who disregards
this is himself disregarded.

So, my brothers, strive to be prophets, and do not oppose speaking with tongues; but let everything be done
properly, in an orderly way.

¶I remind you, brothers, of the gospel which I brought
to you, which you accepted, on which you have stood
fast, by which you are saved; what I said when I brought
the gospel to you, if you retain it still, if you did not
become believers frivolously. To you I handed on what I
had been given to believe which was of the highest importance: that Christ died for our sins, as in the scriptures; and that he was buried, and that he rose on the
third day, as in the scriptures, and that he was seen by
Peter, and then by the twelve. Then he was seen by more
than five hundred brothers all at once, and most of them
are still with us, but some have died. And then he was
seen by James, and then by all the apostles; and last of
all, as to an aborted child, he appeared also to me. For I
am the least of the apostles, who am not fit to be called
an apostle, because I persecuted the church of God. But
by grace of God I am what I am, and his gift of grace to
me has not been vain, but I, not I but the grace of God
which is with me, have worked harder than all of them.

But whether it is I or they, thus we preach and thus you believed.

But if it is preached that Christ rose from the dead, how is it that some among you say that there is no resurrection of the dead? If there is no resurrection of the dead, then neither was Christ raised. But if Christ was not raised, then our preaching is empty, and your belief is empty, and we are found out as false witnesses to God, because we testified against God that he raised up Christ, whom he did not raise up, if, that is, the dead do not rise. For if the dead do not rise, then neither has Christ risen; and if Christ has not risen, your faith is vain, you are still in your sins. And then also those who went to their rest in Christ are lost. If by this life in Christ we are no more than hopeful, then we are the most pitiful of all people.

But in truth, Christ has risen from the dead, the first of the sleepers to rise. For since death came through man, so also resurrection is through man; just as all die in Adam, so in the Christ all will be brought to life. Each in his own appointed place: first Christ, then the Christ's own, at his coming; and then the end, when he hands over his kingdom to his God and Father, when he abolishes every realm and authority and power, for he must be King until he places all his enemies beneath his feet. The last enemy to be abolished is death, for: He has set all things beneath his feet. But when it says that all has been subjected, it means all except the one who subjected all things to him. But when all things are subjected to him, then the son himself will be subjected to him who subjected all things to him, so that God may be all in all.

Otherwise, what will those do who are baptized for

the sake of their dead bodies? If the dead bodies do not rise at all, why are they baptized for their sake? And why do we too go in danger every hour? I die every day; I swear it by the pride I have in you, brothers, through Christ Jesus our Lord. If as a man I fought with beasts in Ephesus, what use is that to me? If the dead do not rise, let us eat and drink, for tomorrow we die. Do not be deceived; bad associations corrupt good characters; be justly sober and sin no more, for there are some who have no knowledge of God. I say this to your shame.

But some one will ask: In what way are the dead raised and with what kind of body do they appear? Foolish man; the seed you sow does not germinate unless it dies. And when you sow it is not the body to come that you are sowing, but the bare seed, whether it be of wheat or any other grain; and God gives it a body according to his will, and to each of the seeds its own body. Not all flesh is the same flesh, but there is one of human beings, and another flesh of beasts, and another flesh of birds, and another of fishes. And there are heavenly bodies and earthly bodies; and the glory of the heavenly bodies is one thing, and the glory of the earthly is another. There is one glory for the sun, and another glory for the moon, and another glory for the stars; star differs from star in glory.

And thus it is also with the resurrection of the dead. The body is sown in corruption and raised in incorruption; it is sown in dishonor and raised in glory; it is sown in weakness and raised in strength. It is sown as a sensual body and raised as a spiritual body. If there is a sensual body, there is also a spiritual body. Thus it is written: The first man, Adam, was created for sensual life; the last Adam is for life-giving spirit. But first comes not the spiritual, but the sensual first, and then the spiritual. The first man is made from earth, the second from heaven. As was the earthly man, so are the earthly ones, and as was the heavenly man, so are the heavenly ones; and as we wore the likeness of the earthly one, so shall we wear the likeness of the heavenly one.

But this I tell you, brothers, that flesh and blood cannot inherit the Kingdom of God, nor shall corruption inherit incorruption. See, I am telling you a mystery. We shall not all die but we shall all be changed, in an instant, in the twinkling of an eye, at the last trumpet; for the trumpet will blow, and the dead will waken uncorrupted, and we shall be changed. For this which is perishable must put on imperishability, and this which is mortal must put on immortality. But when this which is mortal puts on immortality, then will come to pass the word which is written: Death is swallowed up in victory. Where, death, is your victory? Where, death, is your sting? The sting of death is sin, and the power of sin is the law; now thanks be to God who gives us the victory through our Lord Jesus Christ.

So, my beloved brothers, be steadfast, be immovable, surpassing always in the work of the Lord, knowing that your toil is not vain, by reason of the Lord.

¶ Now, regarding the collection for the saints, do you also do as I directed to the churches in Galatia. On every sabbath let each one of you, laying aside money in proportion to his gains, save it, so that there will not have to be collections when I arrive. And when I come to you I will send those whom you have recommended in your letters to convey your charitable gift to Jerusalem; and if it is of any importance for me to go myself, they will travel in my company.

I will come to you when I have passed through Macedonia, for I am going through Macedonia, and perhaps I shall stay with you, or spend the winter, so that you can send me on my way wherever I may be going. For I do not want to see you now only in passing, since I hope to stay for some time with you, if the Lord permits. But I shall stay in Ephesus until Pentecost; for a great and important door has opened for me, and my adversaries are many.

But if Timothy goes to you, see that he has nothing to fear from you, for he does the Lord's work, as I do; let no one treat him with contempt, but send him on his way in peace so that he can come to me, for I am waiting for him with the brothers.

As for our brother Apollos, I have much entreated him to visit you, along with the brothers; but his choice was not to go just now, but he will visit you when the time is right.

Be watchful, be steadfast in your faith, be brave, be strong. Let all be love among you. And I ask this of you, brothers: You know the household of Stephanas, that it was my first conversion in Achaea and that they have given themselves to the service of the saints; I ask you to work under such people, or anyone else who toils and labors with them. And I am happy in the presence here of Stephanas and Fortunatus and Achaicus, because they made up for your absence, since they refreshed my spirit and yours. Give recognition to men like these.

The churches of Asia send you greetings. Aquila and Prisca send many greetings, along with the church at their household. All the brothers send you greetings. Greet each other with the sacred kiss.

This greeting is in the hand of myself, Paul. A curse upon anyone who does not love the Lord. The Lord has come. The grace of the Lord Jesus be with you. My love be with you all, in Christ Jesus.

The Second Letter

to the Corinthians

¶PAUL, APOSTLE OF CHRIST JESUS BY
the will of God; and Timothy our brother; to the church
of God which is in Corinth, together with all the saints
who are in the whole of Achaea: grace and peace to you
from God our Father and the Lord Jesus Christ.

Praised be the God and Father of our Lord Jesus Christ,
the father of the mercies and the God of all consolation,
who comforts us in every affliction of ours, so that we
are able to comfort those who are in every affliction
through the consolation we ourselves received from God.
For as the sufferings of the Christ abound for us, so
through the Christ our consolation abounds. If we are
afflicted, it is for your comfort and salvation; if we are
comforted, it is for your comfort, which works in endurance of those same sufferings which we also undergo;
and our hope for you is firm, since we know that, as you
are sharers in our sufferings, so also you are sharers in
our consolation.

For we do not wish you to be unaware, brothers, of the
affliction which befell us in Asia, how we were burdened
beyond our powers so that we did not know whether we

could survive. For all we could do, we would have got the death sentence; so that our trust had to be not in ourselves but in God, who raises the dead, who rescued us, and will rescue us, from so great a danger of death; in whom we have hope, that he will still protect us, if only you will help with your prayers for us; so that the grace given us because of many persons may be thankfully received by many for our sake.

This is our cause for pride, the testimony of our consciousness that we behaved in the world in the holiness and purity of God, not by fleshly wisdom but by the grace of God, and especially in relation to you. We are not writing you anything except what you can read and understand; and I hope that you will understand us completely, as you have understood us in part; that we are your cause for pride, as you are ours, on the Day of our Lord Jesus.

It was in this spirit of confidence that I wished formerly to visit you, so that you could enjoy me a second time; to visit you on my way to Macedonia, and return from Macedonia to you, so that you could speed me on my way to Judaea. That was what I wished. Then did I turn fickle? Or when I make my plans, do I do it after the way of the flesh, so that I can say both yes yes and no no? Trust God that our message to you is not yes and no. For Christ Jesus the son of God, preached among you by us, myself and Silvanus and Timothy, was never yes and no, but yes is his nature. For all the promises of God through him are yes; and that is why, because of him, the amen is said for the glory of God by us. It is God who confirms us for Christ, along with you; who anointed us, and set his seal upon us, and deposited the first payment of the Spirit in our hearts.

And I invoke God as witness, on my life, that it was to spare you that I gave up coming to Corinth; not that we are in charge of your faith; we work with you to bring you joy, since you have stood firm in your faith.

¶ I told myself that I must not visit you again in painful circumstances. For if I cause you pain, who else is there to gladden me, besides you, whom I caused pain? And I wrote this precisely so that I should not, visiting you, be caused pain by those who ought to bring me joy; being sure that, for all of you, my joy is the joy of you all. I wrote to you in great affliction and anguish of heart, with many tears, not so that you should be grieved, but so that you may know the love I have in surpassing degree for you.

But supposing someone really has caused trouble, he has not caused it for me but in part—not to exaggerate— for you all. For such a one, his punishment by the majority has been enough, so that now you should reverse yourselves and forgive and console him, so that the man I mean will not be overwhelmed by excessive suffering. Therefore I implore you to declare your love for him; since that is why I wrote, to learn of your disposition, whether you are in every way obedient. Whom you forgive I too forgive; and if I have forgiven, what I forgave was for your sake, before the face of Christ, so that we may not be taken advantage of by Satan; for we are not ignorant of what he has in mind.

When I reached Troas, for the gospel of the Christ, and when a door was opened for me by the Lord, I got no relief for my spirit because I did not find Titus, my brother; so I took my leave of the people and went on to Macedonia.

Thanks be to God who constantly leads us in triumph
through Christ and through us manifests the savor of the
knowledge of him in every region; for we are the fra-
grance of Christ for God among those who go the way of
salvation and those who go the way of perdition; to these,
the smell of death for death, to those others the smell of
life for life. Who is qualified for that? We do not, like
most, go about cheapening the word of God, but speak,
as it were, out of purity, from God in the presence of
God through Christ.

¶ Are we beginning to recommend ourselves to you once
again? Or is it that we do not, as some do, need letters
of recommendation to you or from you? You are our letter, written on our hearts, known and read by all men;
because you are displayed as the letter of Christ administered by us, written not in ink but in the Spirit of the
living God, not on tablets of stone but on the heart's
tablets of flesh.

Such is the confidence we have in God through the
Christ; not that we are qualified in ourselves to reason
out anything, as if it came from ourselves, but our qual-
ification is from God, who qualified us to be ministers
of the new covenant, not of the letter but of the Spirit;
for the letter kills, but the Spirit gives life. For if the
ministry of death, engraved in letters on the stone, appeared in such glory that the sons of Israel could not look
upon the face of Moses, which was perishable, because
of the glory of that face; how can the ministry of the
Spirit not be in even greater glory? If the ministry of condemnation is glory, all the more does the ministry of
righteousness excel in glory. For what has been glorified
is no longer glorious insofar as there is a glory that sur-

passes it; for if what is perishable has glory, how much greater is glory in what endures.

Having such hope as this, we speak out very plainly, not as when Moses put the veil over his face because the sons of Israel could not gaze upon the end of a glory that was passing away. But their minds were impenetrable. For until this very day the same veil remains when the old covenant is read and is not taken away, because only with Christ does it come to an end; but until this day when Moses is read the veil lies upon their hearts; but when anyone turns to the Lord the veil is taken away. And the Lord is the Spirit, and where the Lord's Spirit is, there is liberty. And all of us, with faces unveiled seeing as in a mirror the glory of the Lord, are transformed into the same image, from glory to glory, as from the Spirit of the Lord.

¶ We therefore, having this ministry bestowed in mercy upon us, do not weaken; but we have renounced acts which are hidden for shame, not going the way of wickedness or falsifying the word of God, but, by making plain the truth, presenting ourselves to the full consciousness of mankind before God. But if our gospel is hidden at all, it is hidden from those who are on their way to perdition. For them the God of this world has blinded the minds of these unbelievers so that the radiance of the gospel of the glory of Christ, who is the image of God, cannot shine upon them. For we do not preach ourselves, but Christ Jesus the Lord, and ourselves as your slaves for Jesus' sake. For the God who said: Out of the darkness light shall shine, has made a light in our hearts for the radiance of the knowledge of the glory of God in the face of Christ.

We keep this treasure in vessels of clay, so that the
supremacy of power may be God's, not ours; always afflicted but not crushed, bewildered but not despairing,
persecuted but not forsaken, cast down but not destroyed, always carrying the death of Jesus in our bodies
so that the life of Jesus also may be made manifest in
our bodies; for constantly we the living are handed over
to death for Jesus' sake, so that the life of Jesus also may
be made manifest in this mortal flesh of ours. So death
is at work in us, but life in you.

And having the same spirit of faith as in what is written: I believed, therefore I spoke; we also believe, therefore we also speak, knowing that he who raised up Jesus
will also raise us up with Jesus and bring us to him, along
with you. For all is for your sake, so that grace increasing
through greater numbers may make thanksgiving abound
to the glory of God. So we do not weaken, and even if
our outer man is destroyed, our inner man is renewed
day by day. The light momentary affliction builds in us
an ever greater and greater mass of eternal glory, in us
who look not on things visible but on things invisible,
for visible things are of the moment, but invisible things,
eternal.

¶ For we know that if our home in this earthly tabernacle is destroyed, we have from God a home which is a
building not made by hands, and eternal, in heaven. For
while we are in this one we make complaints, longing
to put on above it, like a garment, our habitation in
heaven, if we are to be found still in our bodies covered
and not naked. For we who are still in this tabernacle
groan under our burden, because we wish not to put it
off but to put on the other in addition, so that death may

be swallowed up by life. And he who brought us to this is God, by granting us a deposit of the Spirit.

Always confident then and knowing that while we live in the body we live away from the Lord, for we go by what we believe, not what we see, we are of good courage and satisfied to leave the body and be at home with the Lord. So we aspire, whether in the body or out of it, to be pleasing to him; for we all must be shown for what we are before the tribunal of the Christ, so that each may receive good or evil according to what he did in the flesh.

Knowing then the fear of the Lord, we try to persuade men. To God we are well known; and I hope that we are also well known to you in your own consciences. We are not recommending ourselves to you again, but offering you some cause for pride in us, so that you may have an answer to those whose pride is in appearance and not in the heart. If we are out of our wits, it is for God; if we are in our right minds, it is for you. For the love of the Christ constrains us as we consider that he, alone, died for all (but really all died); and he died for all so that all who live may live, no longer for themselves, but for him who died for them, and was raised from the dead.

Thus from now on we know no one in the flesh. Even if we did know Christ in the flesh, we now no longer know him thus. So that one who is in Christ is a new creature; the old is gone, behold, the new is here; and all is from God, who reconciled us with himself through Christ, and gave us the ministry of this reconciliation, because when God was in Christ he reconciled the world with himself, not counting their sins against them, and establishing in us the word of reconciliation. So we are ambassadors for Christ, as if God were summoning you through us. For Christ's sake, we implore you, be reconciled with God. He made the one who knew no sin into sin for our sake, so that we, in him, may become the justice of God.

¶ Working with him, we implore you not to let God's grace be given in vain. For he says: At a favorable time I heard you, and on the day for salvation I came to your rescue. Behold, now is the favorable time, now is the day for salvation. We say this, giving no offence in any way, lest our ministry be blamed, but in every way showing ourselves to be ministers of God by enduring much; in afflictions, in duress, in anguish; through beatings, through imprisonments, through riots, through labors, through sleeplessness, through starvation; by purity, by understanding, by forbearance, by goodness, by the Holy Spirit, by undissembling love, by the word of truth, by the power of God; with the weapons of righteousness in the right hand and the left hand; through glory and dishonor, through slander and praise; as false and truthful, as unknown and recognized, as dying, and behold, we live, as punished but not with death, as in pain but always joyful, as poor but making many rich, as having nothing and possessing everything.

Our speech has been open to you, people of Corinth; our hearts are open to you. You are not inhibited by us, your inhibitions are in your own vitals. Give us what we give you; I speak to you as my children; and open your hearts also.

Do not be mismated with unbelievers. For what common ground is there for righteousness and lawlessness, or what fellowship between light and darkness? What agreement is there between Christ and Belial, or what is shared by believer and unbeliever? How can the temple of God make truce with idols? For we are the temple of the living God; as God said: I will live with them and walk among them, and I will be their God and they will be my people. Therefore go forth from among those others, and be apart from them, says the Lord; and do not touch what is unclean; and I will welcome you in; and I will be as a father to you, and you shall be as sons and daughters to me, says the Lord Almighty.

¶ Since we have these promises, dear friends, let us purify ourselves from every pollution of the flesh and spirit, completing our sanctification in the fear of God.

Make room for us. We have injured no one, corrupted no one, taken advantage of no one. I do not say this to fault you; I have told you before that you are in our hearts, to live and die together. I have great confidence in you, I take great pride in you; I am filled with comfort, I am overflowing with joy, through all our affliction.

For when we arrived in Macedonia, our flesh got no relief, but we were afflicted in every way; outward quarrels, inward fears; but God, who comforts the downcast, comforted us through the arrival of Titus; not only by his presence, but in the comfort he had received concerning you; for he told us of your longing, your sorrowing, your enthusiasm for me; so that I rejoiced the more. Even if I did grieve you by that letter, I do not regret it, though I did regret it; I see that that letter did grieve you, if only for a while; but now I rejoice: not because you were grieved but because your grief led to repentance, because you were grieved according to God's will, so that you have lost nothing with us. For grief by God's will causes repentance leading to salvation, not to be regretted; but the world's grief causes death. This very fact of your being grieved by God's will—see what activity it has caused in you: what defensiveness, what indignation, what fear, what longing, what zeal, what vindictiveness. In every way you have established your innocence in this matter. But if I wrote to you, it was not for the sake of the wrongdoer, or of the one who was wronged, but in order to make plain to you, in the sight of God, your own concern for us. Therefore, I have been comforted. And in addition to this, I have been all the more filled with joy over the happiness of Titus, because his spirit was set at rest by all of you. If I have ever boasted of you to him, I have not been put to shame for it; but just as everything I said to you was true, so also our boasting before Titus has proved to be true; and his heart is fully given to you as he remembers the obedient spirit in all of you, how you received him with fear and trembling. I am happy that I have full confidence in you.

¶ We would have you know, brothers, of the grace of God which was granted in the churches of Macedonia; that through a great ordeal of affliction the abundance of their joy, even though their poverty was extreme, overflowed into lavish generosity. I bear you witness that, to the extent of their means, and even beyond their means, of their own free will, they begged us with much entreaty to let them share in our ministering to the saints. And this was not as we had expected, but first they gave themselves, by God's will, to the Lord and to us; so that we asked Titus that, as he had originated this gift of grace, he should go to you to bring it to completion. Then, as you are lavishly endowed with faith and eloquence and understanding and every kind of enthusiasm, and in the love we have inspired in you, be lavish also in this work of grace.

In saying this I am not giving you an order; but by the example of others' eagerness I am trying to prove the genuineness of your own love; for you know the graciousness of our Lord Jesus Christ, and how, when he was rich, he made himself poor so that by his poverty you might become rich. And in this matter, here is my opinion. This is to your advantage. You made a good beginning last year, not only in what you did but in your willingness to do it. Now finish the work, so that your willingness to give may be matched by your actual giving, within your means. For the will is acceptable if one gives what he has, not beyond what he has. It should not be relief for others and hardship for you; but as it is now your surplus should be matched against their deficit, so that when they have a surplus it may meet your deficit, and all be made equal. As it is written: He who got much had no excess, and he who got little did not go short.

Thanks be to God, who granted that the same zealous concern for you should be in the heart of Titus, who accepted our plea and, in an excess of zeal, goes of his own accord to you. With him we are sending the brother whose preaching of the gospel is praised in all the churches; in addition to which he was elected by the churches to journey with us on this mission of grace which is being administered by us, for the glory of the Lord and to satisfy our own urge. We have this in mind, to avoid harsh criticism for the lavishness of this contribution administered by us; for we look for honor, not only in the judgment of God but in that of men. With them we are sending one of our brothers whom we have proved often in many circumstances to be enthusiastic, and who will be all the more so, by far, by reason of his great confidence in you. As for Titus, he is my partner and fellow worker for you; as for our brothers, they are apostles of the churches, the glorification of Christ. Give proof of your love for them, and the truth of the claims we made to them about you, in the presence of the congregations.

¶ It would be superfluous for me to write to you concerning contribution for the saints; for I know your great enthusiasm, a thing about which I have boasted to the Macedonians, saying that Achaea has been ready since last year; and your zeal stirred up most of them. But I am sending the brothers, to keep the boasts I have made about you in this matter from being proved empty; so that you may be ready, as I told them you were; to save us, not to mention you, from being embarrassed by your condition, supposing that some Macedonians were to arrive along with me and find you unprepared. So we thought it necessary to ask the brothers to go on to you before us and arrange for that bounty which has already been promised, so that it will be ready as a bountiful gift, not as something extorted. Consider this: He who sows sparingly will reap sparingly, and he who sows abundantly will reap abundantly. Let each give as he thinks right in his heart, not painfully, not forcibly, since God loves a cheerful giver. God has the power to make every grace abound for you, so that, always having full sufficiency in every way, you may have enough for every good work; as it is written: He scattered his bounty abroad, he gave to the poor; his righteousness abides into eternity. He who provides seed for the sower and bread for food will provide and multiply your store of seed and increase the products of your righteousness. You will be rich enough for all that generosity which, through us, brings about thanksgiving to God; because the ministering of this service not only is the supplying of the saints' needs, but also overflows into thanksgiving to God by many. Through the proof of this ministry you will be glorifying God, in addition to the obedience of your confession to the gospel of the Christ, and the generosity of your sharing with them and with all; and to their prayers for your sakes when they love you for the surpassing grace of God in you. Thanks be to God for his indescribable gift.

¶ Now I, Paul, appeal to you by the gentleness and courtesy of the Christ, I who am humble when I am face to face with you, but bold when I am away from you; and what I ask is that I need not be bold when I am with you, not with that boldness of confidence in which I believe I can venture against certain people who charge that we live in the way of the flesh. We do live in the flesh, but our campaign is not according to the flesh. For the weapons of our campaign are not of the flesh, but, with God's help, powerful enough to demolish strongholds. We demolish arguments and everything raised up in pride against the knowledge of God, and lead every thought in captivity to obedience to the Christ, and are ready to punish every disobedience, when your obedience is made complete. Look at what is before your eyes. If anyone is sure in his heart that he belongs to Christ, let him think again and tell himself that, as he belongs to Christ, so do we. Even if I do boast rather too much of our authority, which God gave us, to build you up, not to tear you down, I shall not be put to shame. Let me not be thought to be trying to frighten you by my letters. His letters, says someone, are weighty and powerful; but when he is here he is weak in body and his discourse is insignificant. Let that person realize that we are the same when we are absent and speaking through letters, and when we are present and acting.

We do not dare to rate ourselves or compare ourselves with certain people who put themselves forward; only they do not realize that they are measuring themselves against themselves and comparing themselves with themselves. We shall not go infinitely far in our pride, but only within the measure of what God gave us as our portion, which reaches as far as to you. We are not overextending our authority, as if it did not reach as far as you, for we were the first to come to you with the gospel of the Christ. We do not spread our proud claims infinitely far, where others have done the work, but rather hope that, as your faith grows, we shall become surpassingly great in our own territory, so that we can bring the gospel to places beyond you, without making proud claims to work already done in someone else's territory. Let him who takes pride take pride in the Lord; for it is not the man who commends himself who is approved, but the man whom the Lord commends.

¶ I wish you could put up with a little bit of silliness from me. Please do put up with it; for I am jealous over you as God might be jealous, for I have contracted to bring you like a pure virgin to one bridegroom only: to Christ. But I am afraid that, as the serpent in his knavery seduced Eve, your minds may be corrupted from their innocence and pure devotion to the Christ. For if someone comes along and preaches another Jesus, whom we did not preach, or you receive another spirit which you had not received before, or another gospel which you had not accepted before, you put up with him cheerfully. But I think we do not in any way fall short of the super-apostles; even if I am an amateur in oratory, I am not one in understanding, as we demonstrated to you in each and every way.

Did I make a mistake in lowering myself so that you should be exalted, because we brought you the gospel of God as a free gift? I robbed other churches by accepting stipends from them in order to serve you; when I was with you, and in need, I was never a burden to any one of you, since the brothers who came from Macedonia supplied my needs, and I always kept myself, and shall keep myself, from burdening you. As Christ's truth is in me, I shall not be kept from making this claim in all the region of Achaea. Why? Because I do not love you? God knows I do.

This I do, and this I shall do to cut away the pretexts of those who desire a pretext for boasting that they are found to be our equals. Such people are the false apostles, treacherous workers, disguised as apostles of Christ. And no wonder; even Satan disguises himself as the angel of light, so there is nothing startling if his ministers disguise themselves as ministers of righteousness. Their end will be what their acts have deserved.

I say once again, let no one take me for a fool; but if you do, then accept me as a fool, so that I too can do a little boasting. What I say now has nothing to do with the Lord, but in this state of boastfulness I am speaking, as it were, like a madman. Since many boast about matters of the flesh, I shall boast too. You, being sensible people, cheerfully put up with fools; you put up with anyone who enslaves you, eats you alive, lays hands on you, browbeats you, or hits you in the face. I say to our shame, we are too weak for that; but where one can show his daring, I mean, in madness, I too am daring. Are they Hebrews? So am I. Are they Israelites? So am I. Are they the seed of Abraham? So am I. Are they ministers of Christ? In my madness I say it: I am, more than they. With more labors, more imprisonments, many more beatings, often near the point of death; five times I took the thirty-nine lashes from the Jews, three times I was beaten with rods, once stoned, three times shipwrecked, and spent a day and a night in the water; often on the road, with danger from rivers, danger from brigands, danger from my own people, danger from foreigners, danger in the city, danger in the wilds, danger at sea, danger among false brothers; with toil and hardship, often sleepless, in hunger and thirst, often famished, cold, and naked. Aside from externals, there was the day-by-day pressure on me, my anxious concern for all the churches. Who fails, without my failing with him? Who goes astray, without my burning in sympathy? If I must boast, I will boast about those matters which show my weakness. God, the father of the Lord Jesus, blessed forever and ever, knows that I am not lying. In Damascus the local governor for King Aretas had the city of the Damascenes under guard so as to seize me; but I was lowered in a basket through a window in the wall, and so escaped his hands.

¶ I must make my boast. It does me no good, but I will go on to speak of visions and revelations of the Lord. I know of a Christian man fourteen years ago, who, whether in his body or out of it I do not know, God knows, was caught up into the third heaven. And I know that such a man, whether in his body or out of his body I do not know, God knows, was caught up into paradise and heard secret sayings which it is not lawful for any man to repeat. Of such a man I will boast, but not of myself except in the matter of my weaknesses. If I do choose to boast, I shall not be a fool, because what I say will be true; but I refrain, not wishing anyone to think me better than what he sees and hears, judging me by the greatness of the things revealed to me. Because of these, to keep me from self-conceit, a thorn was stuck into my flesh, an angel of Satan, to hurt me and keep me from self-conceit. Concerning this I called three times upon the Lord to remove it from me; but he said to me: My grace is enough for you; your power is fulfilled in your weakness. Therefore I will boast the more gladly in my weaknesses, so that the power of the Christ may reside in me. So I am well pleased with weaknesses, outrages, duress, pursuit, and hardships, for the sake of Christ; for when I am weak, then I am strong.

I have been a fool. But you forced me to it. I should have been recommended by you. For I have in no way come short of the super-apostles, even though I am nothing; for the signs of the apostle have been demonstrated among you with every kind of patience, by signs and portents and miracles. In what have you been treated worse than the other churches except that I have not been a burden upon you? Pardon me for this injustice.

Here I am ready to visit you for the third time, and I shall not be a burden upon you; for I want you, not your money, since children are not obliged to store up treasures for the parents, but parents for their children. I will most gladly spend and be expended myself for the sake of your lives. If I love you excessively, am I the less beloved? Concede, I did not burden you. But was I really unscrupulous and took you by guile? Could I have taken advantage of you through one of those I sent to you? I asked Titus to go and I sent the brother with him. Surely Titus did not take advantage of you? Do we not go in the same spirit as he? In the same footsteps?

Have you been thinking all this while that we were defending ourselves to you? We are speaking as Christians, before God. And all is for your edification, dear friends, for I am afraid I might arrive and find you not as I would wish you to be, and I myself be found not as you wish me to be; and there will be rivalry, jealousy, rages, ambitions, slanders, whisperings, pretensions, disorderliness. I am afraid God might humiliate me before you once again, and I may have to mourn over many of those who sinned before and did not repent of the viciousness and lechery and unchastity of which they were guilty.

¶ I am coming to you for the third time; and everything said shall be established by the mouths of two, or three, witnesses. As I warned you on my second visit, so I warn you now in my absence, both those who sinned before and all the rest: when I come again I will not spare you, since you demand a proof of the Christ who speaks in me. He is not weak against you but strong among you, since he was crucified because of weakness but lives because of the power of God. We too are weak with him but shall live with him because of the power of God. Test yourselves, whether you are still in the faith, assess yourselves. Do you not know yourselves, and that Jesus Christ is in you? Unless you prove unworthy. I hope you will recognize that we are not unworthy. And we pray to God that you will not do anything wrong, not so that we may appear worthy, but so that you may do what is good and we may be, as it were, the unworthy ones. We cannot do anything against the truth, only on the side of the truth. We rejoice when we are weak and you are strong; that is what we are praying for, your improvement. Therefore I write this while I am still absent from you, so as not to use too sharply, when I am with you, the authority which the Lord gave me (to build you up, not to tear you down).

For the rest, brothers, farewell; improve yourselves, encourage each other, agree, be at peace, and the God of love and peace will be with you. Greet each other with the sacred kiss. All the saints send you greetings. May the grace of our Lord Jesus Christ and the love of God and the fellowship of the Holy Spirit be with you all.

The Letter

to the Galatians

¶PAUL, THE APOSTLE, NOT FROM MEN, nor through man, but through Jesus Christ and God the Father who raised him from the dead; and all the brothers who are with me, to the churches of Galatia: grace to you and peace, from God our Father and the Lord Jesus Christ, who gave himself for our sins, to rescue us from the present age, which is evil; according to the will of our God and Father, whose glory is forever and ever. Amen.

I am amazed that you have so quickly forsaken the man who summoned you by the grace of Christ, for another gospel, which is not another gospel; unless there are some people who are confusing you and trying to upset the gospel of the Christ. But even if anyone, we ourselves or an angel from heaven, announces any gospel that is contrary to the gospel we brought you, let him be damned. I have said it before and I say it again now, if anyone brings you a gospel contrary to the one you have been given, let him be damned.

Am I appealing now to men or to God? Or am I trying to please men? If I were still trying to please men, I should not be the slave of Christ. For I would have you know, brothers, the gospel you received from me is not according to man; nor did I receive it from man, nor was I taught it by man, but by the revelation of Jesus Christ.

For you have heard how I used to act when I was a Judaist, how excessively I persecuted and assailed the church of God, and went further in the Jewish faith than many contemporaries of my own kind, since I was an extreme zealot for the traditions of our fathers. But when he, who had marked me from my mother's womb and summoned me by his grace, was pleased to reveal his son through me, so that I should bring his gospel to the Gentiles, I did not turn at once to any flesh and blood, nor did I go up to Jerusalem to those who were apostles before me, but I went into Arabia and then returned to Damascus. Then after three years I went up to Jerusalem to learn to know Peter, and I stayed with him for fifteen days, but I did not see any other of the apostles except James the brother of the Lord. Behold, before God, what I am writing you is no lie. Then I went to the regions of Syria and Cilicia. But I was not known personally in the churches of Christ in Judaea; they had only heard this: the man who once persecuted us is now preaching the gospel of the faith which he used to assail. And they glorified God for me.

¶ Then after fourteen years I went up to Jerusalem again, with Barnabas, and taking Titus along. I went up in obedience to a vision; and I put before them the gospel which I preach among the Gentiles; but I did it privately, to the men of mark, so that the race I ran should not be run, or have been run, in vain. Even Titus, who was with me and was a Greek, was not forced to be circumcised, but only might have been because of some so-called brothers

who were brought in, who stole in to spy on that freedom which we had in Christ Jesus, and to enslave us.
But we did not for one moment give way and obey them;
so that the truth of the gospel might be preserved for
you. But of those who were thought to have some standing—which ones they were does not matter to me, God
is no respecter of persons—those who were thought to
have some standing did not make any additions to my
gospel. On the contrary, they saw that I had been entrusted with the gospel for the uncircumcised just as Peter had been with the circumcised; for he who had moved
Peter to his mission to the circumcised had moved me
to go to the Gentiles. And realizing the grace that had
been granted to me, James and Peter and John, who are
held to be the pillars of the church, gave Barnabas and
me the right hand of fellowship, that we should go to
the Gentiles and they to the circumcised; only we should
remember their poor, which I have taken pains to do.

Then when Peter came to Antioch, I stood up to him
face to face because he was plainly at fault. Before the
arrival of certain people from James he had been eating
with the Gentiles; but when these came he flinched and
removed himself from them, fearing the representatives
of the circumcised. And the other Jews were hypocrites
along with him, so that even Barnabas followed them in
their hypocrisy, but when I saw that they were deviating
from the truth of the gospel, I said to Peter before them
all: If you, a Jew, live like a Gentile and not like a Jew,
how can you make the Gentiles be like Jews?

We, Jews by birth, not sinners from among the Gentiles, knowing that a man is not justified by doing what
is in the law unless it is through belief in Christ Jesus,
believe, we too, in Christ Jesus, so that we may be jus-

tified by faith in Christ and not by doing what is in the law. It is not from the law that all flesh shall be justified. But if while seeking to be justified in Christ we ourselves are found to be also sinners, then is Christ the minister of sin? Never! But if I rebuild what I tore down, I make myself a transgressor. Because of the law I died in the law to live for God. I have been crucified with Christ. It is no longer I who live, but Christ lives in me. But I who now live in the flesh live in faith in the son of God who loved me and gave himself for me. I do not reject the grace of God. For if righteousness comes through the law, then Christ died in vain.

¶ O foolish Galatians, who bewitched you, before whose eyes Christ was displayed on the cross? I should like to learn this one thing from you: Did you receive the Spirit from doing what is in the law or from listening to faith? Are you so foolish? Did you begin with the spirit and now end with the flesh? Did you undergo all this in vain? If it really is in vain. Does he who provides you with the Spirit and works wonders among you do this because you are doing what is in the law or listening to faith? It is like Abraham, who believed God and it was counted as righteousness in him.

You know that it is those who believe who are the sons of Abraham. For the scripture, foreseeing that God would justify the nations by faith, brought this gospel first to Abraham, saying: In you all the nations shall be blessed. So that those who are of the faith are blessed along with the faithful Abraham. All whose conduct is controlled by the law are subject to a curse; for it is written: Anyone is accursed who does not abide by all things written in the book of the law, that he must do them.

That no one is justified with God by the law is evident, because: The righteous man shall live by faith. But the law is not a matter of faith; rather it says: He who does these things shall live by them. Christ ransomed us from the curse of the law by becoming the thing accursed, for our sake, since it is written: Accursed is everyone who hangs upon the tree; so that, by Jesus Christ, the blessing of Abraham might come to the nations, so that we may receive the promise of the Spirit through our faith.

Brothers, I am speaking in human terms. No one can nullify or add to the testament of a human being when it has been ratified. The promises were spoken to Abraham and his descendant. It does not say, and to his descendants, as for many; but as for one, and to your descendant, that is, Christ. This is what I am saying; that law, which came four hundred and thirty years later, does not disqualify so as to make void the promise, a testament that was ratified before by God. For if the inheritance came from the law, it would not come from the promise; but to Abraham God gave it as a grace through the promise.

What, then, of the law? It was added because of transgressions, until the coming of the descendant to whom the promise was made. It was ordained by angels through the hand of a mediator. But what is one does not have a mediator; and God is one. Then is the law against the promises of God? Never. For if a law which could create life had been given, righteousness would have been in the law. But scripture had everything confined in sin so that the promise could be given, by faith in Jesus Christ, to those who believe.

For before faith came we were in the custody of the law, confined until the coming revelation of faith. Thus the law was our tutor until Christ, so that we could be justified by faith; but since faith came we are no longer under a tutor. For you are all sons of God through your faith in Christ Jesus. All of you who have been baptized in Christ have armed yourselves in Christ. There is neither Jew nor Greek, slave nor free, male nor female; for you are all one in Christ Jesus. And if you are Christ's, then you are the seed of Abraham, heirs by the promise.

¶ But I am saying, that as long as the heir is a child, even if he is head of the whole household he is no better than a slave; he is under guardians and caretakers until the time, set by his father, when he comes of age. So we too when we were children were enslaved to the elements of the world; but in the fullness of time God sent his son, born of a woman, born under the law, to ransom those who were under the law so that we may be given our adoption. Because you are sons, God sent the Spirit of his son to our hearts crying Abba, Father. So you are no longer a slave but a son; and if a son, then heir, because of God.

Now at that time you did not know God and were enslaved to beings which are not by nature gods; but now, when you do know God, or rather are known by God, how is it that you turn back to the weak and beggarly elements, and want to be their slaves once more? You keep count of days and months and seasons and years. I am afraid I may have labored on you in vain.

Be as I am, brothers, I pray you, because I am as you are. You did me no wrong. You know that I was sick in body when I brought you the gospel before; and when I was a trial to you, because of my physical state, you did not despise or reject me, but received me as if I were an angel of God, as if I were Christ Jesus. Where then is your delight in me gone? For I testify to you that if you could have, you would have dug out your eyes and given them to me. Then have I turned into your enemy by telling the truth? They are zealous for your favor, not fairly, but they wish to keep you in seclusion, so that you may be zealous for their favor. To be honorably favored, not only when I am there with you, is always good, my children, whom I am laboring to give birth to once more until Christ takes shape in you. But I wish I could be with you now, and change my way of speaking; because I do not know what to do about you.

Tell me, you who wish to be under the law, do you not listen to the law? It is written that Abraham had two sons, one by the slave girl and one by the free woman. But the one by the slave girl was begotten in the flesh, and the one by the free woman through the promise. These are allegories. For the women are the two covenants: one is from Mount Sinai, breeding for slavery; this is Hagar, and Hagar is Mount Sinai in Arabia, but she corresponds to the present Jerusalem, for she is enslaved along with her children. But the Jerusalem which is above is free, and she is the mother of us. Since it is written: Rejoice, barren woman who bore no child; break forth and shout aloud, woman who had no labor pains; for the children of the deserted one shall be far more than hers who kept the husband.

Now we, brothers, are children by the promise, like Isaac. But just as then the one born in the flesh persecuted the one born in the spirit, so it is now. But what does the scripture say? Cast out the slave girl and her son, for the son of the slave girl shall never inherit with the son of the free woman. Thus, brothers, we are the children not of the slave girl but of the free woman.

¶ Christ liberated us to freedom. Stand fast, then, and do not be caught again under the yoke of slavery.

Behold, I, Paul, tell you that if you become circumcised Christ will do you no good. And I testify once more to every man who is circumcised that he is under obligation to perform all the law. All of you who justify yourselves by the law are lost to Christ; you have fallen from grace. For we are given hope of righteousness by the Spirit, from faith. For in Christ neither circumcision nor uncircumcision has force, but only faith working through love.

You were running well. Who broke your stride, so as to keep you from believing the truth? The temptation was not from him who called you. A little leavening raises the whole mass of dough. I believe in you, that, the Lord helping, you will not take the wrong view; but the one who is confusing you shall bear the blame, whoever he may be. If I, brothers, am still preaching circumcision, why am I still persecuted? Then the difficulty of the cross has been made void. I wish that those who are unsettling you would also castrate themselves.

You were called to freedom, brothers; only not freedom for the impulse of the flesh. Rather be enslaved to each other by love. For the entire law is fulfilled in one saying, that is: You shall love your neighbor as yourself. But if you bite and try to devour each other, beware of being destroyed by each other. But I tell you, follow the spirit and do not fulfill the desire of the flesh. For the flesh has its desires, which oppose the spirit, and the spirit opposes the flesh; for these two are set as opposites to each other, to keep you from doing what you wish to do. But if you are led by the spirit, you are not subject to the law. And the works of the flesh are plain to see. They are lechery, viciousness, unchastity, idolatry, sorcery, hatreds, rivalry, jealousy, rages, ambitions, dissensions, partisanships, envy, drinking bouts, orgies, and that sort of thing. And I warn you, as I warned you before, that those who practice that sort of thing shall not inherit the Kingdom of God. But the harvest of the spirit is love, joy, peace, patience, kindness, goodness, faithfulness, gentleness, temperance. The law is not against such things. But those who belong to Jesus crucify their flesh with its passions and desires. If we live by the spirit, let us also follow the spirit. Let us not be vain-minded, challenging each other, envying each other.

¶ Brothers, if a person is caught in some transgression, you, who are spiritual, must set him right in a spirit of gentleness; examining yourself, for fear you also may be tempted. Take up each other's burdens, and thus fulfill the law of the Christ. For if a man thinks he amounts to something and does not, he is deceiving himself; let each one evaluate his own actions, and then he will have cause for pride in himself alone and not in any other, for each one will carry his own burden.

And let the one who is being instructed in the word share in all good things with his instructor.

Do not be deceived: God is not made light of. For what a man sows, that he will also reap; because if he sows for his own flesh, he will reap, from the flesh, destruction; but he who sows for the spirit will reap, from the spirit, life everlasting. Let us not weaken in doing good, for at our proper time we shall reap, if we do not give out. So then, while we have time, let us do good to all, but especially to those who are of the family of the faith.

See with what big letters I have written in my own hand.

Those who wish to look well in the flesh are the ones who are trying to make you be circumcised, only so that they may not be persecuted for the cross of Christ. For those who are circumcised do not themselves keep the law; but they want you to be circumcised so that they can take pride in your bodies. But for us, let there be no pride except in the cross of our Lord Jesus Christ, through whom the world is crucified for me, and I for the world. For neither circumcision nor uncircumcision means anything; only to be created anew does. And for all who follow this rule, peace and mercy to them, and to God's Israel.

Henceforth, let no one give me trouble; for I carry the stigmata of Jesus on my body.

May the grace of the Lord Jesus be with your spirit, brothers. Amen.

The Letter
to the Ephesians

¶PAUL, APOSTLE OF CHRIST JESUS BY
the will of God, to the saints who are in Ephesus and
who believe in Christ Jesus: grace to you and peace from
God our father and the Lord Jesus Christ.

Blessed be the God and father of our Lord Jesus Christ,
who blessed us in Christ with every spiritual blessing in
heaven, as he chose us in Christ, before the foundation
of the world, to be pure and blameless in love in his presence; preordaining us for adoption to himself as sons
through Jesus Christ, by the favor of his will, for the
praise of the glory of his grace he bestowed on us through
his beloved son. We have our redemption through his
blood, the remission of our sins, by the wealth of the
grace which he made abundant for us, by complete wisdom and intelligence making known to us the mystery
of his will; by the favor which he set forth in him, for
his scheme for the fulfillment of the ages, that everything in heaven and on earth should be summed up in
the Christ. It was he by whom we, preordained, received
our inheritance by the plan of him who works all things
according to the purpose of his will, so that we, the first
to hope in Christ, must praise his glory. You too are with

him; having heard the word of truth, the gospel of your salvation, and believing, you have been sealed by the Holy Spirit of the promise. This is the first installment of our inheritance, for our redemption as his property, and the praise of his glory.

I also, therefore, hearing of your faith in the Lord Jesus and the love you have for all the saints, never cease to give thanks for you; and I remember you in my prayers, praying that the God of our Lord Jesus Christ, the Father of glory, may grant you the spirit of wisdom and revelation in the recognition of him; that the eyes of your hearts may be filled with light, so that you may know what is the hope he calls you to, what is the wealth of glory in the inheritance he grants you among the saints, and what is the surpassing greatness of his power for us who believe, by the working of the supremacy of his strength which he has realized in the Christ. This he did by raising him from the dead, and seating him by his right hand in the heavens, above every realm and authority and power and lordship, and every name that is named not only in this age but in the age to come. And he put everything beneath his feet, and gave him headship entire over the church, which is his body, the fulfillment of him who fulfills all things in all.

¶ You were dead men by reason of your transgressions and sins in which you once walked, following the Presence of this world, the lord of the dominion of the air, the spirit which is now at work in the sons of disobedience. And with you we too, all of us, once followed the desires of our flesh, doing the bidding of our flesh and our senses, and we were natural children of the wrath, like all the rest. But God, being rich in mercy through the great love he has for us, though we were dead by our transgressions, brought us to life along with Christ; you have been saved by grace; and he revived us, along with Christ Jesus, and seated us beside him in the heavens, to show to ages to come the surpassing abundance of his grace in his kindness to us through Christ Jesus. You have been saved by grace through faith. This does not come from you; God's is the gift; not from anything you have done; let no one be proud. We are his handiwork, made in Christ Jesus for the good works for which God readied us so that we should be active in them.

Remember, then, that once you, the Gentiles in the flesh, called uncircumcision by what is called circumcision, a thing done in the flesh by human hands; that at that time you were without Christ, shut out from the community of Israel and strangers to the covenants of the promise, without hope and godless in the world. But now through Christ Jesus you, who were once far off, are now near by the blood of the Christ. He himself is the peace between us. He made the two things one, who broke down the middle partitioning wall, the hatred, with his own body, who abolished the law of the commandments given in ordinances; to make the two men in him into one new man by establishing peace, and reconcile both, in one body, with God, killing the hatred in his own person by the cross. With his coming he announced the gospel of peace to you, who were far off, and peace to those who were near; because through him we have, both alike, access to the Father in a single Spirit.

You are, therefore, no longer foreigners and resident aliens, but you are fellow citizens of the saints and members of the household of God; built upon the foundation of the apostles and prophets, whose capstone is

Christ Jesus himself. By him all construction is made harmonious and grows into a temple sacred in the Lord; into which you also are built as a dwelling place of God in the spirit.

¶ Because of this, I, Paul, prisoner of Christ Jesus for the sake of you, the Gentiles, say this to you. You must have heard of the stewardship of grace which was granted to me to bring to you. Through revelation a mystery was made known to me, as I have already written to you in a brief account; reading which, you can understand my insight into the mystery of the Christ. This was not made known to other generations of the sons of man as it has now been revealed in the Spirit to his holy apostles and prophets; namely, that the Gentiles are co-heirs, incorporate, fellow sharers in the promise by Jesus Christ through his gospel. Of this I became a minister by God's gift of grace granted to me by the working of his power; to me, the least of all the saints, this grace was given, to bring to the Gentiles the gospel of the incalculable bounty of the Christ, and to bring to light the nature of the scheme of the mystery, which was hidden from the ages in God, who created all things; so that now the intricate wisdom of God may be made known, through the church, to all the realms and authorities in heaven. All this is according to the eternal plan which he brought about in Christ Jesus our Lord, in whom we have our confidence and access in trust because of our faith in him.

Therefore I ask you not to lose heart because of my sufferings for your sake. This is your glory.

Because of this, I bend my knees before the father from whom every family in heaven and on earth is named, praying that in the abundance of his glory he may grant that you be confirmed in strength, of the inward man, through his spirit, and that by your faith you make the Christ dwell in love in your hearts; that, rooted and founded, you may, with all the saints, have strength to understand the breadth and length and height and depth of the love of Christ and know it, though it surpasses knowledge; so that you may be filled with all the fullness of God.

To him who can bring to pass all things far beyond what we ask or think of through the power which is at work in us, to him be the glory in the church and in Christ Jesus for all the generations forever and ever. Amen.

¶ I, then, prisoner for the Lord, call upon you to proceed in a way worthy of the calling you received; with all humility and gentleness, with patience, bearing with each other in love, striving to preserve your singleness of spirit by the bond of peace: one body and one spirit, as your calling involved one hope; one Lord, one faith, one baptism; one God and Father of all, who is over all and through all and in all. But to each one of us was given a gift of grace in accordance with the measure of the Christ's giving.

Therefore scripture says: He went up to the height, and took many captives; and he gave gifts to men. But what does: He went up mean, unless he had also gone down to the nether parts of the earth? He who went down is the same as he who went up above all the heavens, to make all things complete. And the same one granted to some to be apostles, some to be prophets, some to be evangelists, some to be pastors and teachers; all these for the training of the saints for the work of ministry, for

the building of the body of the Christ, until we all attain
to singleness of faith and knowledge of the son of God,
to complete manhood and the measure of full maturity
of the Christ. Thus we shall no longer be children storm-
tossed and swept along by every wind of doctrine, at the
mercy of people unscrupulous in contriving our misdirection; but truthfully and with love grow in all ways
toward him who is our head, Christ; dependent on whom
the whole body, harmonized with itself and joined together by every connective sinew, through the measured
activity of every part, brings about the body's development toward its own completeness by love.

I tell you, then, and charge you by the Lord, to live no
longer as the heathens do in the vanity of their minds,
darkened as they are in their perceptions, alienated from
the life of God through the ignorance that is in them
because of the impenetrability of their hearts. In their
insensibility they have given themselves up to debauchery for the practice of every kind of vice, insatiably. This
is not how you learned the Christ, if indeed you did hear
him and were taught in him how the truth is in Jesus:
namely, that you must put off, with your former way of
life, your old person, the one corrupted by desire for pleasure, and be remade anew in the spirit of your minds,
and put on the new person, the one created by God's will
in true righteousness and piety.

Put aside falsehood, therefore, and each of you speak
the truth with your neighbor, because we are members
of each other. Are you angry? Even so, do no wrong. Do
not let the sun set on your anger; do not give the devil
room. Let the thief steal no longer, but rather work hard
with his hands to produce some good, so that he will
have enough to share with one who is in need. Let no

corrupt speech proceed from your mouth, but only what will help where it is needed, to bestow grace on those who hear you. And do not exasperate the Holy Spirit of God by which you have been sealed for the day of redemption. Let all bitterness and anger and rage and loudness and abuse be gone from you, with every kind of malice. Be kind and compassionate toward each other, forgiving each other as God through Christ forgave you.

¶ Make yourselves imitators of God as beloved children, and act in love; as Christ loved you and gave himself as a fragrant sacrificial offering to God for your sake.

Let lechery and every kind of immorality or greed be, as befits saints, not even mentioned among you; avoid also indecent silly facile talk, which is unbecoming. You should rather be giving thanks. For you know well that any lecherous or vicious or greedy person, an idol worshipper, that is, has no share in the Kingdom of the Christ and God.

Let no one deceive you with empty talk. Through this, the anger of God comes against the sons of disobedience. Have nothing to do with these. Once you were darkness, now you are light, through the Lord. Conduct yourselves as children of light, for what issues from light is always goodness and righteousness, and truth. Try to determine what is well pleasing to the Lord; and have no part in the barren works of darkness, but rather expose them, for the things that are done in secret by those people are shameful even to speak of; but everything that is exposed by the light is illuminated, for everything that is illuminated is light. Therefore scripture says: Sleeper, awake, and rise from the dead, and the Christ will give you light.

So watch your behavior carefully, like wise people, not foolish ones, making the most of your time, because these are evil days. Therefore do not be thoughtless but study to know the Lord's will; and do not get drunk on wine, which means dissipation, but fill yourselves with the Spirit, talking to each other in psalms and hymns and spiritual songs, singing and making music for the Lord in your hearts, always giving thanks for all things to God the Father in the name of our Lord Jesus Christ, and subordinating yourselves to each other in awe of Christ. Wives should subordinate themselves to their own husbands as to the Lord, because the husband is the head of the wife as the Christ is the head of the church, the very savior of the body. But as the church is subordinate to the Christ, so wives should be subordinate to their husbands in everything.

Husbands, love your wives as Christ loved the church and gave himself up for her sake, to sanctify her by washing her clean with water in the word, so as to set the church next to himself in glory, with no spot or wrinkle or anything of the sort upon her, but to be holy and without flaw. Thus also husbands ought to love their wives as they love their own bodies. One who loves his wife loves himself, for no one ever hated his own flesh, but one nourishes it and cherishes it, as the Christ does with the church, because we are parts of his own body. For this reason a man will leave his father and mother and cling to his wife and the two of them will be one flesh. This is a great mystery; I am speaking of Christ and the church; but you also should each one of you love his own wife as he does himself, and the wife should be in awe of her husband.

¶ Children, be obedient to your parents; it is right to do so. Honor your father and mother, for this is the first commandment, with the promise: That so it may be well with you, and you will live long upon the earth. And you, fathers, do not try your children's patience, but raise them in the training and precepts of the Lord.

And you, slaves, obey your human masters as you obey the Christ, with fear and trembling and in simplicity of heart, not with service to catch the eye and please people, but as slaves of Christ doing the will of God, doing slave work with good will from the heart, as for the Lord and not for men, knowing that everyone who does what is good will receive good from the Lord, whether he be slave or free. And you, masters, do likewise toward them, sparing your threats, knowing that their master and yours also is in heaven, and that there is no discrimination with him.

Lastly, strengthen yourselves in the Lord and in the supremacy of his might. Put on the full armor of God so that you can stand against the treacherous attacks of the devil; because ours is no struggle against flesh and blood, but against the realms, against the authorities, against the world rulers of this darkness, against the spirits of evil in heaven. Therefore assume the full armor of God so that you can oppose them on this evil day and, over-coming all, stand firm. Take your stand then, belted around the waist with truth, wearing the breastplate of righteousness, and your feet shod with the boots of the gospel of peace, over all holding up the shield of faith with which you will be able to put out all the burning arrows of the Evil One. And take the helmet of salvation, and the sword of the Spirit, which is the word of God. Do this with all prayer and entreaty, praying in the spirit on every occasion. To this end be wakeful with full endurance, and with prayers for all the saints. And pray for me, that the words may come when I open my mouth, to make known boldly the mystery of the gospel whose ambassador, in chains, I am; that I may be able to speak boldly, as I ought to do.

And so that you also will know about me, and how I am faring, Tychicus will tell you everything; my beloved brother and trusted helper in the Lord, whom I send you for this very purpose, so that you may learn about us, and so that he may comfort your hearts.

Peace to the brothers, and love, with faith, from God the Father and the Lord Jesus Christ. Grace be with all who love our Lord Jesus Christ in his immortality.

The Letter

to the Philippians

¶PAUL AND TIMOTHY, SLAVES of
Christ Jesus, to all the saints of Christ Jesus who are
in Philippi, together with their bishops and deacons:
grace to you and peace from God our Father and the Lord
Jesus Christ.

I thank my God for you every time I mention you in
my prayers, in every one of my prayers for all of you. I
make my prayer with joy, because of your sharing in the
gospel from the first day until now; being confident that
he who began the good work among you will go on per-
fecting it until the Day of Jesus Christ. So it is right for
me to feel thus about all of you, because you hold me in
your hearts, and during my imprisonment and my defense of myself and confirmation of the gospel you have
shared in grace with me, all of you. As God is my witness, I long for you with the love of Christ Jesus. And
this is my prayer, that your love may grow more and
more in understanding and all perception, so that you
can determine what is right and wrong; so that you may
be pure and blameless for the Day of Christ, fulfilling
the harvest of righteousness that comes through Jesus
Christ for the glory and praise of God.

I wish you to know, brothers, that what has happened to me has gone toward the advancement of the gospel; so my imprisonment for Christ has become well known in the whole praetorian camp and to everyone else; and most of our brothers, trusting in the Lord, begin to preach the word of God the more fearlessly because of my imprisonment. Some preach the Christ in a spirit of envy and contentiousness, others in good will; these with love, knowing that I lie in prison because of my defense of the gospel; but the others proclaim the Christ out of spite, not sincerely, thinking to cause trouble through my bondage. But what of that? In one way or another, whether in pretense or in truth, Christ is being proclaimed, and in that I rejoice. And I shall continue to rejoice, for I know that this will turn out to be salvation for me, through your prayers and the support of the spirit of Jesus Christ; all this as I hope and eagerly expect that I shall not be put to shame in any way, but that with full freedom of speech, as now and always, Christ will be exalted in this body of mine, whether in life or death.

For me, Christ is life, and to die is a gain. But what if living in the flesh brings some good from the effort? I do not know which to choose. I am caught between the two. My desire is to depart this life and be with Christ, for that is much better; but my staying in the flesh is more useful, because of you. And this I confidently know, that I will stay and stand by all of you for the advancement of your faith and your joy in it, so that your pride in me may abound in Christ Jesus when I am with you once again.

Only live lives worthy of the gospel of the Christ, so that whether I come and see you or hear about you in my absence, I shall know that you are enduring in a single spirit, in a single feeling striving to help the belief in the gospel, in no way frightened by your adversaries. This is the proof of destruction for them and salvation for you, and it comes from God: that with respect to Christ you were given the privilege not only of believing in him but of suffering for him. Your contest is the same one that you have seen as mine, and now hear of as mine.

¶ If, then, there is any encouragement in Christ, any consolation in love, any community of spirit, any compassion and feelings of pity, make my joy complete by being unanimous, sharing the same love, harmonious, one in purpose; without emulation or vanity but in your modesty always thinking that others among you are better than yourselves; not looking each for his own interest but every one for the rest. Keep this purpose in yourselves, one which is also in Christ Jesus. He was in the form of God, but did not think to seize on the right to be equal to God, but he stripped himself by taking the form of a slave, being born in the likeness of a human being; and being found in the guise of a human being, he humiliated himself and was obedient to the death, death on the cross. Therefore God exalted him and graced him with the name which is above every name, so that at the name of Jesus every knee shall bend, of those in heaven and on earth and under the earth, and every tongue shall confess, to the glory of God the Father, that the Lord is Jesus Christ.

So, my beloved people, as you have always been obedient, continue to work out your own salvation in fear and trembling, not only when I am with you but now all the more by far in my absence. For it is God who causes you to wish and to act for the sake of his good will. Do everything without mutterings and disputations, so that you may be blameless and pure, flawless children of God in the midst of a crooked and perverse generation, among whom you shine in the world like stars by holding to the word of life, to make me proud on the Day of Christ because I did not run my course in vain or labor in vain. But even if I am being offered up to the sacrificial service of your faith, I rejoice and share my joy with all of you. Do you likewise rejoice, and share your joy with me.

I hope, if the Lord Jesus is willing, to send Timothy to you soon, so that I myself may learn how things are with you, and take heart. I have here not one with a spirit like his, who would be honestly concerned about you; they are all after their own interests, not those of Christ Jesus. You know how Timothy has proved himself, you know how like a son with his father he has toiled with me for the gospel. So I hope to send him as soon as I can find out what my own future is; and I trust in the Lord that I myself shall come to you soon.

I also thought it necessary to send Epaphroditus to you; my brother and helper and fellow soldier sent by you as an emissary to minister to my needs; since he has been longing to see you and was concerned because you heard that he had been sick. And indeed he was sick, almost to the point of death, but God took pity on him; not only on him, but also on me, so that I should not have one grief on top of another. Thus I send him the more urgently, so that you may see him and be happy again, and I too may be the less troubled. Welcome him, then, with all joy, in the Lord's name, and prize people like him, because in doing the Lord's work he came very close to death, risking his life in order to fill the need you felt to have someone helping me.

¶ For the rest, my brothers, rejoice in the Lord. But I have no hesitation in writing you the same thing once again, and it is safe, as regards you.

Beware of the dogs, beware of evil practitioners, beware of mutilation. It is we who are the circumcised, we who serve the spirit of God and take pride in Christ Jesus and do not put our confidence in the flesh —although I myself do have reason for confidence in the flesh also. Even if another man may think he has reason for confidence in the flesh, yet I have more: circumcised on the eighth day, of the race of Israel, of the tribe of Benjamin, a Hebrew of Hebrews; in law a Pharisee, in zeal, a persecutor of the church, in righteousness according to the law, without fault. But all those things which had been gains for me I now count as loss, because of the Christ. I do then count everything else as loss because of the greater value of knowing of Christ Jesus, my Lord, for whose sake I was deprived of everything; and I count it all as garbage if so I may gain Christ and be found in him, not keeping my righteousness which came from the law but that which came through faith in Christ, the righteousness from God which rests on faith; from knowing him and the power of his resurrection and the sharing of his sufferings, conforming myself to his death, so as somehow to arrive at the resurrection of the dead. Not that I have already got it or am already made perfect, but I pursue it, trying to overtake it, as I was overtaken by Christ. My brothers, I do not count myself as one who has caught it yet, but I do only one thing: forgetting what is behind me and straining on toward what is ahead of me, I pursue my objective, the prize, which is to be summoned aloft by God with Christ Jesus. Let those of us who are mature be so minded; and if you think otherwise on any point, God will make that also clear to you; only let us stand fast at the place we have already reached.

Join in following my example, brothers, and since you have us for a model, observe those who conduct themselves as I do. For there are many people about, of whom I have spoken to you often and now, tearfully, speak of them again: the enemies of the cross of the Christ, whose end is destruction, whose god is their belly and whose glory is in their shamefulness, whose minds are on earthly things. But we have our city in heaven, from which we also await our savior the Lord Jesus Christ, who will transfigure the body of our lowliness to conform to the body of his glory, through the activity of his power and because all things are subject to him.

¶ So, my brothers, longed for, my joy and my crown, be thus steadfast in the Lord, my dear ones. I implore Euodia and I implore Syntyche to agree in the Lord. Yes, and I ask you, my true yoke-fellow, come to their aid; in my evangelism they strove along with me, together with Clement and the rest of my helpers, whose names are in the book of life. Rejoice in the Lord always; I say it again, rejoice. May your goodness be made known to all men. The Lord is near; never be anxious, but in every prayer and entreaty let your requests be communicated with thanksgiving to God; and the peace of God which passes all understanding will keep your hearts and your thoughts in Christ Jesus.

Finally, brothers, all things that are true, that are honorable, that are just, that are pure, that are lovely, that are admirable; if there is any virtue, if there is anything praiseworthy; think upon these things. And all that you have ever learned and taken over and heard and seen in me, so do; and the God of peace will be with you.

I rejoiced greatly in the Lord that your concern for me has flowered once again; after the time when you were concerned, but had no opportunity to help. I do not speak about needing help, since I have learned how to be self-sufficient in whatever circumstances I may be. I know how to do without and how to have plenty; anywhere and in anything I have been initiated into how to be full, how to be hungry, to have more than enough and to have not enough. I have strength for everything through him who fortifies me.

Still you did well to share my suffering with me. And, Philippians, you yourselves know that, in the early time of my mission when I had left Macedonia, not one other church shared in my gains and losses: only you; and that even when I was in Thessalonica once and then again you sent me what I needed. Not that I ask for the gift but what I do ask is that the excess profit be credited to you. I am paid in full, and more; I am fully rewarded in receiving from Epaphroditus the gift from you, a fragrant offering, an acceptable sacrifice, well pleasing to God. And my God will fill every need that you have through his glorious riches in Christ Jesus. Glory be to our God and Father forever and ever. Amen.

Greet every saint in Christ Jesus. The brothers who are with me send you greetings. All the saints send you greetings, especially those of Caesar's household.

The grace of the Lord Jesus Christ be with your spirit.

The Letter

to the Colossians

¶PAUL, THE APOSTLE OF CHRIST JESUS
by the will of God, with Timothy our brother; to the
saints and faithful brothers in Christ who are in Colos-
sae: grace to you and peace, from God our Father.

In all our prayers to God the Father of our Lord Jesus
we give thanks for you, since we have heard of your faith
in Christ Jesus and your love for all the saints, because
of the hope which is laid up for you in heaven, hope of
which you heard before in the word of truth in the gospel which is present among you; the gospel which grows
and bears fruit in all the world, as it does among you,
since the day when you heard it and truly acknowledged
the grace of God; as you learned it from Epaphras our
beloved fellow slave, who acts for us as a trusted minister of the Christ, and who told us of the love you have
in the Spirit. Therefore we also, since the day when we
heard about you, never cease from praying for you. We
pray that you may be fulfilled in your understanding of
his will, in full wisdom and spiritual comprehension; so
as to act in a manner worthy of the Lord and always
pleasing to him, productive in every good work and increasing in your understanding of God; empowered with

every power, by the supremacy of his glory, to be always steadfast and joyfully enduring, thankful to the father who made you fit for your share in the fortune of the saints, in the light. It was he who rescued us from the power of darkness, and removed us to the Kingdom of the son of his love, where we find our redemption, the remission of sins.

He is the image of the invisible God, first-born of all creation, because in him were created all things in heaven and on earth, the visible and the invisible, whether thrones or lordships or realms or authorities. All things have been created through him and for him. And he is before all things and all things come together in him, and he is the head of the body, the church. He is the beginning, first-born from the dead, to be first himself in all things, because all fulfillment has been well pleased to reside in him and through him to reconcile all things to him, establishing peace by the blood of his cross; whether it be the things on earth or the things in heaven. And as for you, who were once estranged and hostile in your minds with your wicked doings, he has now rec- onciled you in his physical body by his death, so as to bring you, holy and blameless and unimpeachable, into his presence; provided that you remain firm-founded and steady in your faith, not shaken from your hope in the gospel you have heard, the gospel preached in all crea- tion under heaven, the gospel of which I, Paul, have been made the minister.

Now I am happy in my sufferings for your sake; and in my own flesh I am filling out what is still lacking in the sufferings of the Christ, for his body, which is the church. Of this I have been made a minister through the dispensation of God granted to me, to bring to completion among you the word of God, the mystery which has been hidden away for ages and for generations. But now it has been revealed to his saints, since God wished to make known to them how rich is the glory of this mystery among the Gentiles. This is Christ in you, your hope for glory. It is he whom we proclaim, admonishing every person and teaching every person by every kind of wisdom, so as to present every person as one complete in Christ. I toil to bring this about, struggling in obedience to his activity, which is powerfully at work in me.

¶ For I wish you to know what a struggle I maintain for the sake of you and the people in Laodicea and all those who have never seen me in the flesh. I do it so that their hearts may be comforted, so that they may be brought together in love and to all the resources of fulfilled comprehension, to the recognition of the mystery of God: Christ, in whom are hidden all the treasures of wisdom and understanding. I say this so that none may mislead you by persuasive argument. For even if I am absent in person, yet in the spirit I am with you, rejoicing as I observe the good order and solidity of your faith in Christ.

So, as you have accepted the Christ, Jesus the Lord, go by him, rooted in him and built upon him, confirmed in your faith as you were taught it and abounding in gratitude. See to it that there shall be no one to steal you away by philosophy and by empty deception according to the tradition of men, according to the fundamentals of the world, and not according to Christ. Because in him resides, physically, all the fulfillment of the divine, and you have been fulfilled in him. He is the head of every realm and authority; in him also you were circumcised with a circumcision not done by human hands, in the putting off of the body of the flesh, in the circumcision of the Christ. You were buried with him in your baptism, and with him you were raised again, through your faith in the working of God, who raised him from the dead. When you were dead because of your sins and the uncircumcision of your flesh, he brought you to life along with himself. He forgave us all our sins, obliterating the unfavorable bond, with its decisions, that went against us, and removed it from our midst by nailing it to his cross; disarming authorities and powers, he made a spectacle of them by leading them captive in his train.

Do not, then, let anyone pass judgment on you over any matter of food or drink or detail of a festival or new moon or sabbath. These are the shadows of things to come; the body belongs to the Christ. Let no one willingly condemn you by excessive humility and adoration of angels, basing himself on his visions. Such a one is irrationally puffed up by the mind in his own body; he does not hold fast to the head, dependent on which the whole body, supported and held together by its joints and sinews, increases as God makes it increase.

If with Christ you are dead to the fundamentals of the world, why are you to be regulated as if you were still living in the world, with *do not handle, do not taste, do not touch?* These prohibitions concern what perishes with use; they accord with the commandments and teachings of man. They have some show of reason through the will to be religious, and humility, and the mortification of the flesh, but they are of no use for preventing carnal indulgence.

¶ If, then, with Christ you were wakened from the dead, look for what is above, where the Christ is, seated by the right hand of God. Think upon the things above, not the things on earth, for you died, and your life has been hidden away in God, with the Christ; when the Christ appears, then so will our life, and you too will appear in glory along with him.

Then put to death those elements in you which are of the earth: lechery, impurity, passion, base desire, and that greed which is idolatry. These are what bring on the anger of God. Once you went the way of these feelings, when you lived by them. Put them off now, all of them, anger, rage, baseness, blasphemy, foul language from your mouths. Do not lie to each other. Strip off the old person with all his doings and put on the new one, renewed in understanding after the likeness of him who created him: where there is no room for Greek or Jew, circumcision or uncircumcision, barbarian, Scythian, slave, free man, but Christ is all in all. As the chosen of God, holy and beloved, take on the feelings of compassion, kindness, humility, gentleness, patience, putting up with each other and forgiving each other when anyone has some fault to find with anyone else. As the Lord has forgiven you, so do likewise. Above all is love, which is what holds perfection together. And let the peace of the Christ, into which you were called in one body, rule in your hearts; and be thankful. Let the word of the Christ live within you abundantly in all wisdom, as you teach and admonish yourselves with psalms, hymns, spiritual songs, with thanks, singing to God in your hearts. And whatever you do, in word or act, do all in the name of the Lord Jesus, giving thanks for him to God the Father.

Wives, subordinate yourselves to your husbands, as is your duty in the Lord. Husbands, love your wives and do not be sharp with them. Children, be obedient to your parents in everything, for this is pleasing to the Lord. Fathers, do not try your children's patience, for fear they may lose heart. Slaves, obey your human masters in all things, not with service to catch the eye and please people, but in simplicity of heart and fearing the Lord. Whatever you do, do it from the heart, as for the Lord and not for men, knowing that you will receive your share of the inheritance as a reward. You are serving Christ the Lord. The wrongdoer will be requited for the wrong he did, and there is no discrimination.

¶ Masters, be just and fair with your slaves, knowing that you also have a master in heaven.

Be constant in your prayers, with wakefulness and thanksgiving; and at the same time pray also for us, that God may open the door of the word to us, to speak of the mystery of the Christ, for which I am in prison; so that I may reveal it in the language I ought to use.

Conduct yourselves wisely toward outsiders, making the most of your time. Let your speech be always gracious, seasoned with salt, so that you know how to talk to each particular person.

Tychicus, my beloved brother and trusted helper and fellow slave in the Lord, will tell you all the news about me. I send him to you for this very purpose, so that you may know about me and so that he may comfort your hearts. He is with Onesimus, my trusted and beloved brother, who is one of you. They will tell you about everything here.

Aristarchus, my fellow prisoner, sends you greetings, as does Mark, the cousin of Barnabas, concerning whom you have received instructions from me; if he comes to you, welcome him. So too Jesus, who is called Justus.

These, of the circumcised, are the only ones who have worked with me for the Kingdom of God, and have been a comfort to me. Epaphras sends you greetings; he is one of you, a slave of Christ Jesus, forever striving for you in his prayers so that you may stand complete and fulfilled in every way God wishes. For I bear him witness that he works very hard for you and for those in Laodicea and Hierapolis. Luke the beloved physician sends greetings, as does Demas. Give greetings to the brothers in Laodicea and to Nympha and the church which is in her house. And when this letter is read before you, arrange to have it read also in the church of the Laodiceans, and see that you also read the one from Laodicea. And say to Archippus: Be sure to carry out the ministry you received from the Lord.

The greeting is written in the hand of myself, Paul. Remember my chains. Grace be with you.

The First Letter
to the Thessalonians

¶PAUL AND SILVANUS AND TIMOTHY
to the church of the Thessalonians, in God the Father
and the Lord Jesus Christ. Grace to you and peace.

We thank God at all times for all of you, as we make
mention of you in our prayers and constantly remember
the work of your faith and the labor of your love and the
endurance of your hope in our Lord Jesus Christ before
our God and Father; knowing, God-beloved brothers, of
your election, because our gospel came to you not in word
alone, but also with power, and the Holy Spirit, and great
assurance; just as you know what we were when we came
to you for your sake. And you followed the example of
us and of the Lord, and received the word, in great affliction, with joy in the Holy Spirit, so that you became
a model for all believers in Macedonia and Achaea.
From you the word of the Lord has re-echoed not only
in Macedonia and Achaea, but your faith in God has gone
forth to every region, so that there is no need for us to
say anything. For they themselves report our visit to you,
what it was like, and how you turned from idols to God,
to serve the true and living God, and to await his son

from the heavens, the son whom he raised, Jesus, our protector from the anger to come.

¶ For you yourselves know, brothers, how our visit to you was not in vain; but after first suffering and being outrageously treated in Philippi we were bold in God to tell you the gospel of God, under great strain. For our appeal to you comes not from error, nor from impurity, nor in deceitfulness, but as we had had God's approval to have the gospel entrusted to us, thus we speak, not trying to please men but God, the examiner of our hearts. For we said nothing by way of flattery, as you know; nor as a pretext for profit, God is our witness; nor looking for honor from men, neither you nor others; though we could have put pressure upon you, as apostles of Christ. But we were innocents among you, as when a mother cherishes her children; so longing for you that we thought it right to share with you not only the gospel of God but also our own lives, because you had become dear to us. You remember, brothers, our toil and labor; how we worked with our hands night and day so as not to lay any burden on you as we preached to you the gospel of God. You and God are our witnesses how piously and justly and blamelessly we acted toward you who are believers, just as you know how, like a father with his children, we urged and advised and reasoned with each one of you, to make you walk in a way worthy of the God who summons you to his Kingdom and his glory.

Therefore we also thank God at all times, that when you received the word of God which you heard from us, you accepted it not as the word of men but the word of God as it really is, which works also in you who believe.

For you, my brothers, followed the example of the churches of God which are with Christ Jesus in Judaea, in that you have suffered the same treatment from your own fellow countrymen as they have from the Jews; who killed the Lord Jesus and the prophets and chased us out; unpleasing to God, against all men; trying to prevent us from speaking to the Gentiles, to save them, and filling up the measure of their own sins, always; and the wrath has overtaken them in the end.

But we, brothers, who have been bereft of you for a space of time, in actual presence not in the heart, have been the more eager and in great longing to see you face to face. Thus we have wished to go to you, I, Paul, again and again, but Satan blocked our way. For what is our hope or joy or crown of exultation, if not you, before our Lord Jesus and at his coming? You are our pride and joy.

¶ Therefore when we could no longer endure it, we decided to stay behind in Athens by ourselves, and we sent Timothy, our brother and the servant of God in the gospel of Christ, to strengthen you and encourage you on behalf of your faith, so that none should weaken in these present sufferings. For you know yourselves that sufferings are our lot; since, when we were with you, we warned you that we must suffer, as has happened and as you know. Therefore when I could no longer endure it, I sent him to find out about your faith, fearing that the tempter might have tempted you and all our labor gone for nothing. But Timothy came back to us from you a little while ago and brought us the good news of your faith and your love for us, and told us that you have a good memory of us and long to see us as we long to see you; and for this, brothers, we have taken comfort in you through all our hardship and suffering, because of your faith, since if you are steadfast in the Lord now, we live. For what thanks can we render to God for you, for all the joy we have in you before our God, as night and day we pray most urgently to see you face to face and to mend any shortcomings in faith? May God our Father himself and our Lord Jesus direct our way to you; and may our Lord multiply and increase your love for each other and for all, as we also love you, to strengthen your hearts so that they are blameless in holiness before our God and Father at the coming of our Lord Jesus with all his saints.

¶ Finally, brothers, we ask you this and urge you, by the Lord Jesus. You were told by us how you should live your lives in a way that would be pleasing to God, and so indeed you are doing. But improve even more. For you know what instructions we gave you, through the Lord Jesus. This, your sanctification, is the will of God; that you should abstain from lechery, and each one know how to keep his own body in sanctity and honor, not in subjection to desire like the heathens who do not know God; not to trespass against any brother and take advantage of him in this matter; since the Lord punishes these things, as we have warned you and attested. For God did not call us to unchastity but to sanctity. Therefore he who refuses this refuses not man but God, who gave us his Holy Spirit.

As for brotherly love, you have no need for me to write you, for you yourselves have been taught by God to love each other; and this you do to all the brothers in all of Macedonia. But we urge you, brothers, to improve further, and to rival each other in keeping the peace, to pursue your own business, to work with your hands, as I have advised you, so that you may be respected by those outside our number and need nothing from anyone else.

Also, we do not wish you to be ignorant, brothers, concerning those who are asleep, nor to be grieved like the rest of mankind, who have no hope. For if we believe that Jesus died and rose again, so also God, through Jesus, will bring back the sleepers along with him. For this we say, by the word of the Lord, that we the living, the survivors, will not join the coming of the Lord before the sleepers do. For at the signal, at the cry of the archangel and the trumpet of God, the Lord himself will come down from heaven, and first those who are dead in Christ will rise up, and then we the living, the survivors, will be caught up with them into the clouds to meet the Lord in the air. And thus we shall be with the Lord forever. So comfort each other by saying this.

¶ Concerning the times and occasions, brothers, you have no need for anyone to write you, for you yourselves know well that the day of the Lord will come like a thief in the night. When they say: Peace and safety, that is when doom will come suddenly upon them, like birth pangs to a pregnant woman, and they cannot escape. But you, brothers, are not in darkness, for the day to catch you like thieves, since all of you are sons of light and sons of day. We are not of the night or the dark; then let us not sleep, as the others do, but be wakeful and sober. For the sleepers sleep at night, and the drunkards are drunk at night; but we who are of the day should be sober, putting on the breastplate of faith and love, with hope of salvation our helmet. For God did not destine us to the anger but to the winning of salvation through our Lord Jesus, who died for us so that, whether we wake or sleep, we shall live with him. Therefore, comfort each other and strengthen one another; as indeed you are doing.

Let us then, brothers, ask you to recognize those who are working for you and acting for you with the Lord and giving you counsel, and hold them in special love because of their work. Be at peace among yourselves. And we implore you, brothers, admonish the disorderly, comfort the faint-hearted, protect the weak, be patient with all. See to it that no one returns evil for evil, but always pursue the good, toward each other and toward all. Be always joyful, pray constantly, be thankful on every occasion; for this is God's will for you, through Christ Jesus. Do not quench the Spirit, do not ignore prophecies. Examine everything, hold fast to the good, keep away from every kind of wickedness.

May the very God of power sanctify you completely, and may your entire spirit and soul and body be kept safe without fault at the coming of our Lord Jesus Christ. Faithful is he who summons you, who will act accordingly.

Brothers, pray for us.

Greet all the brothers with a sacred kiss. I charge you by the Lord to have this letter read to all the brothers.

May the grace of our Lord Jesus Christ be with you.

The Second Letter
to the Thessalonians

¶PAUL AND SILVANUS AND TIMOTHY
to the church of the Thessalonians, in God our Father
and the Lord Jesus Christ. Grace to you and peace from
God the Father and the Lord Jesus Christ.

We must be thankful to God at all times on your account, brothers, as is only right, because your faith increases, and the love of all of you for each other is grow-
ing; so that we also can take pride in you in the churches
of God, because of your endurance and faith in all the
persecutions and sufferings you endure. This is a demonstration of the just judgment of God, for you to be
counted worthy of the Kingdom of God, for whose sake
you suffer; if indeed it is God's justice to repay with affliction those who afflicted you, and to grant to you, the
afflicted, relief with us at the revelation of the Lord Jesus
from heaven with the angels of his power, in flame of
fire; who will bestow punishment on those who do not
know God and do not obey the gospel of our Lord Jesus.
These will pay the penalty of everlasting destruction, far
from the face of the Lord and the glory of his power,
when he comes to be glorified among his saints and ad-
mired among all believers, on the great Day, because our

testimony to you was believed. Until then we pray constantly for you, that our God may consider you worthy
of election, and fulfill all your desire for goodness, and
the work of your faith by his power, so that the name of
our Lord Jesus may be glorified in you, and you in him,
by the grace of our God and the Lord Jesus Christ.

¶ But let us ask you, brothers, in the matter of the coming of the Lord Jesus Christ and our meeting with him,
not to be lightly driven out of your minds or terrified by
any spirit or report, or letter that seems to come from us
saying that the Day of the Lord has arrived. Let no one
deceive you in any way; since first must come the rebellion and the revelation of the man of iniquity, the son of
perdition, who opposes and sets himself above whatever
is called divine and worshipful, so that he seats himself
in the temple of God, displaying himself still as God. Do
you not remember that I told you this when I was with
you? And you know what now restrains him, until he
will be revealed in his own time; for the mystery of iniquity is now at work, only there is one who prevents it
until he is gone from our midst. And then the iniquitous
one will be revealed, but the Lord will kill him by the
breath of his mouth and annihilate him by the manifes-
tation of his coming. But this one's appearance will come
by the working of Satan with all his power, with the signs
and portents of falsehood, with full deception of wrong
for those who perish because they did not accept the love
of truth for their salvation. Therefore God visits them
with the force that makes them go astray, to believe in
the lie; so that all who did not believe in the truth, but
favored unrighteousness, may be condemned.

But we owe constant thanks to God for your sake,

brothers beloved by the Lord, because from the beginning he chose you for salvation by sanctification of the spirit and belief in the truth. He summoned you to this through our gospel, to a share in the glory of our Lord Jesus Christ. Therefore, brothers, be steadfast, and preserve the traditions you were taught by us whether by word of mouth or by letter. May our Lord himself, Jesus Christ, and God our Father, who loves us and gave us everlasting comfort and good hope through grace, comfort your hearts and strengthen you in every good action and word.

¶ For the rest, pray for us, brothers, that the word of the Lord may go forward and gain in glory, as with you, and that we may be kept safe from the wrong and wicked people. For faith is not for all. But the Lord is to be trusted, who will strengthen you and protect you from evil. And we trust in the Lord concerning you, because you do and will do what we tell you. And may the Lord direct your hearts to the love of God and endurance to await the Christ.

And we charge you, brothers, in the name of the Lord Jesus Christ, to keep yourselves from every brother who follows a course that is idle and not in accordance with the tradition you received from us. For you yourselves know how you should copy us, in that we were not idle when we were among you and did not eat food supplied as a gift by anyone else, but plied our trade with hard labor night and day so as not to be a burden on any of you; not that we did not have that right, but so as to present ourselves as a model for you to copy. For when we were with you we taught you that anyone who would not work should not eat. Since we hear that some among you follow an idle course, and do not work but mind the business of others. And these, by the Lord Jesus Christ, we direct and urge to ply their trade in peace and earn their own living. But you, brothers, do not weaken in your good works. And if anyone disobeys our instructions in this letter, mark him and have nothing to do with him, to make him ashamed. But do not count him as an enemy, but counsel him as a brother. And may the very Lord of peace give you peace of every kind, always. The Lord be with you all.

The greeting is by the hand of myself, Paul. This is my signature to every letter. This is my writing. May the grace of our Lord Jesus Christ be with you all.

The First Letter

to Timothy

¶PAUL, APOSTLE OF CHRIST JESUS BY the order of God our savior and Christ Jesus our hope, to Timothy, my own true child in faith: grace, mercy, peace, from God the Father and Christ Jesus our Lord.

As I asked you, when I was setting out for Macedonia, to stay on in Ephesus, it was so that you could tell certain people not to teach heretical doctrines, not to put their minds on myths and interminable genealogies which lead to speculations rather than the plan of God, which is through faith. The aim of my instruction is love, from a pure heart and a good conscience and unfeigned faith, qualities which certain people have missed and turned to talking nonsense, wanting to be teachers of the law without either knowing what they are saying or what those things are about which they are so firm. We know that the law is a fine thing if one uses it lawfully, in the knowledge that the law is not established for the just man, but for the lawless and disobedient, the impious and sinful, the unholy and profane, the parricides and matricides, murderers, lechers, pederasts, kidnappers, liars, oath breakers, or anything else that is opposed to healthy teaching according to the gospel of the glory of the blessed God in whom I believe.

I am grateful to him who gave me power, to Christ Jesus our Lord, because he thought me trustworthy when he established me in my ministry, though before I had been a blasphemer and persecutor and a violent man. But I was given mercy, because I had been acting ignorantly in unbelief, and the grace of our Lord overabounded in love and faith, which is in Christ Jesus. This word is to be believed and worthy of full acceptance, that Christ Jesus came into the world to save sinners; of whom I am the foremost, but for this reason I was given mercy, so that in me, foremost of all, Christ Jesus might display his complete patience, for an example of those to come who will believe in him for everlasting life. To the king of the ages, imperishable, invisible, single God, honor and glory forever and ever. Amen.

I entrust this charge to you, Timothy my child, in accordance with those prophecies which pointed to you before, so that in their spirit you may serve in the good campaign, keeping faith and good conscience. This certain people have rejected and come to grief in the matter of faith. Among them are Hymenaeus and Alexander, whom I consign to Satan to be taught not to blaspheme.

¶ So I ask you first of all to make your prayers, entreaties, intercessions, thanksgivings, for all people, for kings and all who are of high degree, so that we may live a quiet and peaceful life in all piety and dignity. This is good and acceptable in the sight of God our savior, who wishes all people to be saved, and to come to the recognition of the truth. For there is one God, and also one mediator between God and men, a man, Christ Jesus, who gave himself as ransom for all, a testimonial to his own times. To which fact I was appointed herald and apostle —I am speaking the truth, I do not lie—the teacher of the Gentiles in faith and truth.

I wish, therefore, that men in every place should pray, uplifting reverent hands, without anger or disputations. So too I wish women to dress in decorous style with modesty and good taste, not in hairstyles and gold or pearls or expensive fabrics, but as becomes women who profess piety through good works. Let a woman be a learner, quietly and in all obedience; I do not permit a woman to teach, nor to have authority over her husband. She should hold her peace. For Adam was made first, then Eve; and Adam was not deceived but the woman was deceived and went astray; but she will be saved through motherhood, if women are steadfast in faith and love and sanctity, with good behavior.

¶ This word is to be believed. If anyone desires to be a bishop, it is an honorable wish. But then a bishop must be irreproachable, married to one wife, sober, discreet, orderly, hospitable, good at teaching, not given to wine, no brawler, but forbearing, peaceable, not avaricious, a good head of his own household, keeping his children under control in full respectability. If a man does not know how to be head of his own house, how shall he take charge of the church of God? And he should not be a new convert who might become conceited and fall into the devil's damnation. And he must be well spoken of by those who are outside our church, so as not to fall into disrepute and the entrapment of the devil.

So also deacons must be dignified, not two-tongued,

not given to heavy drinking, not shamefully grasping, keeping to the mystery of the faith with a clear conscience. And they must first be examined, and then serve as deacons when they are found to be unimpeachable. So also their wives should be dignified, not gossips, sober, faithful in every way. Let deacons be married to one wife, exercising good authority over their children and their own households. For those who serve well as deacons provide themselves with a good standing and much confidence in faith in Christ Jesus.

I write you these things hoping to come to you speedily, but, in case I am slow in coming, so that you may know how you should conduct yourself in the house of God, which is the church of the living God, which is the pillar and foundation of truth. And, admittedly, great is the mystery of religion. He appeared in the flesh; he was justified in the spirit; he was seen by angels; he was preached among the nations; he was believed in the world; he was taken up to heaven in glory.

¶ The Spirit expressly says that in times to come some will forsake the faith, giving themselves to deceitful spirits and the teachings of demons through the hypocrisy of liars, branded in their own conscience, opposers of marriage, telling us to abstain from food which God created to be partaken of with thanksgiving by believers and those who recognize the truth. Because everything created by God is good, and nothing is to be thrown away which is received with thanksgiving, for it is hallowed by the word of God and prayer.

If you teach these things to the brothers you will be a fine deacon of Christ Jesus, trained in the words of faith and good teaching which you have followed; but reject

the profane old wives' tales. And exercise yourself toward piety. Exercise of the body is good for only a little,
but piety is good for everything, containing the promise
of life now and to come. This that I say is to be believed
and is worthy of full acceptance, for this is what we toil
and struggle for; because our hopes are in the living God,
who is the savior of all people, but most of all of the
believers.

Teach and promote these beliefs. Let no one belittle
you because of your youth, but make yourself a model
of the faithful in speech, in behavior, in love, in faith, in
chastity. Until I come, devote yourself to reading, to exhortation, to teaching. Do not neglect the gift of grace
that is in you, which was given to you through prophecy
by the laying of the council's hands upon you. Give your
mind to these matters, occupy yourself with them, so
that your progress may be visible to all. Attend to yourself and your teaching; keep on with it; for by doing so
you will save yourself and those who hear you.

¶ Do not reprove a man older than yourself, but exhort
him as a father, and the younger men as brothers, older
women as mothers, and younger ones as sisters in complete chastity. Revere widows who are really widows.
And if a widow has children or grandchildren, let these
learn first of all to respect their own household and return to their forebears what they owe them, for this is
acceptable in the sight of God. She who is really a widow
and lives alone has put her hope in God and is constant
in her prayers and entreaties night and day. She who in-
dulges in pleasure is one of the living dead. Impress these
ideas on people so that they may be above reproach. But

if anyone does not take care of his own people, and particularly his own family, that one has denied his faith and is worse than one who never believed.

Let one who is registered as a widow be not under sixty years of age, widow of one husband, attested for good works: whether she cared for children, was hospitable to strangers, washed the feet of the saints, rescued the oppressed, or gave herself to whatever good work. But refuse the younger widows, since when their lusts take them away from the Christ, they want to marry, being open to the charge of breaking their original pledge. And at the same time they learn how to be shiftless, going about from house to house; and not only shiftless but silly and meddlesome and improper in their talk. So I desire that the younger widows marry, have children, run their own houses, thus giving the Adversary no occasion for slander; for already some of them have turned back to follow Satan. If any woman believer has widows in her family, let her take care of them and not let the church be burdened, so that the church may take care of those who are really widowed.

The elders who have been good leaders should be accorded twice as much honor, especially those who work hard at speaking and teaching. For scripture says: You shall not muzzle the ox who treads the grain; and: The laborer is worthy of his hire. Do not accept a charge made against an elder unless it was before two or three witnesses; but convict those who do wrong openly before all, so that the others may be afraid. I charge you before God and Christ Jesus and the chosen angels to keep these commandments without prejudice, doing nothing in partiality. Do not lay hands hastily on anyone or have anything to do with the sins of others. Keep yourself chaste. Do not go on being a water drinker, but take a little wine because of your stomach and your frequent illnesses.

The sins of some men are obvious and lead the way to judgment, but those of others lag behind: so also some good deeds are evident, and those that are otherwise can not remain hidden.

¶ Those who are slaves under the yoke should consider their own masters worthy of full honor, so that the name and teaching of God may not be ill spoken of. Those who have masters who are believers should not therefore treat them with disrespect because they are brothers, but work all the harder as their slaves, because those who have the benefit of their good work are believers, and are beloved.

Teach and urge these principles. If anyone deviates from them in his teaching and does not adhere to wholesome doctrines, those of our Lord Jesus Christ, and teaching that accords with piety, he is conceited, understands nothing, but is sick over controversies and battles of words; from which grow spite, rivalry, blasphemies, base suspicions, the frictions of men who are corrupted in mind and deprived of the truth, who think that piety is gain. And piety, with self-sufficiency, is a great gain; for we brought nothing into the world, and because we can take nothing out of it, and while we have food and covering we shall be satisfied with them. Those who want to be rich fall into temptation and entrapment and many senseless and harmful desires which sink people into ruin and destruction. For the root of all evils is the love of money, in longing for which some have strayed from their faith and transfixed themselves with many pains.

But you, man of God, avoid all this. Pursue righteousness, piety, faith, love, endurance, gentleness. Strive in the good contest of faith, lay hold on everlasting life, to which you were summoned and confessed to the good confession before many witnesses. I charge you before God, who gives life to all things, and Christ Jesus, who testified to the good confession in the time of Pontius Pilate, to keep this commandment stainless and irreproachable until the appearance of our Lord Jesus Christ, which in his own time the blessed and single ruler will display; the King of Kings and Lord of Lords, sole holder of immortality, dwelling in unapproachable light, whom no man has seen or can see: to whom be glory and power everlasting. Amen.

Charge those who are rich in the present time not to be haughty and not to put their hopes in the uncertainty of riches, but in God, who provides us richly with all means for enjoyment, to do good, to be rich in good deeds, to be liberal, sharing, laying away for ourselves a good foundation for the future so that all may partake of what is really life.

Oh, Timothy, guard this which has been entrusted to you, putting aside the profane babblings and antitheses of what is falsely called knowledge; which some have professed, and thus failed in their faith.

Grace be with you.

The Second Letter

to Timothy

¶PAUL, APOSTLE OF CHRIST JESUS, BY
the will of God through the promise of life in Christ Jesus; to Timothy, his beloved son: grace, mercy, peace
from God the Father and Christ Jesus our Lord.

I give thanks to God, whom I serve with the clear conscience which is from my ancestors, as I mention you
continually in my prayers. I long to see you, night and
day, remembering your tears; to make my joy complete
as I am reminded again of the unfeigned faith that is in
you. First it dwelt in Lois your grandmother, and Eunice
your mother; and I believe that it is also in you. For
which reason I am reminding you to rekindle the gift of
God which is in you through the laying on of my hands;
for God did not give us any spirit of cowardice, but of
power and love and discretion.

Do not then be ashamed of your testimony to our Lord,
nor of me his prisoner, but take your share of suffering
for the gospel, with strength from God: God who saved
us and summoned us with a holy summons, not because
of what we had done but according to his own purpose
and his grace, grace in Christ Jesus granted to us countless ages ago, but made evident now through the appear-

ance of our savior Christ Jesus, who abolished death and
spread the light of life and imperishability through his
gospel. Of this I have been appointed the herald and
apostle and teacher; and that is the cause for which I
suffer as I do. But I am not ashamed, but I know whom
I trust, and I am persuaded that he can guard my trust
until the great Day. Preserve the standard of wholesome
precepts which you have heard from me in faith and love
and in Christ Jesus; guard the good which has been entrusted to you through the Holy Spirit which lives in us.

You know this, that all the people in Asia turned away
from me; among them are Phygelus and Hermogenes. But
may the Lord grant mercy to the house of Onesiphorus,
because many times he refreshed me, and was not
ashamed of my chains; rather, when he arrived in Rome
he eagerly sought me out, and found me; may the Lord
grant that he find mercy from the Lord on the great Day;
and you know better than I all the services he did in
Ephesus.

¶ But you, my child, be strong in the grace which is in
Christ Jesus; and what you have heard from me before
many witnesses, pass this on to trustworthy men who
will be able to teach it to others as well. Take your share
of sufferings like a good soldier of Christ Jesus. No soldier in service involves himself in the business of ordinary life, if he is to please the man who enlisted him.
And if an athlete competes, he wins no wreath unless he
competes by the rules. The farmer who does the work
must be first to have his share of the crops. Think upon
what I say, for the Lord will grant you understanding in
all things.

Remember Jesus Christ, of the seed of David, who rose

from the dead, according to the gospel I preach; the gospel for which I am mistreated to the point of chains, like a criminal. But the word of God is not in chains; and through this I endure all for the sake of the elect, so that they also may attain the salvation which is in Christ Jesus with glory everlasting. This word is to be believed: If we die with him, we shall live with him; if we endure, we shall be kings with him; if we disown him, he will disown us; if we lose our belief, he is still to be believed, for he cannot disown himself.

Keep reminding people of this, charging them before God not to fight verbal battles, which are of no use for anything except for the subversion of those who listen to them. Strive to present yourself to God as one who is worthy, a worker with nothing to be ashamed of, drawing a straight line of argument for the truth. But avoid profane and empty words, for they will advance people in impiety and their speaking will spread like gangrene. Among such people are Hymenaeus and Philetus, who have strayed from the truth in saying that the resurrection has already taken place; and so they are upsetting the faith of some. But the foundation of God stands firm, with this seal upon it: The Lord knows those who are his; and: Let everyone who names the name of the Lord abstain from wrongdoing. In a great house there are vessels not only of gold and silver but also of wood and clay; and some are to be prized and others to be despised. If, then, a person purges himself from what I have been speaking of, he will be a vessel to be prized, hallowed, useful to his master, made ready for every good work. But avoid the desires of youth, and pursue righteousness, faith, love, peace, with those who call upon the Lord from a pure heart. Put aside stupid uninstructed speculations, knowing that they breed quarrels. A slave of the Lord must not quarrel but be mild toward all, instructive, patient, gentle, enlightening his opponents; on the chance that God may grant them to repent and recognize the truth, and they come to their senses and escape the entrapment of the devil, though they had been captured by him for his own will.

¶ Know this, that in the final days hard times will set in. For men will be lovers of themselves and lovers of money, pretentious, proud, blasphemous, disobedient to their parents, ungrateful, impious, loveless, implacable, troublemakers, intemperate, wild, with no love for good, treacherous, rash, conceited, lovers of pleasure rather than God, keeping the form of piety but denying its force.

Have nothing to do with these people. For from their number come those who get into houses and captivate women who are overcome by sins, who are seduced by fantastic desires, always learning something but never able to come to the recognition of the truth. As Jannes and Jambres stood up against Moses, so these men will stand up against the truth, being corrupt in mind and unworthy in the matter of faith. But they will progress no further, for their madness will be made evident to all, as was that of those others.

But as for you, you have followed my teaching, my behavior, my devotion, my faith, my patience, my love, my steadfastness; my persecutions, my sufferings, the sort of thing that happened to me in Antioch, in Iconium, in Lystra; such persecutions have I borne, but the Lord rescued me from all of them. And all who desire to live piously in Christ Jesus will be persecuted; bad men and wizards will make progress, for the worse, leading men astray and led astray themselves. But as for you, abide by what you learned and what you came to believe, realizing from what people you learned it, and that even when you were a child you knew sacred scriptures, which have power to make you wise for your salvation through faith in Christ Jesus. Every writing that is divinely inspired is also useful for teaching, for argument, for correction, for education in righteousness, so that the man of God may be complete and equipped for every good work.

¶ I charge you before God and Christ Jesus, who will judge the living and the dead, and by his coming appearance and his Kingdom: preach the word, insist on it in season and out of season; confute, reprove, exhort, with complete patience, with every kind of instruction. For the time will come when people will no longer put up with healthy doctrine, but will get themselves masses of teachers who accord with their own desires; their ears will be flattered, and they will turn their ears from the truth, and go over to myths. But as for you, keep your head at all times, endure your suffering, do your evangelist's work, fulfill your ministry.

For I am now being offered up as a sacrifice, and the hour for my departure is upon me. I have run the good race, I have finished the course, I have kept the faith; for the rest, the wreath for righteousness is set aside for me. The Lord, the just umpire, will award it to me on the great Day; and not to me alone, but to all who have loved his appearing.

Try hard to come to me soon. For Demas has forsaken me, being in love with the present age, and gone to Thessalonica. Crescens went to Galatia and Titus to Dalmatia. Only Luke is with me. Bring Mark along with you; he is helpful in my service. I sent Tychicus back to Ephesus. Bring with you when you come the cloak which I left behind with Carpus at Troas; also the book rolls, especially the parchments.

Alexander the bronzesmith did me a great deal of harm. The Lord will repay him according to his acts. Beware of him, you also, for he has been all too much opposed to our speaking.

In my first defense, no one stood by me but all forsook me. May it not be counted against them. But the Lord was with me and gave me strength, so that through me the message should be completed and all the nations should hear it; and I was rescued out of the lion's mouth. And the Lord will rescue me from every bad action and will save me for his heavenly Kingdom. To him be glory forever and ever. Amen.

Give greetings to Prisca and Aquila and the household of Onesiphorus. Erastus remained in Corinth; I left Trophimus sick in Miletus.

Try hard to come before winter.

Eubulus and Pudens and Linus and Claudia, and all the brothers, send you their greetings.

May the Lord be with your spirit. Grace be with you.

The Letter

to Titus

¶PAUL, THE SLAVE OF GOD, AND APOS-
tle of Jesus Christ in the faith of the chosen of God and
the recognition of the truth which comes by piety in the
hope for life everlasting, which God, who cannot lie,
promised countless ages ago and, in his own time, revealed in the annunciation with which I have been entrusted at the bidding of God our savior; to Titus, my
true child through shared faith; grace and peace from God
the Father and Christ Jesus our savior.

This is the reason that I left you in Crete, so that you
could set right what remains to be done, and institute
elders in every city, as I have instructed you to do. Such
an elder must be unimpeachable, married to one wife,
with children who are believers, not open to the charge
of dissipation, not disobedient. For the bishop, as God's
steward, must be unimpeachable, not self-willed, not
choleric, not given to drinking, no brawler, not shamefully grasping; but hospitable, lover of the good, discreet,
just, pious, temperate, holding fast to the word of faith,
according to doctrine, so that he can have power to exhort men by healthy teaching and confute those who oppose it.

For there are many who are disobedient, speakers of vanities and deceivers of the mind. They come mostly from among the circumcised. One must stop their mouths; for they overturn whole households by teaching as they should not, out of love for shameful gain.

For one of their number, their own prophet, has said: Cretans are always liars, foul beasts, lazy gluttons. That testimony is true. For this reason, confute them sharply, to make them grow healthy in faith, no longer giving their minds to Jewish myths and the commandments of people who reject the truth. To the pure all things are pure; but to the defiled and unbelieving nothing is pure, but their mind and conscience are defiled. They confess that they know God, but in their acts they deny him, being abominable, and disobedient, and unfit for any good work.

¶ Go on telling them, in the way that befits healthy doctrine, that older men should be sober, dignified, discreet, sound in faith, in love, in endurance. So also older women should be, in their behavior, reverent, not troublemakers or enslaved to excessive wine drinking, and teachers of the good; so as to set the young women right and make them love their husbands and their children, be discreet, chaste, housewifely, good, obedient to their own husbands, so that the word of God may not be ill spoken of. So also exhort the younger men to behave themselves. In every case present yourself as an example of good works: in your teaching, integrity, dignity, discourse that is irreproachably sound, so that anyone who opposes you may be put to shame, unable to say anything bad about us. Slaves should be obedient to their own masters in everything, pleasant, not talking back to them, not misappropriating anything, but showing completely good faith, to improve the image of the teaching of God our savior among people in general.

For the saving grace of God was shown forth to all people. It educates us, so that disowning impiety and worldly desires we may live discreetly and righteously and piously in this present age, looking forward to the blessed hope and the appearing of the glory of the great God and our savior Christ Jesus; who gave himself for our sakes, to set us free from all lawlessness and purify for himself a chosen people, making them eager for good works. Keep on speaking thus and exhorting and confuting. Let no one despise you.

¶ Remind them to be submissive and obedient to powers and authorities, ready for every good work, to speak ill of no one, be peaceable and reasonable, showing complete gentleness toward all men. For once we too were thoughtless, disobedient, led astray, enslaved to desires and fantastic pleasures, spending our lives in vice and spite, hateful, hating each other. But when the kindness of God our savior was revealed, and his love for mankind, not because of any things we had done righteously, but through his own mercy, he saved us by the washing of regeneration and the renewal of the Holy Spirit, which he poured abundantly upon us through Jesus Christ our savior, so that, justified by his grace, we may become heirs in the hope of life everlasting. This word is to be believed, and I want you to insist on these principles so that those who believe in God may concern themselves with good works. These are honorable and useful for mankind; but avoid silly speculations and genealogizing and contention and controversies about the law, since these are useless and vain. Banish a heretic after one, and then a second, warning; knowing that such a man is perverted and sinful, since he has condemned himself.

When I send Artemas or Tychicus to you, make haste to come to me at Nicopolis, since that is where I have decided to spend the winter. Send Zenas the lawyer and Apollos on their way, trying to see that they lack for nothing. And let our own people also learn to follow honorable trades, for their essential needs. They must not be unproductive.

All who are with me send you greetings. Greet all who are our friends in the faith.

The grace of God be with you all.

The Letter
to Philemon

¶PAUL, THE PRISONER OF CHRIST JE-
sus, and Timothy our brother; to Philemon, our beloved fellow worker, and Apphia, our sister, and Archippus, our fellow soldier, and to the church which is in
your house: grace to you and peace from God our Father
and the Lord Jesus Christ.

I thank my God at all times as I make mention of you
in my prayers, when I hear of the love and faith you have
for the Lord Jesus and for all the saints. I pray that your
sharing in the faith may work toward understanding all
the good we have in Christ; since I took much joy and
comfort in your love, because, brother, the hearts of the
saints were refreshed through you.

I, therefore, though I have full authority in Christ to
order you to do your duty, because of our love prefer to
entreat you to it, though I am what I am, Paul, ambassador, and now prisoner, of Christ Jesus. My entreaty
concerns my child, Onesimus, whose father I have become while in my chains; who once was worthless to
you, but now is of great worth to you and to me. Now I
send him, the child of my heart, to you. I would have
wanted to keep him with me, to serve me for your sake

in my bondage for the gospel; but I did not wish to do anything without your will, so that your good deed would be done not by constraint but voluntarily. Perhaps this is why he was taken away for a while, so that you could have him back for always, no longer as a slave but more than a slave, a brother greatly beloved by me but so much the more by you, both in the flesh and in the Lord. If, then, you hold me to be your partner, welcome him as you would me. If he did you any injury or owes you anything, charge it to me. I, Paul, write it in my own hand: I will pay. Not to mention that you owe me your very self. Yes, brother, let me have some good of you in the Lord; refresh my heart in Christ.

Confident in your obedience, I write you this, knowing that you will do even more than I ask. At the same time, make ready a guest room for me, since I hope that, because of your prayers, you will be granted a visit from me.

Epaphras, my fellow prisoner, greets you in Christ Jesus, as do Mark, Aristarchus, Demas, and Luke, my fellow workers.

May the grace of the Lord Jesus Christ be with your spirits.

The Letter
to the Hebrews

¶GOD, WHO IN ANCIENT TIME SPOKE
to our fathers in many and various ways through the
prophets, has now in these last days spoken to us through
his son, whom he made the heir to all things and through
whom he also created the ages. He is the gleam of his
glory and the representation of his nature, he carries all
things by his word of power; and when he had caused
purification from sins, he took his seat on the right hand
of the majesty, in the highest; thus proving to be greater
than the angels by as much as the name he inherited is
more exalted than theirs.

For to which of the angels did God ever say: You are
my son, this day I begot you? And again: I will be a father to him, and he will be a son to me?

And when, once more, he introduces his firstborn to
the world, he says: And let all the angels of God fall down
and worship him; and as to the angels he says: He who
makes his angels into winds, and his servants into flame
of fire. But to the son he says: Your throne, O God, is
forever and ever, and the scepter of your uprightness is
the scepter of his Kingdom. You love righteousness and
hate lawlessness; because of which, God, your God,

anointed you with the oil of exultation, beyond your companions. And: In the beginning, Lord, you laid the foundations of the earth, and the works of your hands are the heavens. They will perish, but you endure. And they all will be outworn like a garment, and like a mantle you will roll them up, and like a garment they will be changed; but you are the same, and your years will not give out.

But to which of the angels did he ever say: Sit on my right, so that I may make your enemies a footstool for your feet? Are they not all ministering spirits sent forth into service for the sake of those who are to inherit salvation?

¶ Because of this, we must all the more strongly hold to what we have heard, lest we slip away from it. For if the word spoken by the angels proved certain, and every transgression and disobedience got its just punishment, how shall we escape if we neglect so great a salvation? This began by being proclaimed by the Lord, and was confirmed for us by those who heard it, with God adding his testimony by signs and portents and miracles and apportionments of the Holy Spirit, according to his will.

For he did not make the world to come, of which we are speaking, subject to angels. To this someone bore testimony at one point, saying: What is man, that you are mindful of him, or the son of man, that you consider him? You have made him a little lower than the angels; you have crowned him with glory and honor. And you set him over the works of your hands. You have subjected all things beneath his feet. In subjecting everything he left nothing that was not to be subjected. But now we do not yet see everything subjected to him; but we do see him who was a little below the angels, Jesus, through the suffering of death crowned with glory and honor, that by the grace of God he should taste of death for the sake of all. For it was right for him, by whom and for whom all things are, to lead many sons to glory and make perfect the author of their salvation through suffering. For the consecrator and the consecrated are from a single source; for which reason he is not ashamed to call them brothers, saying: I will announce your name to my brothers; in the midst of the congregation I will hymn you. And again: I will put my trust in him. And again: Here am I and my children, whom God gave me.

Since, then, his children share his flesh and blood, so likewise he too partakes of theirs, so as by his death to abolish the one who has power over death, that is, the devil; and set free those who through fear of death had been condemned to slavery all their lives. For he is not, surely, concerned with angels, but with the seed of Abraham. Hence he needed to be made like his brothers in every way, to be merciful and the faithful high priest for all that concerns God, to expiate the sins of the people; for by the fact that he himself suffered through trial, he can help those who undergo trial.

¶ Therefore, sacred brothers, sharers of a heavenly summons, think upon the apostle and high priest of our belief, Jesus, faithful to him who made him as Moses also was faithful in the house of God. He is worthy of greater glory than Moses, inasmuch as he who made the house has more honor than the house; since every house is made by someone, and he who made all things is God. And Moses was faithful in all the house of God as a servant to witness to things that are to be spoken, but Christ as the son in his own house. We are his house, if we keep our courage and the pride of our hope.

Thus, as the Holy Spirit says: Today, if you hear his voice, do not close your hearts as in the time of rebellion, on the day of trial in the desert, when your fathers made trial of me in a test of me, and they had looked on my works for forty years. And therefore I was enraged with that generation, and said: They always go astray in their hearts, and they do not understand my ways. So I swore in my anger that they shall not come into my rest.

See to it, brothers, that there can never be in any of you a heart evil and faithless in forsaking the living God, but keep encouraging each other every day, while it is still called today, so that no one of you may be hardened by the beguilement of sin; for we are partners of the Christ, if only we can keep our original condition firm to the end.

In the saying: Today, if you hear his voice, do not close your hearts as in the time of rebellion, who heard and rebelled? Was it not all who went out of Egypt led by Moses? And with whom was God enraged for forty years? Was it not with the sinners, whose bodies collapsed in the desert? Against whom, if not the unbelievers, did he swear that they should never come into his rest? And we see that they did not come into his rest, through unbelief.

¶ We should be afraid, then, that, while his promise that we shall come into his rest still remains open, some one of you might be judged to have come short. For we also have received the gospel as those others did, but the word they had heard did them no good, since they had no admixture of faith in what they had heard. For we who do believe are going into his rest; but as he said: So I swore in my anger, that they shall not come into my rest. And yet his works had been done since the beginning of the world; for scripture says at one point concerning the seventh day: And on the seventh day God rested from all his works; and again, in this place: They shall never come into my rest. Since, then, it remains for some to come into it, and those who formerly received the gospel did not come in because of their unbelief, once more he sets a certain day, today; as he says through David after all that time, as has been said here before: Today, if you hear his voice, do not close your hearts.

For if Joshua had given them rest, he would not have spoken about another day after that. But there remains a sabbath for the people of God; since one who comes into God's rest also rests from his works, as God rested from his own works.

Let us then strive to enter into that rest, so that none may fall through the same example of unbelief. For the word of God is alive and active, and sharper than any two-edged sword, and cuts through to the division of soul and spirit, of joints and marrows, and it can judge the thoughts and purposes of the heart; and there is no creature that is hidden from his sight, but all things are naked and helpless before the eyes of him with whom we have to do.

Since, then, we have a great high priest, Jesus the son of God, who has passed through the heavens, let us hold fast to our belief; for the high priest we have is not one who cannot sympathize with our weaknesses, since he has suffered all the trials we have, except that he did not sin. So let us confidently approach the throne of grace, so that we may receive mercy and find grace to rescue us in our time of need.

¶ For every high priest is selected from among men and appointed to perform, on behalf of men, duties before God, to offer gifts and sacrifice for sins committed. He can be moderate with those who are ignorant and go astray because he himself is submerged in weakness, and because of it he is bound to make offerings for sins on his own account also, as well as for the people. And the priest does not take the office upon himself but is called by God, like Aaron. So even the Christ did not do himself the honor of becoming high priest, but rather he who said to him: You are my son, this day I begot you; as he also said in another place: You are priest forever in the order of Melchizedek. And in his days of the flesh he addressed entreaties and supplications to him who could save him from death, with strong outcry and tears; and after being heard because of piety, even though he was the son, he learned obedience from his sufferings; and, made perfect, he became for all who obey him the cause of everlasting salvation, being called by God high priest in the order of Melchizedek.

About him we have much to say which is difficult to explain to you, since you have become dull listeners. For by this time you ought to be teachers, but you need to have someone teach you again the elementary first principles of the oracles of God, and you have come to need milk, not solid food. For anyone who takes milk is ignorant of the study of righteousness, since he is an infant; solid food is for the mature who have their faculties trained through practice to distinguish good from bad.

¶ Let us therefore pass over the elementary study of the Christ and go on to mature study; not once again laying down the foundations of repentance for dead acts, and belief in God, teaching about baptisms and the laying on of hands, the resurrection of the dead and the everlasting judgment. This we shall do, if God permits. For when once men have been enlightened, when they have tasted the gift of heaven and been participators in the Holy Spirit, and known the beautiful language of God and the powers of the age to come, and then fallen away, it is impossible for them to come into a new repentance, since they are crucifying the son of God for themselves and making a spectacle of him. For when the earth drinks the rain constantly falling upon it, and produces an acceptable plant for those by whom it is cultivated, it wins praise from God; but when it bears thorns and thistles it is despised and close to being accursed, and the end is burning.

But concerning you, dear friends, even though we speak as we do, we are convinced of better things, which go with salvation. For God is not unfair, so that he could forget your work and the love you have shown for his name, serving the saints in the past and serving them still. But we desire that each one of you should show the same enthusiasm, to the last, toward the fulfilment of your hope; not to be dull, but to imitate those who, by faith and patience, are given a share in the promise.

For when God made his promise to Abraham, since he had no one greater to swear by, he swore by himself, saying: In my blessing I will surely bless you, and in my multiplying I will multiply you. And thus, after waiting patiently, Abraham gained the promise. For human people swear by one greater than themselves, and the oath is final confirmation in any dispute. God, therefore, wishing to make even plainer to the heirs of his promise how unchangeable was his will, guaranteed it with an oath; so that, by means of two acts in which it is impossible for God to deceive us, we who have taken refuge with him may have strong assurance that we shall grasp the hope that lies before us. This hope we have as an anchor for our life, steady and secure and reaching to the innermost place behind the curtain, where Jesus entered as our forerunner, made high priest forever in the order of Melchizedek.

¶ This Melchizedek, King of Salem, priest of God the all-highest, is the one who met Abraham as he returned from the slaughter of the Kings, and blessed him, the one to whom Abraham allotted a tenth of all the spoils; meaning, when translated, first, King of Righteousness, then King of Salem, that is, King of Peace, fatherless, motherless, without genealogy, with neither a beginning of his days nor an end of his life, in the likeness of the son of God, he remains as priest for all time.

Consider how great was this one to whom Abraham the patriarch gave a tenth of his spoils. And those from among the sons of Levi who assume the priesthood are commanded by the law to collect a tenth from the people, that is, from their brothers, even though these are the issue of the loins of Abraham; but the one with no genealogy took a tenth from Abraham, and blessed the holder of the promises. Beyond any argument, it is the lesser who receives the blessing of the greater. And here, it is men who perish who take the tenth; but there, it is he of whom it is testified that he lives. And, so to speak, Levi also, who received the tenths, paid his tenth also, through Abraham, being still in the loins of his fore-father when Melchizedek encountered him.

If, then, there could be perfection through the Leviti-cal priesthood, through which the people received the law, what use would there be in having another priest raised up in the order of Melchizedek rather than his being called in the order of Aaron? For when the priest-hood is changed, of necessity there comes a change of the law. He of whom these things are said belonged to a different tribe, no member of which approached the al-tar; for it is evident that our Lord originated from the tribe of Judah, which Moses never mentioned in connec-tion with priests. And the case is still clearer when an-other priest is raised up in the order of Melchizedek, and has become priest not by decree of human law but through the power of imperishable life; for it is attested: You are priest forever in the order of Melchizedek. The former commandment is canceled because of its weak-ness and uselessness, since the law brought nothing to perfection; but a better hope is introduced by which we draw near to God. And inasmuch as it was not without an oath sworn; for these others became priests without an oath sworn, but he with an oath sworn by the one who said to him: The Lord swore, and he will not change his word, you are priest forever; by so much the more is Jesus the guarantee of a greater covenant. Those priests were many because death prevented any one of them from enduring; but he, because he endures forever, holds a priesthood in which none can succeed him. He can, therefore, forever save those who through him come be-fore God, since he lives forever to intercede for them.

It was fitting that our high priest should be such a one, holy, without evil, without stain, removed from sinners and made higher than the heavens. He has no day-by-day need, as the high priests do, to offer sacrifices first for his own sins and then for those of the people. For he did this once for all in offering up himself. For the law appoints as high priests human beings who have their weaknesses; but the word of the oath sworn since the law appoints the son, perfect forever.

¶ To summarize what has been said, such is the high priest we have, one who sits at the right of the throne of greatness in the heavens, minister of the sanctuary and of the true tabernacle which the Lord, not man, set in place. Now every high priest is appointed to offer gifts and sacrifices; so he too would have to have something to offer. If he were on earth, he would not even be a priest, since there are those who offer gifts according to the law. These serve the imitation and the shadow of the things in heaven, as Moses was directed to do when he was about to complete the tabernacle; for see to it, God said, that you make everything on the model of what was shown you on the mountain. But Christ has been given a higher ministry, inasmuch as he is mediator of a greater covenant, which is made law on the strength of greater promises. For if that first covenant had been without fault, no place would have been needed for a second; but he does find fault with them when he says: Behold, the days are coming, says the Lord, when I will compact a new covenant with the house of Israel and the house of Judah, not like the covenant which I made with their fathers on the day when I took them by the hand to lead them out of the land of Egypt. Because they did not keep to my covenant, and I have put them out of my mind, says the Lord. For this is the covenant which I

will make with the house of Israel after those days, says
the Lord, giving them my laws for their understanding,
and I will inscribe them on their hearts; and I will be
their God, and they shall be my people. And they must
not instruct each other, each man saying to his fellow
citizen or his brother: Know the Lord; because all of
them, from small to great, will know me; because I shall
be merciful to their wrongdoings, and I shall no longer
remember their sins.

In speaking of a new covenant he has made the old one
antiquated; but what is antiquated and grows old is close
to disappearing.

¶ The first covenant did have its rules for service and a
sanctuary on earth. A tabernacle was set up, the first one,
in which were the lampstand and the table and the display of the showbread; this is called the Holy. And beyond the next curtain is the tabernacle which is called
the Holy of Holies, containing a golden altar of incense
and the ark of the covenant, entirely overlaid with gold;
and there is a golden jar containing the manna, and Aaron's rod which budded and the tablets of the covenant,
and above it the cherubim of glory overshadowing the
seat of mercy; concerning which things it is not now
possible to speak in detail. Such being their arrangement, the priests enter the first tabernacle constantly in
the performance of their duties; but only the high priest
enters the second, once a year, not without blood offering which he brings for his own errors and those of the
people. And this is what the Holy Spirit shows us: that
while the first tabernacle is still in place the way to the
sanctuaries is not revealed. It is a symbol for our present
time, when gifts and sacrifices are brought which cannot

make the worshipper conscious of perfection, but it is only a matter of things eaten and drunk and various washings, regulations for the flesh applied until the time of the new order.

But Christ arrived as high priest of all the good things which have come about through the greater and more final tabernacle not made by human hands, that is, not of this world; and not by the blood of goats and calves but by his own blood he entered once for all into the holy place, having found everlasting redemption. For if the blood of goats and bulls and the sprinkled ashes of a heifer can hallow those who are defiled for the lustration of their flesh, how much more will the blood of the Christ, who through his everlasting spirit offered himself without fault to God, purify our conscience, away from dead acts to the service of the living God. And for this reason he is the mediator of a new testament, so that, with his death coming for absolution from their sins under the first covenant, those who are called may receive the promise of an everlasting inheritance. For in the case of a testament, the death of the testator must be involved; since a testament has force after death has occurred, but it has no force while the testator is still living.

Even the first covenant, therefore, was not established without blood; for when the whole commandment had been declared by Moses to all the people, according to the law, he took the blood of calves and goats, with water and scarlet wool and hyssop, and sprinkled the book itself and all the people, saying: This is the blood of the covenant which God decreed for you. And in the same way he sprinkled the tabernacle and all the articles of service. And, by the law, practically everything is purified by blood, and without bloodshed there is no remission.

It must be, then, that while the copies of things in heaven are purified by these means, the actual things in heaven must be purified by sacrifices greater than these. For Christ did not enter a sanctuary made by human hands which was a copy of the real thing, but he entered heaven itself, to appear before the face of God for our sake. Not to offer himself again and again, as the high priest enters the sanctuary once every year with blood that is not his own, since then he must have suffered again and again since the beginning of the world; but now, once for all at the conclusion of the ages, he has appeared, to abolish sin by the sacrifice of himself. And as it is the lot of man to die once, with the judgment coming after that, so the Christ was offered once for the taking away of the sins of many, and will appear a second time, without relation to sin, to those who look for his coming, for their salvation.

¶ The law, possessing the shadow of the good things to come, not the actual form of the things, cannot, by the same sacrifices which they offer, continually year by year, ever bring to perfection those who come to God. Otherwise, would not these have ceased to be offered? Since, once absolved, the worshippers would no longer have any consciousness of sin. But in these sacrifices is the yearly remembrance of sins, for it is impossible for the blood of bulls and goats to take sins away.

So, coming into the world, Christ says: You did not want sacrifice and offering, but you prepared a body for me. In whole burnt offerings even for sin, you took no delight. Then I said: Behold, I come; in the scroll of a book it is written concerning me; to do, O God, your will. And, while he said above that you did not want sacrifices and offerings and whole burnt offerings even for sin, which are offered according to the law, nor take delight in them, then he said: Behold, I come to do your will. He takes away the first so that the second may stand. By which will we are sanctified by the offering of the body of Jesus Christ, once for all.

And every priest stands day by day performing services and again and again offering the same sacrifices, which can never take away sins. But he, after offering for sins one sacrifice for all time, sat down on the right hand of God, waiting henceforth for his enemies to be made a footstool for his feet; for with one offering he has made those who are consecrated perfect for all time. And our witness to this is the Holy Spirit; for after saying: This is the covenant I will make with them after those days, says the Lord, giving them my laws for their hearts, and I will inscribe them upon their understanding. And I shall no longer remember their sins and their transgressions. But where there is remission of these, there is no longer any offering for sins.

Having therefore confidence, brothers, for entrance into the sanctuary by the blood of Jesus, the new and living way he has made for us through the curtain, that is, his flesh, and having a great priest set over the house of God, let us approach with true heart in abundance of faith, our hearts purged of bad conscience, our bodies washed in pure water. Let us hold fast to our belief in the hope, for he who gave us the promise is to be trusted. And let us study each other to stimulate love and good works, not failing to attend our own meetings, as is the way of some, but encouraging each other, all the more so inasmuch as you see the Day coming nearer.

For when we willingly sin after having received perception of the truth, there is no longer left any sacrifice for sin, only the terrible expectation of judgment, and of fire eager to devour its opponents. If one has broken the law of Moses he dies without pity on the word of two or three witnesses; how much worse do you suppose will be the punishment accorded to one who has trampled down the son of God, and called unclean the blood of the covenant by which he was sanctified, and outraged the spirit of grace? We know who it was who said: Mine is the vengeance, I will repay. And again: The Lord will judge his people. It is a terrible thing to fall into the hands of the living God.

Remember the days that have been, when you, the enlightened ones, underwent a hard struggle with sufferings, both when you were publicly exposed to revilements and afflictions, and when you shared them with those who were so treated; for you suffered along with those who were imprisoned, and you accepted the seizure of your property with joy, knowing that you have a greater possession and one that endures. Do not lose your courage, which brings a great reward, for you have need of endurance in order to do the will of God and win the promise. For (it is written): In a very little time he who is coming will come, and he will not delay; the one who is righteous will live by faith and if anyone falters, my soul is not well pleased with him. We do not belong to faltering, for destruction, but to faith, for the saving of the soul.

¶ Faith is the substance of things hoped for, the proof of things unseen; for by it our forebears were attested. By faith we understand that the ages were formed by the word of God, so that what is seen did not come from things that appear. By faith Abel brought to God a better offering than Cain, and by this he was proved righteous, with God himself bearing witness to his gifts; and by faith, though he died, he still speaks. By faith Enoch was taken up aloft, so as not to look on death, and he was never found because God had taken him; since it is attested that before his taking up he was pleasing to God, and without faith it is impossible to please him; for one who approaches God must believe that he exists and that he is the rewarder of those who seek him out. By faith Noah, divinely warned of things not yet apparent, took careful thought and built the ark for the salvation of his household; and by this he refuted the world, and became heir to that righteousness that comes through faith. By faith Abraham obeyed when he was called to go forth into that region which he was to receive as his inheritance, and he went forth not knowing where he was going. By faith he moved to the land of the promise as to a foreign land, living in tents as did also Isaac and Jacob, who shared with him the inheritance of the same promise; for he was waiting for the city with foundations, of which the architect and designer is God. By faith also Sarah herself found strength to give birth, though past her time of life, since she thought the giver of the promise was to be believed; so that from one man, even from one far gone, there came a number like the stars in the sky, or like the innumerable sands at the edge of the sea.

All of these died in faith without winning the promise,

but seeing it from far off and hailing it, and confessing that they were strangers and visitors on earth. They who say such things make it clear that they are searching for their own country. If they had been remembering the country from which they came, they would have had occasion to turn back; but as it is they long for a better one, that is, the one in heaven. Therefore God is not ashamed to be called their God, for he has made ready a city for them.

By faith Abraham offered up Isaac when he was put to the test, and accepting the promise, offered up his only son, the one of whom it had been said: Your seed shall be called after Isaac; reasoning that God can even raise men from the dead; therefore symbolically he did recover him. By faith even in things to come Isaac blessed Jacob and Esau. By faith Jacob, dying, blessed each of the sons of Joseph and prayed for them over the end of his staff. By faith Joseph, dying, remembered the exodus of the sons of Israel and gave instructions concerning his bones. By faith when Moses was born he was hidden for three months by his parents, because they saw that the baby was a fine one, and they were not frightened by the edict of the King. By faith Moses, grown big, refused to be called the son of Pharaoh's daughter, choosing to suffer with the people of God rather than have the temporary enjoyment of sinfulness, considering the despised estate of the Christ a richer thing than the treasures of Egypt, since he looked forward to his reward. By faith he left Egypt, not fearing the anger of the King, for he endured as if he saw him who cannot be seen. By faith he established the Passover and the sprinkling of blood so that the destroyer of the firstborn might not strike them. By faith they walked across the Red Sea as if on dry land,

which the Egyptians tried to do and were engulfed. By
faith the walls of Jericho fell down when they were cir-
cled for seven days. By faith Rahab the harlot did not
perish with the unbelievers, because she had received the
spies in peace.

Why should I say more? My time will run out as I tell
about Gideon, Barak, Samson, Jephthah, David and Samuel and the prophets. By faith they overthrew kingdoms,
did works of righteousness, won promises, stopped the
mouths of lions, quenched the force of fire, escaped the
edge of the sword, grew strong out of weakness, proved
mighty in battle, routed the lines of their opponents.
Wives recovered their resurrected dead. But others were
tortured, refusing release so as to win a greater resurrection; others again accepted the ordeal of mockery and
whippings and even of chains and prison. They were
stoned, tortured, sawn in two, slaughtered by the sword.
They went about in the skins of sheep and goats, in want
and affliction and abuse. The world was not worthy of
them as they wandered in deserts and mountains and
caves and holes in the ground.

Yet all of these, though proved through their faith, did
not achieve the promise, since God for our sake contem-
plated something better: that they should not be per-
fected apart from us.

¶ Let us also, therefore, surrounded by such a cloud of
witnesses, putting aside every obstacle and the sin that
easily besets us, run with tenacity the course that lies
before us, looking to the originator and perfecter of faith,
Jesus; who, instead of the joy that lay ready before him,
endured the cross, despising the shame of it, and has sat
down to the right of the throne of God. Consider him

who endured so great a rebellion by sinners against himself; so that you may not falter, weakening in your spirits. You have not yet gone to the point of bloodshed in
your struggle against sinfulness, and you have forgotten
that appeal that speaks to you as sons: My son, do not
think lightly of the Lord's discipline, and do not lose heart
when you are punished by him; for whom the Lord loves
he disciplines, and he whips every son whom he acknowledges. Put up with discipline. God treats you as
sons. Where is there a son whose father does not discipline him? If you go without the discipline which all are
born to share, you are bastards, not sons.

Also, we had the fathers of our flesh to discipline us,
and we have let them; should we not far rather submit
to the father of our spirits, and live? For they disciplined
us for a few days, as it seemed right to them, but he does
it for our good so that we can participate in his sanctity.
All discipline, for the moment, seems to belong not with
pleasure but with pain; but later, to those who have been
through it, it yields a peaceful harvest of righteousness.
So straighten up the slack arms and the tottering knees,
and take straight steps with your feet, so that your lame-
ness may not put you off, but rather be set right.

Seek to be at peace with all, and seek sanctification,
without which no one will see the Lord; taking care that
no one of you who lacks the grace of God, some root of
bitterness pushing up among you, cause you trouble so
that all are polluted by it; someone lewd or profane, like
Esau, who sold his birthright for a single meal. You know
that afterward he wished to inherit the blessing but was
rejected, for he found no place for repentance, though he
begged for it in tears.

You have not come to the place that is felt, which

burns with fire, to the gloom and darkness and storm and the clamor of the trumpet and voice speaking, which those who heard it begged not to have to hear it again; for they could not bear the commandment: If even a beast touches the mountain, it shall be stoned to death. And so frightful was the apparition that Moses said: I am terrified and shaking.

But you have come to Mount Zion and the city of the living God, heavenly Jerusalem, to myriads of angels, the festal gathering and assembly of the firstborn whose names are written down in heaven, and to God the judge of all, and the souls of the just made perfect, and Jesus the mediator of the new covenant, and his blood sprinkled which speaks louder than the blood of Abel. See to it that you do not ask not to hear him who speaks to you; for if those others who asked not to hear did not escape him who warned them on earth, even less shall we escape if we turn from him who speaks from heaven. At that time his voice shook the earth; now he has given a promise, saying: One more time I will shake not only the earth but also heaven. The words: One more time, mean the abolition of the shaken things as things that had been made, so that what was not shaken may remain. So, taking over a kingdom unshaken, let us keep our gratitude and in it serve God with piety and fear so that he may be well pleased; for our God is a consuming fire.

¶ Let brotherly love abide. Do not forget your hospitality, for through this some have entertained angels without knowing it. Remember the prisoners as if you were in prison with them, the abused as if you were so in body. Honorable is marriage among all, and the undefiled bed, for God condemns lechers and adulterers. Let your living be without avarice, making do with what is on hand; for he himself said: I will never let you go, I will never forsake you. So that we can be confident and say: The Lord is my aid, I shall not fear. What can man do to me?

Remember your leaders, who spoke the word of God to you, and as you consider the end of their life, imitate their faith. Jesus Christ is the same yesterday and today and forever. Do not be carried away by strange and complex teachings; it is good to strengthen the heart with grace, not foods, by which those who followed that way have not been helped. We have an altar from which those who serve the tabernacle are not allowed to eat. For the beasts whose blood is offered at the sanctuary for sin by the high priests, their bodies are burned outside the camp. Jesus, therefore, to sanctify the people by his own blood, suffered outside the gate. Let us therefore go to him outside the camp and bear the abuse he bore, since we have no enduring city here but are looking for the one to come. For him let us offer a sacrifice of praise to God continually, that is, the product of lips which confess to his name. And do not forget to do good, and to share, for with such sacrifices God is well pleased.

Obey your leaders and give way to them, for they go sleepless for the sake of your souls, since they will be accountable for them; so that they may do this with joy and not grieving, for that would be unprofitable for you.

Pray for us, for we believe that we have a good conscience, trying always to conduct ourselves well. And I ask you to do this all the more so that I may be restored to you the sooner. May the God of peace who brought back from the dead the great shepherd of the flock through the blood of the everlasting covenant, that is, our Lord Jesus, confirm you in all good for the doing of his will; working in us what is pleasing in his sight, through Jesus Christ, to whom be the glory forever and ever. Amen.

And I ask you, brothers, to be patient with my message of exhortation, for I have written to you in only a few words.

Know that our brother Timothy has been released, and if he arrives soon, I will see you in his company.

Give greeting to all your leaders and all the saints. Those from Italy send you greetings. May grace be with you all.

The General Letter
of James

¶JAMES, SLAVE OF GOD AND THE LORD Jesus Christ, to the twelve tribes in their dispersion. Greetings.

Count it all as cause for joy, my brothers, when you are forced into various trials, knowing that the proved quality of your faith engenders fortitude; but let your fortitude have complete scope, so that you may be complete and blameless, lacking in nothing. But if any one of you does lack in wisdom, let him ask for it from God who gives to all simply and without reproach, and it will be given to him. But let him ask with faith and without any doubt, since one who doubts is like the sea waves blown and tossed; let such a one not suppose that a man who is of two minds and uncertain in all his ways will receive anything from the Lord.

Let the humble brother glory in his exaltation and the rich brother in his humiliation, because he will be gone like the flower of the grass. The sun rises with its burning heat and shrivels the grass, and the flower falls to the ground and the beauty of its face is destroyed. Just so the rich man in his comings and goings will wither away.

Blessed is the man who endures trial, because when he passes the test he will win the wreath of life which the Lord promised to those who love him. Let no man who is tempted say: I am being tempted by God. For God is not tempted by evil things, and he himself tempts no one. Each man is tempted when he is attracted and seduced by his own desire. Then the desire conceives and gives birth to sin, and the sin when it is full-grown brings forth death. Do not be deceived, my beloved brothers. Every good giving and every perfect gift comes from above, descending from the father of lights, in whom there is no change, nor any shadow of variation. He willed it and brought us forth by the word of truth, for us to be a kind of first fruits of his creatures.

Know this, my beloved brothers: every man should be quick to listen, slow to speak, slow to anger, for the anger of a man does not effect the righteousness of God. Putting aside, therefore, all filthiness and any excess of baseness, meekly accept the implanted word which can save your souls. Be practitioners of the word, not mere self-deceiving listeners. Since if one listens to the word but does not practice it, he is like a man who looks at his natural face in a mirror; for he looks at himself and then goes on his way and forgets what he looked like. But one who gazes into the perfect law of freedom and abides by it; not a listener to something to be forgotten, but one who performs an act; that man will be blessed in his activity. If one believes that he is religious, but does not curb his tongue, and if he deceives himself, his religion counts for nothing. This is the pure and undefiled worship before our God and Father: to care for orphans and widows in their affliction, and to keep oneself untarnished by the world.

¶ My brothers, surely the faith you have in the glory of our Lord Jesus Christ does not go with discrimination among persons? If a man wearing golden rings and shining clothes comes into your synagogue, and there also comes in a poor man in filthy clothes, and you look at the man wearing shining clothes and say: Sit here, in a place of honor, but say to the poor man: Stand, or else sit down there below my footstool, are you not discriminating among yourselves and being judges who give vicious opinions? Listen, my beloved brothers. Did not God choose out those who are poor in the things of the world but rich in faith and heirs to the kingdom which he promised to those who love him? But you despised the poor man. Are not the rich lords over you, and is it not they who drag you into the law courts? Is it not they who insult the noble name which has been bestowed upon you? If you fulfill the kingly law accordingly as scripture says: You shall love your neighbor as yourself; you are acting well. But if you discriminate among persons, you are committing a sin, and are convicted by the law as transgressors. For anyone who obeys all the rest of the law but fails in one respect is guilty in all respects. He who said: You shall not commit adultery; also said: You shall not murder. But if you do not commit adultery but do murder, you are breaking the law. Speak and act as if you were about to be tried by the law of freedom. For him who acts without mercy, judgment is merciless. Mercy triumphs over judgment.

What good does it do, my brothers, if someone says that he has faith but does not have the acts of faith? Surely his faith will not save him? If a brother or a sister is naked and short of daily nourishment, and one of you says to them: Go in peace, keep warm and eat, but you do not give them what they need for their bodies, what good does it do? So even faith, if it does not have the acts of faith, is a dead thing in itself. But someone will say: You have faith, but I have actions. Show me your faith apart from your actions, and I will show my faith from my actions. You believe that there is one God? You do well to do so. Demons also believe this, and they shudder. But are you willing to understand, O empty man, that faith without acts is idle? Was not Abraham our father justified by his actions, when he offered up Isaac, his son, on the sacrificial altar? You see that his faith worked with his actions and through his actions his faith was made a thing complete, and so the scripture was fulfilled which says: Abraham believed God, and it was counted as righteousness in him, and he was called the friend of God. You see that a person is justified by his acts and not by faith alone. So likewise was not even Rahab the harlot justified by her action when she received the messengers and sent them off by the wrong way? As the body without spirit is a dead thing, so also faith without acts is a dead thing.

¶ My brothers, not many of you should become teachers. We know that we teachers shall be given a stricter trial; for we all make many mistakes. But if a man makes no mistakes in what he says, he is a complete man and able also to control his entire body. If we put bits in the mouths of horses to make them obey us, we can also control the entire body. Consider also ships, which, big as they are and driven by severe winds, are directed by a very small rudder wherever the impulse of the steersman chooses. So also the tongue is a small part of the body but makes a big noise. Consider how small a fire ignites

how great a forest. The tongue too is a fire; the tongue
is appointed among the parts of our bodies as a whole
world of wickedness, which stains the entire body and
sets fire to the wheel of creation, and which itself is
burned by Gehenna. For the whole world of beasts and
birds and reptiles and sea creatures is subjected, and has
been made subject, to the world of men. But no man can
make a subject of the tongue. It is an evil that is never
still, full of deadly poison. With it we praise the Lord and
Father, and with it we curse men, who were born in the
likeness of God; out of the same mouth come praise and
cursing. This, my brothers, should not be so. Surely the
spring does not run sweet and bitter from the same opening? Surely, my brothers, a fig tree cannot grow olives,
nor a grape vine figs? Neither can a salt spring give sweet
water.

Who among you is wise and knowledgeable? Let him
show, with the gentleness that comes from wisdom, the
actions of his good disposition. But if you have bitter envy
and ambition in your hearts, do not be boastful, do not
lie about the truth. That is not the wisdom which comes
from above, but it is earthly, sensual, demonic; for where
there is envy and ambition, there there is disorder and
everything that is bad. But the wisdom which comes from
above is, first of all, pure; it is also peaceful, forbearing,
open to persuasion, filled with mercy and a good harvest,
impartial, not hypocritical; the harvest of righteousness
is sown in peace by those who make peace.

¶ Where do these hostilities come from, where do these
quarrels, which take place among you? Is it not from here,
from the pleasures that go to war inside your bodies? You
want, and do not have. You covet and murder, and can-

not get; you quarrel and are at war. You do not have, because you do not ask; you do ask and do not receive, because you ask badly: for means to spend on your pleasures. Adulterous people, do you not know that love of the world is hatred of God? He who wishes to be a friend of the world becomes an enemy of God. Or do you think it is meaningless when the scripture says: He has jealous longings over the spirit which he lodged in us? But the grace he gives is stronger than that. Therefore scripture says: God is set against the proud but gives favor to the humble.

Submit, then, to God; stand up against the devil and he will run away from you. Come to God and he will come to you. Wash your hands clean, you sinners, and purify your hearts, you doubters. Be miserable and mourn and lament; let your laughter turn to sorrow and your joy to dejection. Humble yourselves before the Lord, and he will exalt you.

Brothers, do not speak against each other. The man who speaks against his brother or judges his brother is speaking against the law and judging the law. But if you judge the law you are not one who carries out the law, but its judge. But there is one lawgiver and judge, the one who can save you and who can destroy you. Who are you to judge your neighbor?

Come now, you who say: Today or tomorrow we shall go to a certain city and spend a year there and do business and make money. But you do not know about tomorrow or what your life will be like then. For you are a mist that appears for a little while and then disappears. You should rather have said: If the Lord wills it and we are alive we shall also do this or that. But as it is, you are boasting in your arrogance. All such boasting is bad.

If one knows how to do right and does not do it, that is a sin in him.

¶ Come now, you rich men: Lament, bewailing the miseries that are advancing upon you. Your wealth has rotted away and your clothes are eaten by moths, your gold and silver have rusted and their rust will testify against you and feed on your flesh. You have stored away treasures for the fire in the final days. Behold, the unpaid wages of the laborers who mowed your fields cry out against you, and the cries of the harvesters have reached the ears of the Lord of the hosts. You reveled and luxuriated upon the earth, you fed your hearts on the day of slaughter. You condemned and murdered the righteous man. Is he not against you?

Be patient then, brothers, until the coming of the Lord. Behold, the farmer looks for the precious harvest of his land when he watches patiently over it until it gets the early and the late rain. Be patient, you also, strengthen your hearts, because the coming of the Lord is near.

Do not complain, brothers, against each other, for fear you may be judged; behold, the judge stands before your doors. As your example of suffering and patience, brothers, take the prophets who spoke in the name of the Lord. Behold, we call blessed those who have endured. You have heard of the endurance of Job, and you know what the Lord did in the end, because the Lord is generous and takes pity.

Before all else, my brothers, do not swear, neither by heaven nor earth, nor any other oath. Let your yes be yes and your no, no, for fear you may be brought to judgment.

Is one of you in distress? Let him pray. Is anyone

happy? Let him sing praises. Is one of you sick? Let him call in the elders of the church, and let them pray over him, anointing him with oil in the name of the Lord; and the prayer of faith will save the sufferer, and the Lord will restore him; and if he has committed sins, they will be forgiven him. So confess your sins to each other and pray for each other, that you may be healed. The prayer of a righteous person at work has great strength. Elijah was human, with the same nature as ours; and he asked in his prayer that it should not rain, and it did not rain on the land for three years and six months; and again he prayed, and the sky gave its rain, and the land grew a flourishing harvest.

My brothers, if one among you is led astray from the truth, and someone else brings him back to it, be sure that the man who brought back the sinner from the error of his ways will save his own soul from death, and cover up a multitude of sins.

The First General Letter

of Peter

¶PETER, APOSTLE OF JESUS CHRIST, TO the chosen exiles in their dispersion through Pontus, Galatia, Cappadocia, Asia, and Bithynia, according to the predestination of God the Father, by the consecration of the Spirit to the service of Jesus Christ and through the sprinkling of his blood. May grace and peace be multiplied for you.

Blessed is the God and Father of our Lord Jesus Christ. Through his great mercy he granted us to be born again into living hope through the resurrection of Jesus Christ from the dead, and into an inheritance which is imperishable and stainless and cannot fade, which has been kept in heaven for you who are held safe in the power of God through your faith in the salvation which is ready to be revealed in the final time. Rejoice over this, even if for a little while, when it had to be, you have been hurt by all kinds of trials; this was so that the quality of your faith might be found far more precious than gold— which, though perishable, is proved by fire—for praise and glory and honor at the revelation of Jesus Christ. You have not seen him but you love him, and now, not seeing him but believing in him, rejoice, with a joy which is inexpressible and glorious, as you win what is the end of faith, the salvation of your souls. Concerning this salvation, the prophets, who prophesied about the grace that would be yours, studied and sought for answers, trying to determine the time for which the spirit of Christ within them foretold the sufferings of Christ and his glory thereafter; and it was revealed to them that they were serving not themselves but you in these matters which have now been announced to you by those who have brought you the gospel through the Holy Spirit sent from heaven; secrets into which angels long to look.

Accordingly, gird up the loins of your mind, in complete sobriety, and put your hopes in the grace which is brought to you in the revelation of Jesus Christ. As children of obedience, do not conform to the desires you had before in your ignorance, but, like the holy one who summoned you, be yourselves holy in all your behavior; because it is written: You shall be holy, because I am holy. And if you invoke as Father the one who judges without prejudice according to what each has done, then spend the time of your exile here in fear; knowing that it was not by perishable things, silver or gold, that you were ransomed from the vain way of life you inherited from your fathers, but by precious blood, as of a blameless unblemished lamb, Christ. He was foreknown before the establishment of the world but revealed at the end of the ages, for you, who because of him believe in God who raised him from the dead and gave him glory, so that your faith and hope is in God.

Sanctifying your souls in obedience to the truth toward unfeigned brotherly affection, love each other from the heart, constantly, since you have been reborn not from a perished seed but from one that is imperishable, through the word of God which lives and endures. Thus: All flesh is like grass, and all its glory is like the flower of the grass. The grass withers and its flower falls to the ground, but the word of the Lord endures forever.

¶ This is the word which was brought to you as gospel. Putting aside, therefore, all malice and all treachery and hypocrisy and envious thoughts and calumnies, crave, like newborn babies, the guileless milk of reason, so that by it you may grow to salvation, if you have tasted and know that the Lord is good. Come to him, a living stone, rejected by men but selected for honor by God; and yourselves, like living stones, be built into a spiritual house for sacred priestly service, to offer up through Jesus Christ spiritual sacrifices which are well pleasing to God. As it says in scripture: Behold, I lay down on Zion a stone that is select and prized at the uttermost corner; and he who believes in it shall not be put to shame. It is a thing prized by those who believe; but for those who do not believe, it is: The stone which the builders rejected has come to be at the head of the corner, and a stone to stumble on and a rock of catastrophe. On which they stumble, by disbelieving in the word; to which end they were appointed. But you are a race elect, a royal priesthood, a sacred nation, a people to be preserved, so that you may proclaim the virtues of him who summoned you from darkness into his own wonderful light; who once were no people but now are the people of God, who received no mercy but now have been granted mercy.

I call upon you then, dear friends, as resident aliens and transients in this world to refrain from carnal desires, which take up arms against the soul. And keep your behavior among the heathens good, so that, whereas they now speak against you as evildoers, they may learn from your good works and glorify God on the Day of Visitation.

Be obedient to all human authority for the sake of the Lord; to a king, as one who is above you; to governors, because they are sent by him to punish the evildoers and to praise the doers of good; since this is the will of God, that by doing right you should suppress the unwisdom of thoughtless men; as free men, having your freedom not as a covering up of baseness, but as slaves of God. Give honor to all; love the brotherhood; fear God; honor the King.

Servants should be obedient with all respect to their masters, not only when they are good and kind, but also when they are unjust. For it is grace when, through consciousness of God, one endures pain when suffering unfairly; but what honor is there when you endure punishment for doing wrong? But when you do good and suffer and endure it, there is grace with God. It was to this that you were called, because Christ also suffered, for your sake, leaving you his example so that you might follow in his footsteps. He did no wrong, nor was any treachery found in his utterance; he was reviled and did not revile in answer; he suffered and spoke no threats but gave himself up to him who judges justly; he took up our sins in his own body onto the cross, so that, dying for sins, we might live for righteousness. You were healed by his wound. For you were like sheep gone astray, but now you have turned to your shepherd and the guardian of your souls.

¶ So likewise you wives should be submissive to your husbands, so that, even if some husbands do not believe in the word, they may, even without the word, be won over by their wives' way of life as they observe how chastely you live out of respect for them. Your beauty should not be the outward kind, in the arrangement of your hair or addition of gold ornaments or the clothes you wear, but the person hidden in the heart, in the incorruptibility of a peaceful and gentle spirit, which is greatly prized in the sight of God. It was thus that, long ago in the old days, the sainted women whose hopes were in God made themselves beautiful, by subordinating themselves to their husbands, as Sarah was submissive to Abraham. She called him lord; and you are her daughters, so long as you do good works and fear no threat. So likewise, you husbands, live with them understandingly, giving them due honor as to the weaker feminine vessel, and as heirs together to the grace of life, so that your prayers may not be stopped.

Finally, be, all of you, as one in your thoughts and feelings, full of brotherly love, compassionate, humble. Do not repay evil with evil or insult with insult but, on the contrary, give a blessing, because it was to this that you were called, to be the inheritors of a blessing. For if one desires to love life and look upon good days, let him keep his tongue from evil and his lips from uttering treachery; and let him turn aside from evil and do good, and seek out peace and pursue it. Because the eyes of the Lord are on the righteous, and his ears are for their prayer. But the face of the Lord is set against the doers of evil.

And who will do you harm if you are zealous for good? Yet even if you suffer for righteousness, you are blessed. Do not fear their terror and do not be shaken, but hallow the Lord Christ in your hearts, always ready to answer anyone who demands that you give a reason for the hope that is in you; but with gentleness and respect, with good conscience, so that those who attack your good life in Christ may be shamed in their slander. For if it is God's will that you suffer, it is better to suffer for doing good than for doing evil. Since even Christ once died for sins, the just for the unjust, to bring you to God. He was put to death in the flesh and brought to life in the spirit; in which he went even to the spirits in prison and preached to them. They had been disobedient once when the patience of God waited for them, in the days of Noah when the ark was being built and in it few souls, eight that is, were saved in the flood. This flood as baptism, its antitype, saves you now. This is not a riddance from the filth of the body, but a plea to God for good conscience, through the resurrection of Jesus Christ, who went to heaven and is at the right hand of God with angels and authorities and powers subjected to him.

¶ Since Christ suffered in the flesh, arm yourselves also with the same understanding, since he who suffers is relieved of his sinfulness, to live out his time in the flesh no longer by the desires of mankind but by the will of God. The time that has gone by has been enough to do the will of heathens, going the way of unchastity, desire, wine tippling, revelries, drinking parties, and disgraceful idolatry. Herein they are surprised if you do not rush to join them in the same excess of dissipation, and speak ill of you. They will have to answer for it to him who will presently judge the living and the dead. Since it was for this that the gospel was brought even to the dead, that they must be judged in the flesh like men but live in the spirit according to God.

The end of all things is at hand. Be temperate, then,

and sober for your prayers. Above all, be constant in your love for each other, since love covers up a multitude of sins. Be hospitable to each other without grumbling; as you have individually been given a gift of grace, dispense it to each other like good stewards of the complex grace of God. If anyone speaks, let it be as if he were quoting the sayings of God; if he serves, as if from the strength which God assigns; so that God may be glorified among all, through Jesus Christ, to whom be the glory and the power forever and ever. Amen.

Dear friends, do not be surprised at the trial by fire which comes to you as if it were some strange thing that happened to you, but as you share in the sufferings of the Christ, rejoice so that in the revelation of his glory you may rejoice and be glad. If you are blamed in the name of Christ, you are blessed, because the spirit of glory and of God comes to rest on you. None of you must suffer punishment for being a murderer or thief or malefactor, or as a troublemaker; but if he suffers for being a Christian, let him take no shame, but glorify God for this name. For it is time for the beginning of the judgment with the household of God; and if it begins with us, what will the end be for those who refuse to believe in the gospel of God? And if the righteous man is barely saved, where will the impious and sinful man be found? Thus even those who suffer by the will of God should, by doing good, entrust their souls to God, their good creator who is to be trusted.

¶ To the elders among you, I, your fellow elder and witness to the sufferings of the Christ and sharer in the glory which is to be revealed, send this appeal: Be shepherds to God's flock that is with you, not under constraint but willingly, not for shameful greed but freely; not as over-lords of your charges but making yourselves models for the flock; and when the chief shepherd appears, you will win the unfading wreath of glory. In the same way, you younger men, be obedient to your elders. And all, gird yourselves with humility, because God is set against the proud and gives favor to the humble.

Humble yourselves, therefore, to the mighty hand of God, so that in time he may exalt you. Cast all your trouble upon him, because he cares for you. Be sober, be watchful. Your adversary, the devil, prowls like a lion, roaring and looking for what he may devour. Stand up against him, firm in your faith, knowing that the same sufferings are befalling your brothers in the world. But the God of all grace, who called you to his everlasting glory in Christ, will, after you have suffered a little while, himself make you whole and firm and strong. To him be the power forever. Amen.

Through Silvanus, a faithful brother as I believe, I have written you thus briefly, appealing to you and testifying that this is the true grace of God. Stand fast by it.

My fellows among the chosen in Babylon send you greetings, as does Mark my son. Greet each other with the kiss of love.

Peace to all of you who are in Christ.

The Second General Letter
of Peter

¶SIMON PETER, SLAVE AND APOSTLE
of Jesus Christ, to those who have been granted faith like
ours in the righteousness of our God and savior Jesus
Christ: may grace and peace be multiplied for you in the
recognition of God and Jesus our Lord. His divine power
has bestowed upon us everything that leads to life and
piety through the knowledge of him who called us in
glory and virtue. By this the greatest and most precious
promises have been given to us; so that you may become
sharers in the divine nature, escaping the world's corruption that comes through lust. For this very reason, bringing all your energy to bear, provide, by your faith, virtue;
and by virtue understanding, by understanding continence, by continence steadfastness, by steadfastness piety,
by piety brotherliness, by brotherliness love. All these
qualities, being yours and in abundance, will cause you
to be not useless or unproductive toward the knowledge
of our Lord Jesus Christ; but one who does not have them
is myopic and blind, forgetful of how he has been purified from his former sins. For this reason, brothers, try
the more strenuously to make sure of your calling and
your election. By so doing you cannot ever fail, for thus

your entrance into the everlasting Kingdom of our Lord and savior Jesus Christ will be generously provided for you.

So I shall constantly remind you of these matters, even though you know and are firm in the truth that is with you. For I think it is right, as long as I am still in this tabernacle of the flesh, to keep you wakeful by reminding you, knowing as I do that the putting off of this tabernacle of mine will come soon, as our Lord Jesus Christ has made clear to me; and I shall try to see to it that you will always remember these things after my departure. For it is not by following artfully constructed myths that we have made known to you the power and the presence of our Lord Jesus Christ, but because we were eyewitnesses to his greatness. For when he received honor and glory from God the Father, a voice like this came to him from the magnificent glory: This is my son, whom I love, in whom I am well pleased. And we heard this voice coming to him from heaven while we were with him on the holy mountain. We have the prophetic word, which is certain; you do well to hold to it, as to a lamp shining in a dingy place, until the day dawns in light and the morning star rises in your hearts. But first, know this, that no prophecy in scripture is subject to personal interpretation; for prophecy did not ever come by the will of man, but men, carried along by the Holy Spirit, have spoken from God.

¶ There were also false prophets among the people, as among you also there will be false teachers, who will bring in destructive heresies, even disowning the master who bought their freedom and bringing swift destruction upon themselves. But many will follow their vicious practices, and because of them the way of truth will be blasphemed; and in their greed they will exploit you with made-up stories; but, long since, the judgment against them has not been inactive, and their destruction has not been sleeping.

For if God did not spare the angels who sinned but consigned them to the lower depths of darkness where they are kept for judgment; and if he did not spare the ancient world, but did protect Noah, the herald of righteousness, with seven others, while he let loose the flood on the world of the impious; and if he doomed the cities of Sodom and Gomorrah to ashes, making them an example of what is in store for the impious; and if he rescued the righteous Lot, who was afflicted by the vicious behavior of these lawless people (for, righteous as he was and living among them, by what he saw and heard day after day he was tormented in his righteous soul by their lawless behavior); then the Lord knows how to rescue the pious from their ordeal and to keep the unrighteous under punishment until the Day of Judgment; especially those who follow the flesh in lust for corruption, and who despise high authority. Daring, headstrong, they do not tremble before glorious creatures, but insult them; whereas angels, who are greater in strength and power than they, do not insult them as they demand judgment against them.

But these men, like unreasoning beasts, creatures of nature bred to be caught and slaughtered, insulting what they do not understand, will be slaughtered as such beasts are slaughtered, damaged for the damage they have done. They think of happiness as the luxury of the day, they are blots and blemishes who revel in their own beguilements as they share your feasts. They have eyes that are full of adultery, insatiable in sinning, and they seduce unstable souls since their hearts are well practiced in serving their greed. Children of the curse, they left the straight road and went astray, following the course of Balaam the son of Beor, who longed for the wages of wickedness but was reproved for this transgression; a dumb beast spoke in a human voice and stopped the madness of the prophet.

These men are waterless springs, clouds before the whirlwind; the dark of hell is in store for them. For speaking loud in their lewdness they seduce, through the lusts of the flesh, through depravity, some who are barely escaping from the wrong way of life. They promise them freedom, being themselves the slaves of corruption; for anyone is the slave of one to whom he has lost. If they once escaped from the defilements of the world by recognizing the Lord and savior Jesus Christ, and then once more are involved in these and overcome, what happened to them last is worse than what happened first. For it would have been better for them not to have known the way of righteousness than, having known it, to turn back from the holy commandment that was handed down to them. What has happened to them is what is in the true proverb: The dog returns to his vomit; and: The sow washed clean goes back to roll in the mud.

¶ This, dear friends, is the second letter I have written you, to quicken the pure purpose in you by reminding you: that you should remember the words spoken of old by the holy prophets, and the commandment of the Lord and savior from your apostles. But first understand this, that in these final days mockers will come with their mockery, people who go the way of their own desires, who will say: Where is the promise of his coming? For since our fathers were laid to rest, all things remain as they have been since the original creation. But they are unaware, as they wish to be, that the skies existed from of old, and the earth formed from water and standing in the water, by the word of God; and through these waters the earth was flooded with water and perished. And by the same word the skies that are now and the earth that is now are stored away for the fire, kept for the Day of Judgment and the destruction of impious people.

Do not forget this one thing, dear friends; that with the Lord one day is like a thousand years, and a thousand years like one day. The Lord is not slow with his promise, as some think it is slowness; but he is patient with you, because he does not want any to be destroyed, but all to come to repentance. But the day of the Lord will come like a thief, and on it the heavens will disappear with a sizzling noise, and the heavenly bodies will fall apart in flames, and the earth and the things inside it will be laid open. When all these things break up, how great is the need for you to keep to the saintly and pious life, expecting and urging on the coming of the day of God, when the heavens will fall apart in fire and the heavenly bodies melt in the flames. Then, according to his promise, let us look for new heavens and a new earth, in which righteousness resides.

So, dear friends, in this expectation, strive to be found spotless and blameless in his peace, and believe that your salvation is the patience of our Lord; as our beloved brother Paul has also written to you in the wisdom that has been granted to him, even as he speaks of these matters in all his letters; but places in them are hard to understand, and these the ignorant and unstable distort, as

they do the other scriptures; but to their own destruction. But for your part, dear friends, being forewarned,
keep yourselves from being carried along in the devia-
tion of the iniquitous, and from falling away from your
own firm position; but grow in grace and the knowledge
of our Lord Jesus Christ. To him be the glory now and
to the day of eternity.

The First General Letter

of John

¶WHAT WAS FROM THE BEGINNING, what we have heard, what we have seen with our eyes, what we have watched and our hands have felt, concerning the word of life; and the life was revealed, and we have seen and attest and announce to you the life everlasting which was with the Father and was revealed to us; what we have seen and heard we announce to you also, so that you also may share it with us; and our sharing is with the Father and with his son Jesus Christ. And we write you this so that your joy may be complete.

And this is the message which we heard from him and announce to you, that God is light and there is not any darkness in him. If we say that we have a share in him, and yet walk in darkness, we are lying and not enacting the truth; but if we walk in the light, as he is in the light, we share with each other, and the blood of Jesus his son washes us clean of all sin. If we say that we have no sin, we are deceiving ourselves and the truth is not in us. If we confess our sins, he is righteous and to be trusted to forgive us our sins and wash us clean of all guilt. If we say that we have not sinned, we are making him a liar and his word is not in us.

¶ My little children, I write you this so that you will not sin. And even if one does sin, we have a just advocate before the Father, Jesus Christ; and he himself is an expiation for our sins, and not for ours alone but for those of all the world. And by this we know that we have come to know him, if we keep his commandments. The man who says: I know him, and does not keep his commandments, is a liar, and the truth is not in him. But if a man obeys his word, truly in that man the love of God is fulfilled. By this we know that we are with him; the man who says that he abides with him must walk in the ways in which he walks.

Dear friends, I am not writing you any new commandment, but the old one which you have had from the beginning. The old commandment is the word to which you listened. Yet, again, I am writing you a new commandment, which is the truth in him and in you, that the darkness is passing away and the true light is now shining. The man who says he is in the light and hates his brother is in the dark even now. The man who loves his brother remains in the light, and there is no offense in him; but the man who hates his brother is in the dark and walks in the darkness, and does not know where he is going, because the darkness has blinded his eyes.

I am writing to you, little children, because your sins are forgiven through his name. I am writing to you, fathers, because you know him who was from the beginning. I am writing to you, young men, because you have overcome the evil one. I wrote to you, children, because you know the Father. I wrote to you, fathers, because you know him who was from the beginning. I wrote to you, young men, because you are strong and the word abides in you and you have overcome the evil one.

Do not love the world, nor the things in the world. If one loves the world, love of the Father is not in him; because all that is in the world, the lust of the flesh and the lust of the eyes and the vainglory of life, is not from the Father but from the world. And the world and its lust are passing away, but he who does the will of God endures forever.

Children, this is the final hour; and as you have heard that antichrist is coming, even so there are now many antichrists. From this we know that it is the final hour. They went forth from us, but they were not of our number (for if they had been of our number they would have remained with us); they went forth from us so that it might be made clear that they are not of our number. And you have been anointed by the holy one; and all of you have knowledge. I do not write to you because you do not know the truth, but because you do know it, and because no lie comes from the truth.

Who is the liar, if not the man who denies that Jesus is the Christ? This is the antichrist, the one who denies the Father and the Son. Anyone who denies the Son also fails to have the Father. He who acknowledges the Son has the Father also. Let that which you have heard from the beginning abide in you; and if that which you have heard from the beginning abides in you, you also will abide in the Son and the Father. And this is the promise which he promised us, the life that is everlasting.

I write you this concerning those who are trying to lead you astray. As for you, the anointing which you received from him abides in you, and you have no need for anyone to teach you; but as his anointing teaches you concerning all things, and is the truth and no lie, and as he himself taught you, abide in him. And now, little children, abide in him, so that if he is revealed to us we may feel confident and not be shamed by him at his coming. If you know that he is righteous, realize that every one who acts righteously is sprung from him.

¶ See what love the Father has bestowed on us, that we should be called God's children; and we are. This is why the world does not know us; because it did not know him. Dear friends, we are God's children now; what we shall be has not yet been revealed. We know that when he is revealed we shall be like him, because we shall see him as he is. And everyone who has this hope in him makes himself pure, as God is pure.

Everyone who commits sin commits lawlessness, and sin is lawlessness. And you know that he was revealed to take sins away, and there is no sin in him. Anyone who abides in him does not sin; anyone who sins has not seen him and does not know him. My little children, let no one deceive you. Everyone who acts righteously is righteous, as the Lord is righteous. Everyone who acts sinfully is from the devil, because the devil is a sinner from the beginning. This is why the Son of God was revealed, to undo the work of the devil.

Anyone sprung from God does not sin, because God's seed endures in him, and he is unable to sin, because he is sprung from God. By this it is clear which are the children of God and which the children of the devil; anyone who does not act righteously is not from God, nor is the one who does not love his brother. Since this is the message we have heard from the beginning, that we should love each other. We should not be like Cain, who came from the evil one and murdered his brother. And why did he murder him? Because his own actions had been evil, and his brother's had been righteous.

Brothers, do not be surprised if the world hates you. We know that we have crossed over from death to life, because we love our brothers. He who does not love remains in death. Anyone who hates his brother is a manslayer, and you know that no manslayer has life everlasting lodged within him.

We know of the Lord's love by this, that he laid down his life for us; and we have a duty to lay down our lives for our brothers. But when a man has worldly means and sees his brother in need and closes his heart against him, how can the love of God be in that man? Little children, let us love, not with talk and the tongue, but in action and truth.

By this we shall know that we are on the side of the truth, and in his presence persuade our hearts that, if our heart condemns us, God is greater than our heart, and knows all. Dear friends, if our heart does not condemn us, we have confidence before God, and what we ask for we receive from him, because we keep his commandments and do what is pleasing in his sight. And this is his commandment, to believe in the name of his son Jesus Christ, and love each other, as he commanded us to do. And he who keeps his commandments abides in him and he abides in that man. And we know that he abides in us from the Spirit which he gave us.

¶ Dear friends, do not believe every spirit, but test the spirits to see if they are from God, because many false prophets have gone out into the world. The spirit of God is known by this: every spirit which acknowledges that

Jesus Christ has come in the flesh is from God, and every spirit which does not acknowledge Jesus is not from God. And this is the spirit of the antichrist. You have heard that he was coming, and now he is already in the world.

But you are of God, little children, and you have overcome these false prophets, because he who is in you is greater than he who is in the world. They are of the world; they speak, therefore, from the world and the world listens to them. But we are of God; the man who knows God listens to us, the one who is not of God does not listen to us. From this we know the spirit of truth and the spirit of error.

Dear friends, let us love each other, because love is from God, and everyone who loves is sprung from God and knows God. One who does not love does not know God, because God is love. The love of God was revealed among us by this, that God sent his only-begotten son into the world so that we might live through him. Love is in this, not in that we have loved God, but in that he loved us and sent his son as propitiation for our sins. Dear friends, if God so loved us we also have a duty to love each other. No one has ever seen God; if we love each other, God abides in us and his love is made perfect in us. We know that we abide in him, and he in us, by this fact, that he has given to us from his spirit. And we have seen and we testify that the Father sent his Son to be the savior of the world. If one acknowledges that Jesus is the Son of God, God abides in him and he in God. And we know and believe the love that God has for us.

God is love, and he who abides in love abides in God, and God in him. By this love is made perfect in us, so that we may have confidence on the Day of Judgment, because as he is in this world so also are we. There is no fear in love, but love that is perfect casts out fear; because fear involves punishment, but one who is afraid is not made perfect in love. We love, because he loved us first. If a man says: I love God, and hates his brother, he is a liar. For one who does not love his brother, whom he has seen, cannot love God, whom he has not seen. And we have this commandment from him, that he who loves God should also love his brother.

¶ Everyone who believes that Jesus is the Christ is begotten from God; and everyone who loves the begetter loves the one begotten from him. By this we know that we love the children of God, when we love God and carry out his commandments. For this is the love of God, to keep his commandments; and his commandments are not burdensome, because everything which is sprung from God overcomes the world. And this, our faith, is the victory that overcomes the world. Who is it who overcomes the world if not he who believes that Jesus is the Son of God? This is he who came through water and blood, Jesus Christ; not in water alone but in water and blood. And the Spirit is what testifies, because the Spirit is the truth. Since there are three who testify, the Spirit and the water and the blood, and the three are at one. If we accept the testimony of men, the testimony of God is stronger, because it is God's testimony where he testified concerning his son. He who believes in the Son of God has the testimony within him; one who does not believe God makes him a liar, because he has not believed in the testimony of God concerning his son. And this is the testimony, that God gave us life everlasting, and that life is in his son. He who has the son has the life; he who does not have the Son of God does not have the life.

I write you this so that you may know that you have life everlasting, you who believe in the name of the Son of God. And this is the confidence we have in his presence, that if we ask him for something that accords with his will he listens to us. And if we know that he listens to us, whatever we ask, we know that we are given what we ask him for. If one sees his brother committing a sin which is not a deadly sin, he shall ask, and God will grant him his life. This is for those whose sin is not deadly. There is a sin which is deadly. I am not saying that he should pray for that kind. Every wrong is a sin, but there is sin which is not deadly.

We know that anyone born of God does no sin, but one who is born of God obeys him, and the evil one does not touch him. We know that we are from God, and our whole world lies in the power of the evil one. We know that the Son of God has come, and he has given us the wit to know who is the true one. And we are under the true one, under his son Jesus Christ. He is the true God and life everlasting.

Little children, keep yourselves from idols.

The Second General Letter of John

¶THE ELDER TO THE CHOSEN LADY and her children, whom I love in truth, and not I alone, but so also do all who know the truth, through the truth which abides in us and will be with us forever. Grace, mercy, and peace will be with us from God the Father, and from Jesus Christ the Son of the Father, in truth and love.

I was overjoyed to find that some of your children were going the way of truth as we have been commanded by the Father to do. And now I ask you, lady, as one who writes you no new commandment but the one we have had from the beginning, that we should love each other. And this is love, to go according to his commandments; this is the commandment, as you have heard from the beginning, to follow love. For many deceivers have come forth into the world, who do not acknowledge the coming of Jesus Christ in the flesh; such is the deceiver and the antichrist. Look to yourselves, so as not to lose what we have done but receive your full reward. Whoever breaks forward and does not abide by the teaching of the Christ does not have God; the one who abides by his teaching has the Father and the Son. If anyone comes to you and does not bring this doctrine, do not take him into your house and do not give him any greeting; for anyone who gives him a greeting shares in his evil deeds.

Though I have much to write you about, I would rather not do it with paper and ink, but hope to be with you and speak to you face to face, so that our joy may be complete. The children of your chosen sister send you greetings.

The Third General Letter

of John

¶THE ELDER TO HIS BELOVED GAIUS, whom I love in truth. I pray, dear friend, that you are in good health and that all your condition is as good as is the condition of your soul. For I was overjoyed when some brothers arrived and testified to your true life, as you do indeed follow the truth. I have no greater joy than this, to hear that my children are following the truth. Dear friend, you are acting faithfully in what you are doing for our brothers, even those who are foreigners. They have testified to your love before the congregation. You will do well to help them on their way as God would wish you to; since they set out for the sake of his name, without taking any funds from pagans. So we have a duty to support such people so that we can all work together for the truth.

I wrote something to the church; but Diotrephes, their would-be leader, does not accept us. For that reason, if I come, I shall speak of the things he has been doing, talking wicked nonsense about us; and not content with that, he refuses to welcome brothers himself, and prevents those who wish to do so and drives them out of the church.

Dear friend, do not imitate evil but good. He who does good is from God; he who does evil has not seen God. Demetrius has testimonials from all and from the truth itself; and we also testify to him, and you know that our testimony is true.

I had much to write you about, but I do not want to write it out for you with pen and ink. But I hope to see you soon, and we shall talk face to face. Peace be with you. Our friends send you greetings. Greet our friends each by name.

The General Letter

of Jude

¶JUDE, SLAVE OF JESUS CHRIST AND
brother of James, to those who are loved by God the Father and kept safe for Jesus Christ, the chosen ones. May
mercy, peace, and love be multiplied for you.

While making all haste to write to you, dear friends,
concerning our common salvation, I found it necessary
to write to you entreating you to fight for the faith which
was, once for all, handed down to the saints. For some
persons have slipped in among us who had been marked
out long in advance for this judgment, impious men, who
turn the grace of our God into licentiousness, and deny
our sole master and Lord, Jesus Christ. And I wish to
remind you, although you once knew it all, that the Lord,
after rescuing his people out of Egypt, then later destroyed those who did not believe; and those angels who
did not obey their government but forsook their proper
dwelling place he stored away in everlasting chains deep
in the darkness to await judgment on the great Day. Just
so Sodom and Gomorrah and the cities around them, who
like those angels debauched themselves and strayed after
unnatural sex, lie before us as an example, submitting to
the punishment of everlasting fire.

Like them, these people also in their dreaming defile the flesh, deny high authority, and insult glorious creatures. And yet the archangel Michael, when he was matched against the devil and disputing for the body of Moses, did not have the audacity to pronounce an insulting judgment, but said: May the Lord punish you. But these people insult what they do not understand; and what they do understand, in a physical way like dumb beasts, is what destroys them. Woe to them, because they have gone the way of Cain, and given in, for a price, to the error of Balaam, and perished in the rebellion of Corah. It is these who are blemishes on your love feasts when they join you in them, shamelessly looking after themselves: rainless clouds driven by on the gales, autumn trees without fruit uprooted and dying twice, wild sea waves foaming their own shame, wandering stars with the dark of hell in store for them.

Enoch, seventh from Adam, prophesied about these, saying: Behold, the Lord comes with his sainted tens of thousands, to pass judgment upon all, and to convict all the impious for all the acts of impiety they have committed, and for all the harsh things the impious sinners have said about him. These people are grumblers, complainers, going the way of their desires, and their mouths talk loud, flattering personages to do themselves good.

But as for you, dear friends, remember the words of prophecy spoken by the apostles of our Lord, Jesus Christ. Because they told you: In the final time there will be mockers, impious men going the way of their desires. These are the causers of divisions, sensual men without spirit. But as for you, dear friends, building yourselves up on your most holy faith and praying in the Holy Spirit, keep yourselves in the love of God, looking forward to the mercy of our Lord Jesus Christ for everlasting life. And pity some who are in doubt and save them by snatching them out of the fire; but pity others with fear, hating even the garment stained by their flesh.

To him who has the power to keep you from stumbling and set you blameless in exultation in the presence of his glory; to the only God our savior through Jesus Christ our Lord; glory, greatness, power, and authority before all time, and now, and through all the ages forever. Amen.

Notes

6.1　"Hellenists." These would be Greek or Greek-speaking Jews, not Hebrews but converted to Judaism or descended from such converts, and now converted to Christianity. They are to be sharply distinguished from the Gentiles, who do not accept Judaism.

7.2–53　This is *all* a continuous speech of Stephen's.

7.60　"he fell asleep." That is, he died; but the choice of this expression for a death in such violent circumstances is surely deliberate.

9.36　"which translated means Dorcas." Dorcas means "gazelle."

12.17　"James." The reference is to James the brother of Jesus Christ. See Galatians 1.19.

13.9　"Saul, who is also Paul." After this point, "Paul" is regularly used in Acts, as elsewhere.

14.19　"from Antioch and Iconium." The Antioch meant here is the city in Pisidia previously visited by Paul, not the great city in Syria.

15.14　"Simon." Properly, "Symeon." The reference is to Saint Peter.

16.6　"Asia." This signifies, not the whole continent or even the whole of what we call Asia Minor, but the Roman province of Asia.

16.10　"We." This first person plural, which comes in so abruptly, will reappear from time to time in *Acts*, ostensibly indicating that the author himself was present during some of Paul's travels.

17.19   "Areopagus." "The Hill of Ares" in Athens, and the court or council located on top of it.

19.9   "Way of God." The Greek has simply "the Way."

19.31   "Asiarchs." This apparently means members of the governing council of the Province of Asia.

20.28   "guardians." Or "bishops" (*episkopoi*).

23.8   "and neither angel nor spirit." The probability is that the Sadducees disbelieved in resurrection either *as* (in the form of) angel or as spirit.

25.13   "King Agrippa and Bernice." This is Herod Agrippa II, son of the Herod whose death is recorded in 12.23. Bernice (it should really be Berenice) was his sister, also his mistress.

25.25   The terms "Augustus," "our master" (26), and "Caesar" (11, 21) all refer to the Emperor Nero.

28–30   "listen . . . He remained." Omitting verse 29, which reads: "When he said this, the Jews went away with much discussion among themselves."

33–35   "Sent them . . . But Paul." Omitting verse 34, which is doubtful and uncertain.

36–38   "baptized . . . So he ordered." Omitting the suspect verse 37, which reads: "Philip said to him: If you believe with all your heart, it is permitted. He answered and said: I believe that Jesus Christ is the son of God." Even here there are variations.

ROMANS

2.12   "outside the law." Paul here continues the contrast of Greeks, or Gentiles (outside the law), and Jews (inside the law).

9.16   "But that is not a matter of wish or effort but of God's mercy."

Literally: "But that does not belong to him who wishes or him who runs, but to God, who has mercy."

10.14 "preach." Literally: "announce," "proclaim."

12.6–8 "We have . . . graciousness." The original is one long sentence which has no main verb or any independent clause at all. The translator has to fabricate some structure.

15.11 "All nations, praise the Lord." The word *ethne*, usually translated as "Gentiles," here seems to indicate *all* the nations of the world.

1 CORINTHIANS

1.12 "Christ is partitioned!" Or "Is Christ partitioned?"

2.14 "sensual." The sensual man is contrasted to the spiritual, as being alive, but animated by the earthly *psyche* rather than the unearthly *pneuma*, which is the word used for the Holy Spirit.

7.25 "unmarried." The word is *parthenoi*, generally used of girls, but what follows is obviously directed to the unmarried of both sexes.

10.11 "end of the world." Or "the ends of the ages."

11.4 "prophesies." This is not here introduced as if it were an activity requiring extraordinary gifts, and presumably may mean nothing more than reading, quoting, or interpreting scripture. See also 14.1 ff.

11.10 "Therefore a woman should take care of her head, because of the angels." Translation and exact bearing are uncertain.

12.7 "to his advantage." Or "for the common good."

14.1 In what follows, "prophesying" is contrasted with "speaking with tongues." The latter describes an attested phenomenon, "the broken speech of persons in religious ecstasy." By contrast, prophecy is reasoned, comprehensible utterance. See 11.4 and note.

15.19   "If by this life in Christ we are no more than hopeful." Or "If our hopes in Christ are for this life only."

2 CORINTHIANS

2.5   "supposing someone really has caused trouble." A particular case is obviously being referred to.

5.3   "Still in our bodies covered and not naked." The reference may possibly be to those who are found still alive on the Day of Judgment.

12.7   "a thorn." The Greek is *skolops,* a stake or spike.

GALATIANS

1.18   "Peter." Here, as always except for Galatians 2.7, Paul uses the Hebrew form, "Cephas." See John 1.42.

2.4   "but only might have been" is not in the text. I have supplied it, provisionally, for the sake of sense and syntax. An occasional unconstructed sentence is characteristic of Saint Paul.

4.13   "You know that I was sick in body when I brought you the gospel before." Or "You know that it was because of bodily sickness that I brought you the gospel before." This is better (Greek) grammar but poorer sense.

5.20   "envy" (Greek *phthonoi*). But the Latin has *homicidia* (Greek *phonoi*), that is, murder.

EPHESIANS

3.1   "say this to you." Conjecturally supplied; there is no main verb, or any independent clause at all.

4.11   "pastors." Literally, "shepherds."

4.26   "Are you angry? Even so, do no wrong." The simplest literal translation would be: "Be angry and do not sin."

NOTES

PHILIPPIANS

3.5   "a Hebrew of Hebrews." Or "a Hebrew with Hebrew parents."

4.12   "do without." The word here usually means "be humble," but we seem to need something that will contrast with having plenty.

1 THESSALONIANS

4.13   "those who are asleep." These sleepers are, of course, the Christian dead or "those who are dead in Christ" (16).

5.5   "catch you like thieves." Or "come upon you like a thief" (alternate readings).

2 THESSALONIANS

1.10   "because our testimony to you was believed." If the text is sound, as it probably is not, "because" must refer back to the just reward of the Thessalonians, because they believed.

1.12   "our God and the Lord Jesus Christ." Or "our God and Lord Jesus Christ."

1 TIMOTHY

5.5   "lives alone." Or "has been left desolate."

5.16   Text and sense uncertain.

2 TIMOTHY

3.3   "troublemakers." The word is *diaboloi*.

TITUS

1.10   "from among the circumcised." From Jews, that is, rather than Gentiles.

[285]

1.12   "their own prophet." The allusion is not to any contemporary but to the almost mythical Epimenides of Crete (sixth century B.C.).

2.10   "among people in general." Or "in every way."

2.13   "the great God and our savior." Or "our great God and savior."

3.10   "heretic." Or perhaps merely a factious man, a causer of dissensions.

HEBREWS

2.7   "a little lower than the angels." Or "for a little while lower than the angels."

3.11   "rest." Or "resting place."

JAMES

1.9   "Let the humble . . . humiliation." A variation on the familiar theme that God can easily bring down the rich and powerful and exalt the poor and weak.

1.12–13   "trial," "tempted." We pass from one to the other sense of the Greek *peirazō, peirasmos.*

3.6   "wheel of creation." Or "round of existence."

5.6   "Is he not against you?" Or, without the question mark: "He does not resist you."

1 PETER

3.1   "even without the word." The hope is that they may be influenced to act like Christians without being actually converted. But the sense may be "without a word being spoken."

5.13   "Babylon." That is, Rome.

NOTES

2 PETER

1.13   "of the flesh" is not in the text. Supplied for the sake of clarity.

2.14   "full of adultery." The Greek *moichalis* properly means, however, an adulterous woman; but this is hard to construe with "full of." The phrase might be wrested into meaning "on the lookout for an adulterous woman."

1 JOHN

3.7   "the Lord." Greek: "he." So also in 3.16.

4.2   "The Spirit of God is known." Or "You know the Spirit of God."

5.8   "the three are at one." Or "the three agree."

2 JOHN

1   "lady." She is surely not a person; this is a letter from the elder (leader) of one church to another church.